Gender and the European Court of Human Rights

In applying an intersectional feminist legal analysis of the European Court of Human Rights' case law in a variety of human rights issues, this book reveals a different and nuanced understanding of the gender issues.

Case law within the ECtHR, which does not explicitly raise gender issues, may have gendered consequences. Profound developments have occurred in Europe in several related areas, including gender equality case law in the context of the prohibition of discrimination under Article 14 of the European Convention on Human Rights; non-conventional parenting rights; discrimination on grounds of sexual orientation and gender identity; rights of asylum seekers; and family reunification rights in the past few decades. The analysis reveals the extent to which the Court considers an applicant's gender, intersectional inequalities, and the concept of 'vulnerability' in its case law. This book contributes to existing literature on gender equality, gender and judging in supranational courts. Furthermore, it highlights the intersectional discrimination experienced by women and diasporic or minoritised groups by uncovering new dimensions of vulnerabilities.

This book will be of interest to researchers in the field of European human rights law, gender, and intersectional issues.

Sanna Elfving is Senior Lecturer at Lincoln Law School, University of Lincoln, the United Kingdom. She was awarded a PhD in Law with minor corrections from the University of Surrey in 2014. Sanna's research focuses on European Union (EU) law and the European Convention on Human Rights. She has published a co-authored research monograph *Gender and the Court of Justice of the European Union* (Routledge 2018). Sanna is an elected Convenor of the EU and Competition Law subject section of the Society of Legal Scholars (2023–2026).

Gender and the European Court of Human Rights

Sanna Elfving

Routledge
Taylor & Francis Group
LONDON AND NEW YORK

First published 2025
by Routledge
4 Park Square, Milton Park, Abingdon, Oxon OX14 4RN

and by Routledge
605 Third Avenue, New York, NY 10158

Routledge is an imprint of the Taylor & Francis Group, an informa business

British Library Cataloguing-in-Publication Data
A catalogue record for this book is available from the British Library

ISBN: 978-1-032-56351-0 (hbk)
ISBN: 978-1-032-63330-5 (pbk)
ISBN: 978-1-003-43509-9 (ebk)

DOI: 10.4324/9781003435099

Typeset in Times New Roman
by Deanta Global Publishing Services, Chennai, India

Dedicated to my sister and my mother

Contents

Foreword

The European Convention on Human Rights has been central to human rights protection in Europe, providing a foundation for safeguarding fundamental freedoms since the end of the Second World War. The Court overseeing the Convention has issued thousands of influential judgments that have significantly shaped our understanding of human rights and generated substantial academic discussion. Frequently cited as the most successful human rights treaty, its importance in shaping the international human rights legal terrain cannot be overstated.

However, a scintillating new wave of scholarship is offering a more critical perspective on the judgments of the European Court of Human Rights and the Convention itself. *Gender and the European Court of Human Rights* is a timely and welcome addition to this discourse. Offering the first systematic analysis of the interplay between gender and the Court's decisions, this book highlights the impact of gender on a vast array of case law in key areas, including parenthood, gender recognition, and asylum claims. A key argument that emerges from this important study is that, despite the Convention's lack of explicit reference to gender, it is far from gender-neutral. The Court's judgments are revealed to be deeply gendered in ways that merit closer examination. As our understanding of gender evolves, it becomes increasingly important to examine how this foundational document addresses and adapts to these changing perspectives. This book reveals the significant practical consequences, especially for marginalised and vulnerable groups, that result from inattention to gender inequality and gender-based discrimination.

The author illuminates both the achievements and limitations of the Court in its (dis)engagement with gender. What follows is a sharp, critical, and nuanced analysis of landmark cases and the Court's evolving approaches to gender within the ECHR framework. Most notably, it underscores that the struggle for equality is ongoing, with women's bodies and gender-non-conforming individuals frequently subjected to over-regulation, violence, and oppression. It also flags the resistance and reluctance of some States to embrace gender equality fully. This book should perhaps come with the following health warning: the questions it provokes may result in sleepless nights. When it comes to gender, the Court is shown all-too-frequently failing to rise to the challenge, to be overly deferential, at times ambivalent and/or lacking in awareness. Nonetheless, the reader is also offered reason for hope; a number of important recent developments in the Court's case law suggest a positive shift in the Court's case-law and greater sensitivity to, and awareness of, gender as a source of structural oppression, discrimination, and inequality.

Innovative in its scale and ambition, this book provides essential insights for scholars, practitioners, and policymakers. It demands that the reader reflects on the dynamic interplay between gender and human rights law and the ongoing efforts needed to realise the principles of equality and justice for all individuals. It stands as both a scholarly achievement and a call to action for those dedicated to advancing human rights and gender equality. Brace yourself to be challenged and inspired.

Loveday Hodson
University of Leicester
September 2024

Acknowledgements

I would like to thank my editors and my mentors for their support during the final stages of the writing and editing process.

List of Acronyms and Abbreviations

Alternative Law Journal	Alt LJ
American Journal of International Law	AJIL
Assisted Reproductive Technology	ART
Cambridge Law Journal	CLJ
Cambridge University Press	CUP
Child and Family Law Quarterly	CFLQ
Common Market Law Review	CML Rev
Convention on the Elimination of All Forms of Discrimination against Women	CEDAW
Council of Europe	CoE
Court of Justice of the European Union	CJEU
Current Legal Problems	CLP
European Convention on Human Rights	ECHR
European Court of Human Rights	ECtHR
European Human Rights Law Review	EHRLR
European Journal of Criminology	EJC
European Journal of International Law	EJIL
European Journal of Migration and Law	EJML
European Law Journal	ELJ
European Law Review	EL Rev
European Union	EU
Female Genital Mutilation	FGM
Feminist Legal Studies	Fem LS
Human Rights Law Journal	HRLJ
Human Rights Law Review	HRL Rev
International Journal of Constitutional Law	ICON
International Journal of Discrimination and the Law	IJDL
International Journal of Human Rights	IJHR
International Journal of Law in Context	Intl JLC
International Journal of Law, Crime and Justice	IJLCJ
International Journal of Law, Policy and the Family	IJLPF
International Journal of Refugee Law	IJRL
International Journal of the Legal Profession	IJLP
International Legal Materials	ILM

In-vitro Fertilisation	IVF
Journal of European Public Policy	JEPP
Law Quarterly Review	LQR
Legal Studies	LS
Leiden Journal of International Law	LJIL
Lesbian, Gay, Bisexual, and Transgender	LGBT
Medical Law International	Med L Intl
Medical Law Review	Med L Rev
Netherlands Quarterly of Human Rights	NQHR
New Journal of European Criminal Law	NJECL
Oxford Journal of Law and Religion	OJLR
Oxford University Press	OUP
Particular Social Group	PSG
United Kingdom	UK
United States	US
Violence against women	VAW

1 Introduction

This book focuses on a substantial body of case law of the European Court of Human Rights (ECtHR) and the former European Commission of Human Rights, which existed until 1998. It aims to offer a critical examination of the case law through different theoretical lenses, including intersectional feminist legal scholarship[1] and queer[2] and trans theories.[3] The book specifically concentrates on the rights of women, considering that they make up over half the global population. An extensive body of case law built up over the years focuses on systemic and systematic violations of human rights suffered across the Council of Europe (CoE) by identifiable groups, such as, asylum seekers and members of diasporic or minoritised groups.[4] One of the aims of this research is to assess the question whether the Court takes gender and other intersecting externally perceived identities, such as, religious beliefs, race, sexual orientation, and gender identity, and legally assigned identity characteristics, such as, age[5] into account in its case law. The judgments of the ECtHR are considered vitally important for the development of European human rights standards within the CoE.[6] Even judgments, which do not explicitly

1 See generally Kimberlé Crenshaw, 'Demarginalizing the Intersection of Race and Sex: A Black Feminist Critique of Antidiscrimination Doctrine, Feminist Theory, and Antiracist Politics' (1989) U Chi Legal F 139; Patricia Hill Collins, *Intersectionality as Critical Social Theory* (Duke UP 2019); Loveday Hodson, 'A Feminist Approach to *Alyne da Silva Pimentel Teixeira (Deceased) v Brazil*' in Damian Gonzalez-Salzberg and Loveday Hodson, *Research Methods for International Human Rights Law: Beyond the Traditional Paradigm* (Routledge 2019).

2 Queer theory facilitates analysis of the lived experiences and narratives of the lesbian, gay, bisexual, and transgender (LGBT) community, focusing on the intersections of gender, sexuality, law, and society. See eg Alexander Maine, 'Queer(y)ing Consummation: An Empirical Reflection on the Marriage (Same Sex Couples) Act 2013 and the Role of Consummation' (2021) 33(2) CFLQ 143, 148.

3 See eg Dean Spade, *Normal Life: Administrative Violence, Critical Trans Politics, and the Limits of Law* (Duke UP 2015).

4 While the exclusionary framing of individuals as members of racial, ethnic, religious or sexual 'minorities' sets minoritised groups apart from the European mainstream, the concept of diaspora is more inclusive. See Elisabeth Becker, 'Theorizing "New Ethnicities" in Diasporic Europe: Jews, Muslims and Stuart Hall' (2024) 47(9) Ethnic and Racial Stud 1858.

5 Loveday Hodson, 'Sexual Orientation and the European Convention on Human Rights: What of the "L" in LGBT?' (2019) 23(3) J Lesbian Studies 383. See also Kate Malleson, 'Equality Law and the Protected Characteristics' (2018) 81 MLR 598.

6 Kanstantsin Dzehtsiarou, 'The United Kingdom and the European Convention on Human Rights: Together Until the End?' (2024) 5(1) ECHR L Rev 1.

DOI: 10.4324/9781003435099-1

raise gender issues, may still have gendered consequences. Applying a gender lens to the jurisprudence of the Court might lead to a different understanding of the issues, if not a different outcome. Reading case law of the Court as an aggregate tends to provide lawyers a reasonable intuition, over time, of trends or patterns in the reasoning of the members of the judiciary and of a court as a whole.[7] Yet, it is often impossible to predict how the judges decide a given case before them as the reasoning of the ECtHR is often materially different from that of the national courts, even if the outcome is the same. The complaints brought to the ECtHR are likely to involve not only the most complex and nuanced issues but also multiple different issues to which there is rarely one obvious answer.

Gender discrimination and inequality continues to impact on the lives of millions of people in Europe,[8] including women, girls, trans men, and trans women. Yet, it has been argued that cases concerning gender discrimination under Article 14 of the European Convention on Human Rights[9] (ECHR), which prohibits discrimination in the enjoyment of Convention rights, constitute a minority of complaints lodged within the Court's registry.[10] Nor are the complaints raising human rights violation claims brought by women or lesbian, gay, bisexual, and transgender (LGBT) applicants frequently addressed by the Court, despite the fact that these complaints often raise a fundamental gender dimension.[11] Quantifying the percentages of the Court's cases that relate to any particular area is challenging due to the absence of statistics relating to case applications or applications ruled inadmissible or struck out of the register at an early stage.[12] It has been argued that nearly half of the Court's case law focuses on concerns under Article 6 ECHR (The right to a fair trial), including systemic deficiencies in access to justice, lengthy proceedings before national courts, non-enforcement of national courts' judgments, and the independence of the national judiciaries.[13]

7 CJS Knight, 'A Court of Specialists: Judicial Behaviour on the UK Supreme Court by Chris Hanretty' (2022) 138(Oct) LQR 684.

8 Natalie Alkiviadou and Andrea Manoli, 'The European Court of Human Rights Through the Looking Glass of Gender: An Evaluation' (2021) 11(1) Goettingen J Intl L 191.

9 Convention for the Protection of Human Rights and Fundamental Freedoms (European Convention on Human Rights, as amended), art 14 prohibits discrimination in the enjoyment of Convention rights on grounds of 'sex, race, colour, language, religion, political or other opinion, national or social origin, association with a national minority, property, birth or other status'.

10 Lisa McIntosh Sundstrom, Valerie Sperling and Melike Sayoglu, *Courting Gender Justice: Russia, Turkey and the European Court of Human Rights* (OUP 2019) 228.

11 Athanasia Petropoulou, 'Gender, Migration and Human Rights in the Case Law of the European Court of Human Rights' Mogens Chrom Jacobsen, Emnet Berhanu Gebre, and Drago Župarić-Iljić (eds), *Cosmopolitanism, Migration and Universal Human Rights* (Springer 2020).

12 McIntosh Sundstrom, Sperling and Sayoglu (n 10) 228; Elisabeth Lambert Abdelgawad, 'The Practice of the European Court of Human Rights When Striking Out Applications' (2018) 36(1) NQHR 7.

13 Başak Çalı, 'Does the Practice of the European Convention on Human Rights Fit the Practical Conception of Human Rights?' (2024) 24(1) HRL Rev 1, 10.

1.1 Research Focus

In terms of the research focus, there is a paucity of research that has examined the ECtHR from a gendered point of view. In fact, there is no recent systematic analysis of the Court's case law in a variety of human rights issues dealt with by the Court's case law from a gendered perspective.[14] Most scholarly commentary on the Court's gender-related jurisprudence to date has focused on the prohibition of manifestation of religious beliefs, most notably in the context of case law focusing on so-called headscarf bans,[15] discrimination on grounds of sexual orientation and gender identity,[16] prohibition of gender discrimination under Article 14 ECHR,[17] and gender stereotypes.[18] The book builds specifically on the extant scholarship focusing on the ECtHR's case law concentrating on the parental rights of LGBT persons[19] and the rights of migrants under the Convention.[20] Scholarly engagement in the latter context has focused specifically on the restrictive national

14 For an overview, see eg Alkiviadou and Manoli (n 8). For scholarly work focusing on gender equality, see eg Ivana Radacic, 'Gender Equality Jurisprudence of the European Court of Human Rights' (2008) 19(4) EJIL 841; Eva Brems, *Diversity and European Human Rights: Rewriting Judgments of the ECHR* (CUP 2013).

15 Demir Gürsel, 'Regulating Women's Bodies in the Jurisprudence of the European Court of Human Right' in Niamh Reilly and Stacey Scriver (eds), *Religion, Gender, and the Public Sphere* (Routledge 2013); Effie Fokas and James T Richardson (eds), *The European Court of Human Rights and Minority Religions: Messages Generated and Messages Received* (Routledge 2020).

16 Jens T Theilen, 'Beyond the Gender Binary: Rethinking the Right to Legal Gender Recognition' (2018) 3 EHRLR 249; Damien A Gonzalez-Salzberg, 'The Accepted Transsexual and the Absent Transgender: A Queer Reading of the Regulation of Sex/Gender by the European Court of Human Rights' (2014) 29 Am U Intl L Rev 797; Claerwen O'Hara, 'Consensus, Difference and Sexuality: Que(e)rying the European Court of Human Rights' Concept of 'European Consensus' (2020) 32 (1) Law & Crit 91.

17 Sandra Fredman, 'Emerging from the Shadows: Substantive Equality and Article 14 of the European Convention on Human Rights' (2016) 16 HRL Rev 273; McIntosh Sundstrom, Sperling and Sayoglu (n 10).

18 See eg Alexandra Timmer, 'Judging Stereotypes: What the European Court of Human Rights Can Borrow from American and Canadian Equal Protection Law' (2015) 63(1) Am J Comp L 239; Isobel Renzulli, 'Discrimination and Gender Stereotypes in Judicial Decisions: The Jurisprudence of the European Court of Human Rights in Light of *JL v Italy*–A Retreat Into The Shadows?' (2023) 41(3) NQHR 155.

19 The focus of this body of scholarly work is to critique the slow phase of recognition of the rights of Europe's LGBT community and the doctrine of margin of appreciation through the lens of queer theory. See eg Elwood D Carlson, Stuart Gietel-Basten, and Marie Digoix, *Same-Sex Families and Legal Recognition in Europe* (Springer 2020); Damian A Gonzalez Salzberg, *Sexuality and Transsexuality Under the European Convention on Human Rights: A Queer Reading of Human Rights Law* (Hart 2020).

20 See in general, Amanda Spalding, *The Treatment of Immigrants in the European Court of Human Rights: Moving Beyond Criminalisation* (Hart 2022); Başak Çalı, Ledi Bianku, and Iulia Motoc (eds), *Migration and the European Convention on Human Rights* (OUP 2021); Marie-Bénédicte Dembour, *When Humans Become Migrants: Study of the European Court of Human Rights with an Inter-American Counterpoint* (OUP 2015).

family reunification policies,[21] racial discrimination in migration policies,[22] and violence against women in the context of women's asylum claims.[23] Reference will also be made to scholarly literature that centres on the ECtHR as a legal and political institution,[24] its case law and other outcomes of its work, such as, the monetary compensation awarded,[25] and domestic implementation of the Court's judgments.[26]

The aim of the book is to evaluate the Court's engagement with selected Convention rights, particularly in Article 3 (Prohibition of torture), Article 8 (Right to respect for private and family), Article 9 (Freedom of thought, conscience, and religion), and combination of each these provisions with Article 14 (Prohibition of discrimination). Additional reference is made to Article 5 (Right to liberty) and Article 4 of Protocol 4 (Prohibition of collective expulsion) in the context of the Court's asylum case law. The book also considers the impact that the Court's case law might have on wider equality overall, especially in the context of sexual orientation, gender identity, ethnic or racial discrimination, and religious discrimination. In terms of women's rights and gender equality, the ECtHR has referred to the significance of gender equality on several occasions in its jurisprudence.[27] Even though gender equality is not explicitly mentioned in the ECHR, the Court has stated that it is 'one of the key principles underlying the Convention'.[28] Additionally, in its judgments the Court has made it clear that: '[t]he advancement of the equality of the sexes is today a major goal in the member States of the Council of Europe and very weighty reasons would have to be put forward before such a difference

21 For analysis of the impact of gender in family reunification case law concerning the Netherlands, see eg Sarah van Walsum, 'Against All Odds: How Single and Divorced Migrant Mothers Were Eventually Able to Claim Their Right to Respect for Family Life' (2009) EJML 295.

22 Karin de Vries and Thomas Spijkerboer, 'Race and the Regulation of International Migration: The Ongoing Impact of Colonialism in the Case Law of the European Court of Human Rights' (2021) 39(4) NQHR 291.

23 For critical analysis of migration and violence against women before the ECtHR, see Janna Wessels, 'The Boundaries of Universality: Migrant Women and Domestic Violence Before the Strasbourg Court' (2019) 37(4) NQHR 336.

24 Jonas Christoffersen and Mikael Rask Madsen (eds), *The European Court of Human Rights between Law and Politics* (OUP 2011); Kanstantsin Dzehtsiarou, *European Consensus and the Legitimacy of the European Court of Human Rights* (CUP 2015); Angelika Nussberger, *The European Court of Human Rights* (OUP 2020); Rory O'Connell, *Law, Democracy and the European Court of Human Rights* (CUP 2020).

25 Sarah Maringele, *European Human Rights Law: The Work of the European Court of Human Rights Illustrated by an Assortment of Selected Cases* (Anchor Academic Publishing 2014); Patricia Popelier, Sarah Lambrecht, and Koen Lemmens (eds), *Criticism of the European Court of Human Rights* (Intersentia 2016); Octavian Ichim, *Just Satisfaction Under the European Convention on Human Rights* (CUP 2015).

26 Dia Anagnostou, *The European Court of Human Rights: Implementing Strasbourg's Judgments on Domestic Policy* (Edinburgh UP 2013).

27 Alkiviadou and Manoli (n 8).

28 *Leyla Şahin v Turkey* App no 44774/98 (ECtHR, 10 November 2005), para 115. See also Alkiviadou and Manoli (n 8) 193.

of treatment could be regarded as compatible with the Convention'.[29] Of course, it is important to note that the term gender has been interpreted extensively by the Court as it has recognised that trans women and trans men are able to benefit from protection enshrined in the provisions concerning equality of sexes.

Case law under the various Convention provisions encompasses a range of different issues. For instance, many of the cases concerning alleged violation of Article 3, which prohibits torture, inhuman or degrading treatment and punishment, relate to forced sterilisation,[30] racial violence and discrimination,[31] police violence,[32] and ill-treatment in detention.[33] Another area where Article 3 plays an important role is the cases concerning the return of unsuccessful asylum seekers to their countries of origin where they may face various human rights violations.[34] Similarly, the ECtHR has interpreted Article 8 as a broad provision that protects, eg, the right to seek to have same-sex relationships acknowledged,[35] the right to enjoy protection of the authorities against violence perpetrated against women in the context of intimate partner relationships,[36] and to obtain gender recognition under the Convention without compromising one's bodily integrity.[37] It is also relevant in the area of family reunification as has been established, including admission of family members to the territory of a CoE State, regularisation of their residence in the State, and expulsion of a settled or irregular migrant from the State.[38]

1.2 The Structure of the Book

The book is structured as follows: The first two chapters following this introduction examine the ECtHR as a legal institution (chapter 2) and the arguments for diversity on the bench (chapter 3). The substantive areas of law on which the case law analysis in this book focuses concern gender equality case law in the context of the prohibition of discrimination under Article 14 (chapter 4); gendered parenting rights (chapter 5);[39] gendered rights of asylum seekers (chapter 6),[40] and

29 *Schuler-Zgraggen v Switzerland* App no 14518/89 (ECtHR, 24 June 1993), para 67.
30 *NB v Slovakia* App no 29518/10 (ECtHR, 12 June 2012).
31 *BS v Spain* App no 47159/08 (ECtHR, 24 July 2012); *Allouche v France* App no 81249/17 (ECtHR, 11 April 2024).
32 *Ebru Dinçer v Turkey* App no 43347/09 (ECtHR, 29 January 2019).
33 *Dilek Aslan v Turkey* App no 34364/08 (ECtHR, 20 October 2015).
34 *B and C v Switzerland* App nos 889/19 and 43987/16, para 5 (ECtHR, 17 November 2020).
35 See eg *Koilova and Babulkova v Bulgaria* App no 40209/20 (ECtHR, 5 September 2023).
36 See eg *Bevacqua and S v Bulgaria* App no 71127/01 (ECtHR, 12 June 2008), para 84 (noting the State's failure to adopt sufficient legal protections against intimate partner violence violated its obligations under art 8).
37 See eg *YY v Turkey* App no 14793/08 (ECtHR, 10 March 2015).
38 Adel-Naim Reyhani and Gloria Golmohammadi, 'The Limits of Static Interests: Appreciating Asylum Seekers' Contributions to a Country's Economy in Article 8 ECHR Adjudication on Expulsion' (2021) 33 (1) IJRL 3.
39 See eg *CE and Others v France* App nos 29775/18 and 29693/19 (ECtHR, 24 March 2022).
40 See eg *MA v Italy* App no 70583/17 (ECtHR, 31 August 2023).

gendered family reunification rights (chapter 7).[41] These areas are of specific interest to the research topic as the ECtHR is thought to have an important role 'in positively contributing to the advancement of substantive equality'.[42] They have been specifically chosen for critical analysis with a view to challenging the CoE States' restrictive approach towards access to non-conventional parenthood (eg, access to assisted reproductive technologies and second parent adoption), asylum, and family reunification. These areas are often considered controversial because the Court has customarily afforded the States a wide margin of appreciation in policies and legislation pertaining to family formation, removal of non-citizens, or refusal of their entry.[43] The chapters will also consider the legal recognition of same-sex unions and recognition of new gender identity after transition where these issues are relevant, for instance, in the context of family formation.

Chapter 2, while focusing on the Court as a legal institution, explains the theoretical framework adopted in this book. It also elaborates on the principal research method, the doctrinal legal analysis, and the theoretical lenses through which the Court's case law is analysed. Various theoretical perspectives in political science are useful when analysing the Court as a legal institution.[44] The Court has been studied through various lenses concerning the limits of judicial power as well as the prisms of its apparent judicial activism and judicial self-restraint.[45] Due to the application of the doctrine of margin of appreciation, the Court has traditionally been cautious to intervene only when the established case law does not allow it to defer the matter to the national authorities or where it is necessary to intervene for the protection of vulnerable people.[46] In cases where it is necessary and important for the Court to intervene, it has avoided overstepping the legitimate boundaries of such interference based on the Court's respect for the respondent State's local expertise.[47] Arguably, the ECtHR demonstrates the greatest level of deference to

41 See eg *Biao v Denmark* App no 38590/10 (ECtHR, 24 May 2016).

42 Renzulli (n 18) 173.

43 Dia Anagnostou, 'Does European Human Rights Law Matter? Implementation and Domestic Impact of Strasbourg Court Judgments on Minority-Related Policies' (2010) 14(5) IJHR 721, 732.

44 See eg Fabio Wasserfallen, 'The Judiciary as Legislator? How the European Court of Justice Shapes Policy-Making in the European Union' (2010) 17(8) JEPP 1128, 1131.

45 See eg Ezgi Yildiz, 'A Court with Many Faces: Judicial Characters and Modes of Norm Development in the European Court of Human Rights' (2020) 31(1) EJIL 73; Steven Greer and Andrew Williams, 'Human Rights in the Council of Europe and the EU: Towards "Individual", "Constitutional" or "Institutional" Justice?' (2009) 15 ELJ 462; Pierre Thielbörger, 'Judicial Passivism at the European Court of Human Rights' (2012) 19(3) MJ 341, 345.

46 Francesca Romana Ammaturo, 'The Council of Europe and the Creation of LGBT Identities through Language and Discourse: A Critical Analysis of Case Law and Institutional Practices' (2019) 23(4) IJHR 575, 578. See also Dzehtsiarou, 'The United Kingdom' (n 6).

47 Juan-Pablo Pérez-León-Acevedo, 'The European Court of Human Rights (ECtHR) vis-à-vis Amnesties and Pardons: Factors Concerning or Affecting the Degree of ECtHR's Deference to States' (2022) 26(6) International Journal of Human Rights 1107. See also Ammaturo (n 45) 578; Dzehtsiarou, 'The United Kingdom' (n 6).

the democratic States that are perceived to be important for the system of human rights protection at the European level.[48]

The doctrine of margin of appreciation plays a role in a significant number of the ECtHR's judgments.[49] It has been argued to have been developed to maintain the delicate balance between the ECtHR's role to highlighting problems in the human rights protection of the CoE States and the ability of the States to develop policies of major importance.[50] The usage of the doctrine has nevertheless proven controversial. The Court has previously noted that the scope of the margin of appreciation to be accorded to the competent national authorities varies in the light of the nature of the issues, circumstances, and background to the case, and the seriousness of the interests at stake.[51] This doctrine has been subject to criticism as the Court's approach to the margin of appreciation is argued to be conflicting.[52]

Chapter 3 discusses the judicial diversity and how the presence or absence of women judges in the ECtHR overall enhances the Court's social legitimacy of legal process, representativeness, inclusiveness, and procedural fairness.[53] Although the election of its judges has been widely discussed in legal and political science literature,[54] there are arguments that the diversity of judges' professional backgrounds and specialism in human rights law and equality law has received only limited academic attention.[55] There appears to be a diversity of opinions around the need to have more women judges in the ECtHR. Some scholars have argued that the legal culture of the judges and the other personnel working in the Court functions as a place where the differences in judges' backgrounds become irrelevant after they have been selected to work in the ECtHR as they share the same fundamental approach towards human rights.[56] Others are of the opinion that it is difficult to justify the continued under-representation of women judges at the

48 Dzehtsiarou, 'The United Kingdom' (n 6).

49 James A Sweeney, 'Margin of Appreciation in the Internal Market: Lessons from the European Court of Human Rights' (2007) 34(1) Legal Iss Econ Integ 27, 30.

50 See eg Dzehtsiarou, 'The United Kingdom' (n 6).

51 See eg William A Schabas, *The European Convention on Human Rights: A Commentary* (OUP 2015) 567.

52 Bart van der Sloot, 'Between Fact and Fiction: An Analysis of the Case Law on Article 12 ECHR' (2014) 4 CFLQ 397.

53 See eg Françoise Tulkens, 'Parity on the Bench: Why? Why Not?' (2014) 6 EHRLR 587, 588–591; Stéphanie Hennette Vauchez, 'More Women: But Which Women? The Rule and the Politics of Gender Balance at the European Court of Human Rights' (2015) 26(1) EJIL 195, 195–197; Michal Bobek (ed), *Selecting Europe's Judges: A Critical Review of the Appointment Procedures to the European Courts* (OUP 2015) 226.

54 See eg Erik Voeten, 'The Politics of International Judicial Appointments: Evidence from the European Court of Human Rights' (2007) 61(4) Intl Org 669; Kanstantsin Dzehtsiarou and Donal Coffey, 'Legitimacy and Independence of International Tribunals: An Analysis of the European Court of Human Rights' (2014) 37 Hastings Intl & Comp L Rev 271; Bobek (n 52).

55 Kanstantsin Dzehtsiarou and Alex Schwartz, 'Electing Team Strasbourg: Professional Diversity on the European Court of Human Rights and Why it Matters' (2020) 21(4) German LJ 621.

56 Nina-Louisa Arold, 'The European Court of Human Rights as an Example of Convergence' (2007) 76(2/3) Nord J Intl L 305, 320.

ECtHR, considering that there are so few women on the bench.[57] There are opinions that a critical mass cannot be achieved without stronger forms of affirmative action, such as, gender quotas.[58] There are also arguments that rather than aiming to appoint an equal number of women and men to the Court, a more pertinent question to be asked may involve what should, or what can, women judges do once they are appointed.[59] Considering that judges' room for manoeuvre in their roles is controlled by institutional and normative constraints, it may not be possible for them to engage in judging that would lead to genuinely life-changing outcomes for the aggrieved applicants.[60] The diversity and gender composition continue to be subject to academic debates, specifically when there are so few women judges on the bench and when the judges' views on fundamental rights are very divergent. Previous research has, indeed, found both liberal and conservative branches in the Court.[61]

Chapter 4 is the first chapter in a series of chapters covering substantive law areas worthy of a closer examination through a gender and queer lens. It is appropriate to start the case law analysis with Article 14, which is the Convention's main provision prohibiting discrimination, as the discussion of discrimination against women, minoritised and diasporic groups, and individuals with protected identity characteristics can frame the conversation that is to follow in the other substantive chapters focusing on parenthood, asylum, and family reunification. Case law under Article 14 has arguably produced most gender equality case law.[62] Although the Court has considered case law concerning gender equality most often by applying Article 14 in conjunction with a relevant substantive Convention Article, in other cases concerning equality issues applicants may have only alleged violation of Article 8 without alleging direct discrimination.[63] It is appropriate to analyse the rights of women belonging to minoritised or diasporic groups in the context of the Court's gender equality case law under Article 14.[64] This is because intersectional

57 See eg Helen Keller, Corina Heri, and Myriam Christ, 'Fifty Years of Women at the European Court of Human Rights: Successes and Failures of the Council of Europe's Gender Agenda' in Freya Baetens (ed), *Who Is the Judge? Identity and Diversity on the International Bench* (OUP 2020) 198. See also Rosemary Grey, Kcasey McLoughlin and Louise Chappell, 'Gender and Judging at the International Criminal Court: Lessons from "Feminist Judgment Projects"' (2021) 34(1) LJIL 247 248; Andreas Føllesdal, 'How Many Women Judges Are Enough On International Courts?' (2021) 52(4) J Social Philosophy 436, 442; Loveday Hodson, 'Gender and the International Judge: Towards a Transformative Equality Approach' (2022) 35 LJIL 913.

58 Margaret Thornton, 'Otherness on the Bench: How Merit Is Gendered' (2007) 29 Sydney L Rev 406.

59 Rosemary Hunter, 'Can Feminist Judges Make a Difference?' (2008) 15(1) IJLP 7, 7. See also Hodson, 'Gender' (n 56) 927.

60 Hunter (n 59).

61 Voeten (n 54).

62 See eg Radacic (n 13) 842; McIntosh Sundstrom, Sperling and Sayoglu (n 10) 136.

63 See eg Svitlana Karvatska, Ivan Toronchuk, and Alyona Manyk, 'Gender Equality Principle: Application in ECtHR's Practice' (2021) 9 Logos Universality Mentality Education Novelty Section Law 83, 86.

64 See ch 4.

discrimination may be an issue in some cases even when the applicants have not invoked Article 14, or the Court has found it unnecessary to rule on Article 14, if it has found a violation of one of the substantial Convention Articles. This may be an issue in the Court's jurisprudence focusing on the prohibition of manifestation of religious beliefs, most notably in the context of case law concentrating on so-called headscarf bans,[65] or discrimination against trans women and trans men. The book also addresses the case law concerning violence against women in the context of Article 14 as the Court has recognised that violence against women constitutes a specific form of gender discrimination.[66]

The focus of chapter 5 is the case law that concerns legal recognition of parenthood. The Court has decided several complaints where parents, who have separated from their former partners, have faced difficulties to be recognised as having parental rights. The case law also concerns the ability of single men and women to adopt a child; legal recognition of parental relationship between, for instance, intended or social parents and children born as a result of donor insemination; *in vitro* fertilisation (IVF); cross-border surrogacy agreements; as well as adoption and the *kafala*, a legal guardianship arrangement in place in the legal systems of many Muslim countries.[67] Many of the judgments and decisions concern parenting rights of single parents and the LGBT community, including trans women and trans men. There are some arguments that the Court's approach in this area is largely inconsistent and incoherent.[68] Although the Court has held that national authorities cannot use an individual's sexual orientation as a reason for rejecting an adoption application, some States maintain restrictive second-parent adoption laws, which have in some cases meant that only opposite-sex married couples may adopt their spouse's genetic children. Additionally, in many cases concerning legal recognition of filial links when the children have been born through donor insemination, it has been challenging for a non-genetic parent to obtain a legal recognition of the parent-child relationship.[69] Many recent cases have also concerned recognition of filial links between the intended parents and children born through cross-border surrogacy agreements. These cases highlight the significance of genetic ties between the parents and their children, prompting scholars to accuse the Court of reinforcing the idea of a traditional heteronormative two-parent family consisting of an opposite-sex married couple with biological children.

65 Gürsel (n 15); Fokas and Richardson (n 15).

66 *Opuz v Turkey* App no 33401/02 (ECtHR, 9 September 2009). See also McIntosh Sundstrom, Sperling and Sayoglu (n 10).

67 *Kafala* is defined as a voluntary undertaking to provide for a child's welfare, education, and protection under Islamic law. See eg *Harroudj v France* App no 43631/09 (ECtHR, 4 October 2012), para 16.

68 Brian Tobin, 'The European Court of Human Rights' Inconsistent and Incoherent Approach to Second-Parent Adoption' (2017) 1 EHRLR 59.

69 See eg *CE* (n 39).

Chapter 6 applies a gendered reading to the Court's asylum case law. Although no right to political asylum exists as such in the Convention or its Protocols,[70] the ECtHR has considered issues whether the CoE States violate asylum seekers' rights under the Convention in the context of extradition, expulsion, or deportation of an unsuccessful asylum seeker to the country of origin under Articles 2 or 3.[71] As the removal of an individual engages the CoE State's responsibility under the ECHR, the State must ensure that no substantial grounds exist for believing that the individual, if expelled, faces a real risk of being subjected to torture, inhuman or degrading treatment, punishment, or loss of life.[72] In the past, the Court's approach to many such cases has been restrictive, with only a handful of cases concluding that an asylum-seeking woman cannot return to their country of origin.[73] The same conclusions can be drawn from the ECtHR's case law concerning LGBT asylum seekers. More recent cases concern asylum-seeking women, who have alleged violation of their rights under the Convention due to inadequate reception conditions, confinement on border transit zones, or inability to submit an asylum application in the first place. In some of these cases, the ECtHR appears to take an approach which is consistent with the principles of the CoE Istanbul Convention,[74] even if it does not specifically reference the provisions of this Convention or the Convention on the Elimination of All Forms of Discrimination against Women[75] in its judgments. The Istanbul Convention is likely to play a significant role within the ECtHR's asylum case law in the future as it establishes the obligation for the Signatory States to introduce gender-sensitive procedures, guidelines, and support services in the asylum process. Therefore, it seems that the Court is slowly developing more gender sensitive asylum case law.

Chapter 7 discusses the Court's family reunification case law where a more inclusive approach is increasingly applied to cases involving migrant women as well as same-sex couples. The case law on Article 8 has progressively imposed some limitations on State discretion regarding allowing entry and residence to immigrants.[76] It has been argued that on the whole, the ECtHR has adopted a more liberal approach towards non-citizens already present in the State at the time of their application for family reunification, as opposed to individuals seeking to enter the territory of a State where their family members lawfully live.[77] The CoE States

70 See eg *Salah Sheek v Netherlands* App no 1948/04 (ECtHR, 13 January 2007), para 135.

71 See eg *AA and Others v Sweden* App no 12470/21 (ECtHR, 4 July 2023).

72 *OM and DS v Ukraine* App no 18603/12 (ECtHR, 15 September 2022). See also ECtHR, 'Guide on the case-law of the European Convention on Human Rights: Immigration' (Updated on 31 December 2021) 21 (Guide on case-law of the Convention: Immigration).

73 *N v Sweden* App no 23505/09 (ECtHR, 20 July 2010).

74 Council of Europe Convention on preventing and combating violence against women and domestic violence (adopted 11 May 2011) CETS No 210 (Istanbul Convention).

75 (adopted 18 December 1979; entry into force 3 September 1981) 1249 UNTS 13.

76 Anagnostou, 'Does European Human' (n 43) 732.

77 Hélène Lambert, 'The ECtHR and the Rights of Refugees and Other Persons in Need of Protection to Family Reunion' (1999) 11(3) IJRL 439; Mark Klaassen, 'Between Facts and Norms: Testing Compliance with Article 8 ECHR in Immigration Cases' (2019) 37(2) NQHR 157.

have experienced profound developments in this regard in the past several decades. The developments are particularly visible when the case law of the Court is compared to that of the European Commission of Human Rights. Many States have maintained national immigration legislation giving priority to unmarried, cohabiting opposite-sex couples until relatively recently, while excluding same-sex couples,[78] reflecting the restrictive stance adopted by the Commission in many of its decisions in the late 1980s and early 1990s. The Commission previously concluded that as no family life existed between an unmarried, cohabiting same-sex couple, the fact that they lived together did not prevent the expulsion of the unmarried same-sex partner to their country of origin after the latter's visa had expired.[79] This has changed with the judgments of the ECtHR in 2016.

Chapter 8 aims at providing some overall insights as well as sets out directions for future research. It specifically highlights the existing judicial dialogue between the two regional courts, the ECtHR and the Court of Justice of the European Union (CJEU), considering that the European Union enjoys increasing importance in the human rights sphere[80] in Europe and arguably beyond its borders in the States with which the EU had developed close cooperation through its external engagement. In the past decade or so similar developments have occurred in relation to human rights in CoE States that are subject to the jurisdiction of both the CJEU and the ECtHR and those that are only subject to the jurisdiction of the latter. There is a visible convergence between the case law of these two courts in several related areas that are subject to case law analysis in this book, including LGBT rights, legal recognition of children born through donor insemination and surrogacy, same-sex unions, asylum, and family reunification.

1.3 Conclusion

Although several judgments of the ECtHR have contributed to the recognition of gender equality and equality beyond gender in Europe, some of the judgments and inadmissible decisions are problematic due to the States' wide margin of appreciation as well as the absence of recognition of the structural and systematic discrimination against women and minoritised and diasporic groups. It is often assumed that the ECtHR has contributed significantly to the recognition of equal rights, however, such an assumption is based on re-litigation over the years concerning the same issues against often the same CoE States. Scholars have raised concerns that some States that are seen as having a long-standing commitment to human rights have been unwilling to change their policies after the Court has found that the State has repeatedly violated the rights of individuals bringing similar issues to

78 *Pajić v Croatia* App no 68453/13 (ECtHR, 23 February 2016).

79 See eg *B v UK* App No 16106/90 (Commission Decision, 10 February 1990).

80 Katja S Ziegler, Elizabeth Wicks and Loveday Hodson, *The UK and European Human Rights: A Strained Relationship?* (Hart 2015).

its attention.[81] Despite accumulating extensive case law condemning discrimination against women in various areas of life, the Court needs to move away from a focus on the margin of appreciation to fully embrace fundamental human rights codified in the Convention as well as complementary international and European human rights instruments. To facilitate such a move adopting a more inclusive and intersectional approach is the first major step in that direction. Although the ECtHR has made many more inclusive judgments in more recent years, other judgments demonstrate limited awareness of the wider equality issues, including making a simple change, such as, addressing trans men and trans women with their preferred gender pronouns. Therefore, the ECtHR needs more judges who are open to interpreting and applying the Convention rights in a gender-sensitive way, taking into account the fact that law is likely to advance already privileged individuals, while the impact on others may be the exact opposite.[82] In the words of Ichim, it is important for the ECtHR to have judges who 'can persuasively employ methods and concepts that go beyond a mechanical application of the Treaty'.[83] A more diverse judiciary ultimately is one that reflects the society it serves. This, in turn, hopefully translates into more inclusive and equal judgments.

References

Alkiviadou N and Manoli A, 'The European Court of Human Rights Through the Looking Glass of Gender: An Evaluation' (2021) 11(1) Goettingen J Intl L 191.

Ammaturo FR, 'The Council of Europe and the Creation of LGBT Identities Through Language and Discourse: A Critical Analysis of Case Law and Institutional Practices' (2019) 23(4) IJHR 575.

Anagnostou D, 'Does European Human Rights Law Matter? Implementation and Domestic Impact of Strasbourg Court Judgments on Minority-Related Policies' (2010) 14(5) IJHR 721.

Anagnostou D, *The European Court of Human Rights: Implementing Strasbourg's Judgments on Domestic Policy* (Edinburgh UP 2013).

Arold NL, 'The European Court of Human Rights as an Example of Convergence' (2007) 76(2/3) Nord J Intl L 305.

Becker E, 'Theorizing "New Ethnicities" in Diasporic Europe: Jews, Muslims and Stuart Hall' (2024) 47(9) Ethnic and Racial Stud 1858.

Bobek M (ed), *Selecting Europe's Judges: A Critical Review of the Appointment Procedures to the European Courts* (OUP 2015).

Brems E, *Diversity and European Human Rights: Rewriting Judgments of the ECHR* (CUP 2013).

Çalı B, Bianku L, and Motoc I (eds), *Migration and the European Convention on Human Rights* (OUP 2021).

Çalý B, 'Does the Practice of the European Convention on Human Rights Fit the Practical Conception of Human Rights?' (2024) 24(1) HRL Rev 1.

Carlson ED, Gietel-Basten S, and Digoix M, *Same-Sex Families and Legal Recognition in Europe* (Springer 2020).

81 Greer and Williams (n 45) 468.
82 Grey, McLoughlin and Chappell (n 57) 247–248 and 251.
83 Ichim (n 25) 56.

Christoffersen J and Madsen MR (eds), *The European Court of Human Rights between Law and Politics* (OUP 2011).
Crenshaw K, 'Demarginalizing the Intersection of Race and Sex: A Black Feminist Critique of Antidiscrimination Doctrine, Feminist Theory, and Antiracist Politics' (1989) 1989 U Chi L F 139.
de Vries K and Spijkerboer T, 'Race and the Regulation of International Migration: The Ongoing Impact of Colonialism in the Case Law of the European Court of Human Rights' (2021) 39(4) NQHR 291.
Dembour M-B, *When Humans Become Migrants: Study of the European Court of Human Rights with an Inter-American Counterpoint* (OUP 2015).
Dzehtsiarou K, *European Consensus and the Legitimacy of the European Court of Human Rights* (CUP 2015).
Dzehtsiarou K, 'The United Kingdom and the European Convention on Human Rights: Together Until the End?' (2024) 5(1) ECHR L Rev 1.
Dzehtsiarou K and Coffey D, 'Legitimacy and Independence of International Tribunals: An Analysis of the European Court of Human Rights' (2014) 37 Hastings Intl & Comp L Rev 271.
Dzehtsiarou K and Schwartz A, 'Electing Team Strasbourg: Professional Diversity on the European Court of Human Rights and Why it Matters' (2020) 21(4) German LJ 621.
Fokas E and Richardson JT (eds), *The European Court of Human Rights and Minority Religions: Messages Generated and Messages Received* (Routledge 2020).
Føllesdal A, 'How Many Women Judges Are Enough on International Courts?' (2021) 52(4) J Social Philosophy 436.
Fredman S, 'Emerging from the Shadows: Substantive Equality and Article 14 of the European Convention on Human Rights' (2016) 16(2) HRL Rev 273.
Gonzalez Salzberg DA, 'The Accepted Transsexual and the Absent Transgender: A Queer Reading of the Regulation of Sex/Gender by the European Court of Human Rights' (2014) 29 Am U Intl L Rev 797.
Gonzalez Salzberg DA, *Sexuality and Transsexuality Under the European Convention on Human Rights: A Queer Reading of Human Rights Law* (Hart 2020).
Greer S and Williams A, 'Human Rights in the Council of Europe and the EU: Towards 'Individual', 'Constitutional' or 'Institutional' Justice?' (2009) 15 ELJ 462.
Grey R, McLoughlin K and Chappell L, 'Gender and Judging at the International Criminal Court: Lessons from "Feminist Judgment Projects"' (2021) 34(1) LJIL 247.
Gürsel D, 'Regulating Women's Bodies in the Jurisprudence of the European Court of Human Right' in Reilly N and Scriver S (eds), *Religion, Gender, and the Public Sphere* (Routledge 2013).
Hill Collins P, *Intersectionality as Critical Social Theory* (Duke UP 2019).
Hodson L, 'A Feminist Approach to *Alyne da Silva Pimentel Teixeira (Deceased) v Brazil*' in Gonzalez-Salzberg D and Hodson L (eds), *Research Methods for International Human Rights Law: Beyond the Traditional Paradigm* (Routledge 2019).
Hodson L, 'Gender and the International Judge: Towards a Transformative Equality Approach' (2022) 35 LJIL 913.
Hodson L, 'Sexual Orientation and the European Convention on Human Rights: What of the "L" in LGBT?' (2019) 23(3) J Lesbian Studies 383.
Hunter R, 'Can Feminist Judges Make a Difference?' (2008) 15(1) IJLP 7.
Ichim O, *Just Satisfaction Under the European Convention on Human Rights* (CUP 2015).
Karvatska S, Toronchuk I, and Manyk A, 'Gender Equality Principle: Application in ECtHR's Practice' (2021) 9 Logos Universality Mentality Education Novelty Section Law 83.
Keller H, Heri C, and Christ M, 'Fifty Years of Women at the European Court of Human Rights: Successes and Failures of the Council of Europe's Gender Agenda' in Baetens F (ed), *Who Is the Judge? Identity and Diversity on the International Bench* (OUP 2020).

Klaassen M, 'Between Facts and Norms: Testing Compliance with Article 8 ECHR in Immigration Cases' (2019) 37(2) NQHR 157.
Knight CJS, 'A Court of Specialists: Judicial Behaviour on the UK Supreme Court by Chris Hanretty' (2022) 138(Oct) LQR 684.
Lambert Abdelgawad E, 'The Practice of the European Court of Human Rights When Striking Out Applications' (2018) 36(1) NQHR 7.
Lambert H, 'The ECtHR and the Rights of Refugees and Other Persons in Need of Protection to Family Reunion' (1999) 11(3) IJRL 439.
Maine A, 'Queer(y)ing Consummation: An Empirical Reflection on the Marriage (Same Sex Couples) Act 2013 and the Role of Consummation' (2021) 33(2) CFLQ 143.
Malleson K, 'Equality Law and the Protected Characteristics' (2018) 81 MLR 598.
Maringele S, *European Human Rights Law: The Work of the European Court of Human Rights Illustrated by an Assortment of Selected Cases* (Anchor Academic Publishing 2014).
McIntosh Sundstrom L, Sperling V, and Sayoglu M, *Courting Gender Justice: Russia, Turkey and the European Court of Human Rights* (OUP 2019).
Nussberger A, *The European Court of Human Rights* (OUP 2020).
O'Connell R, *Law, Democracy and the European Court of Human Rights* (CUP 2020).
O'Hara C, 'Consensus, Difference and Sexuality: Que(e)rying the European Court of Human Rights' Concept of 'European Consensus' (2020) 32 (1) Law & Crit 91.
Pérez-León-Acevedo JP, 'The European Court of Human Rights (ECtHR) *vis-à-vis* Amnesties and Pardons: Factors Concerning or Affecting the Degree of ECtHR's Deference to States' (2022) 26(6) International Journal of Human Rights 1107.
Petropoulou A, 'Gender, Migration and Human Rights in the Case Law of the European Court of Human Rights' in Jacobsen MC, Gebre EB, and Župarić-Iljić D (eds), *Cosmopolitanism, Migration and Universal Human Rights* (Springer 2020).
Popelier P, Lambrecht S, and Lemmens K (eds), *Criticism of the European Court of Human Rights* (Intersentia 2016).
Radacic I, 'Gender Equality Jurisprudence of the European Court of Human Rights' (2008) 19(4) EJIL 841.
Renzulli I, 'Discrimination and Gender Stereotypes in Judicial Decisions: The Jurisprudence of the European Court of Human Rights in Light of *JL v Italy*–A Retreat Into The Shadows?' (2023) 41(3) NQHR 155.
Reyhani AN and Golmohammadi G, 'The Limits of Static Interests: Appreciating Asylum Seekers' Contributions to a Country's Economy in Article 8 ECHR Adjudication on Expulsion' (2021) 33 (1) IJRL 3.
Schabas WA, *The European Convention on Human Rights: A Commentary* (OUP 2015).
Spalding A, *The Treatment of Immigrants in the European Court of Human Rights: Moving Beyond Criminalisation* (Hart 2022).
Sweeney JA, 'Margin of Appreciation in the Internal Market: Lessons from the European Court of Human Rights' (2007) 34(1) Legal Iss Econ Integ 27.
Theilen JT, 'Beyond the Gender Binary: Rethinking the Right to Legal Gender Recognition' (2018) 3 EHRLR 249.
Thielbörger P, 'Judicial Passivism at the European Court of Human Rights' (2012) 19(3) MJ 341.
Timmer A, 'Judging Stereotypes: What the European Court of Human Rights Can Borrow from American and Canadian Equal Protection Law' (2015) 63(1) Am J Comp L 239.
Tobin B, 'The European Court of Human Rights' Inconsistent and Incoherent Approach to Second-Parent Adoption' (2017) 1 EHRLR 59.
Tulkens F, 'Parity on the Bench: Why? Why Not?' (2014) 6 EHRLR 587.
van der Sloot B, 'Between Fact and Fiction: An Analysis of the Case Law on Article 12 ECHR' (2014) 4 CFLQ 397.
van Walsum S, 'Against All Odds: How Single and Divorced Migrant Mothers Were Eventually Able to Claim Their Right to Respect for Family Life' (2009) 11 EJML 295.

Vauchez SH, 'More Women: But Which Women? The Rule and the Politics of Gender Balance at the European Court of Human Rights' (2015) 26(1) EJIL195.
Voeten E, 'The Politics of International Judicial Appointments: Evidence from the European Court of Human Rights' (2007) 61(4) Intl Org 669.
Wasserfallen F, 'The Judiciary as Legislator? How the European Court of Justice Shapes Policy-Making in the European Union' (2010) 17(8) JEPP 1128.
Wessels J, 'The Boundaries of Universality: Migrant Women and Domestic Violence Before the Strasbourg Court' (2019) 37(4) NQHR 336.
Yildiz E, 'A Court with Many Faces: Judicial Characters and Modes of Norm Development in the European Court of Human Rights' (2020) 31(1) EJIL 73.
Ziegler KS, Wicks E, and Hodson L, *The UK and European Human Rights: A Strained Relationship?* (Hart 2015).

2 The ECtHR as a Legal Institution

2.1 Introduction

The system of protection for human rights and fundamental freedoms created by the European Convention on Human Rights[1] (ECHR) has been argued to have evolved into 'authoritative final arbitrator of human rights questions in Europe'[2] in its 75 years of existence. The European Court of Human Rights (ECtHR), together with other bodies of the Council of Europe (CoE), particularly the Parliamentary Assembly, has an important role in highlighting persistent problems in national human rights protection of the 46 Signatory States to the Convention.[3] Under the Convention, the mission of the Court is 'to ensure the observance of the engagements undertaken by the High Contracting Parties in the Convention and the Protocols thereto'.[4] As a regional adjudicatory body, with binding authority over the CoE States, the ECtHR has the ability to deliver judgments that find that domestic laws violate provisions within the ECHR.[5] Moreover, as States in most cases comply with judgments, the case law is widely perceived to have significant influence in the national legal systems of most CoE States.[6] One aspect that has been suggested to be truly unique about the human rights protection under the ECHR is that individual applicants are able to bring their complaints directly before the ECtHR and if successful, obtain reparation.[7] By conferring such a fundamental right on individuals, the ECHR has made the individual a subject of international law.[8] This is exceptional as no other

1 Convention for the Protection of Human Rights and Fundamental Freedoms (European Convention on Human Rights, as amended) (ECHR).
2 Oddný Mjöll Arnardóttir, 'Cross-fertilisation, Clarity and Consistency at an Overburdened European Court of Human Rights: The Case of the Discrimination Grounds under Article 14 ECHR' (2015) 33(3) Nord J Hum Rts 220, 221.
3 Kanstantsin Dzehtsiarou, 'The United Kingdom and the European Convention on Human Rights: Together Until the End?' (2024) 5(1) ECHR L Rev 1.
4 ECHR, art 19.
5 Mareena George, 'Using the European Court of Human Rights to Expand Access to In Vitro Fertilization for Straight Women and Lesbian Couples in Europe' (2021) 53(2) Geo Wash Intl L Rev 321, 324.
6 Robert Blackburn and Jörg Polakiewicz (eds), *Fundamental Rights in Europe: The European Convention on Human Rights and its Member States, 1950–2000* (OUP 2001).
7 Octavian Ichim, *Just Satisfaction Under the European Convention on Human Rights* (CUP 2015) 57.
8 ibid.

DOI: 10.4324/9781003435099-2

international human rights court affords private persons direct access to defend their rights.[9]

This chapter is structured the following way: Section 2.2 outlines the research method adopted in this book. Section 2.3 examines theories aiming to explain the functioning of the Court and the behaviour of its judiciary. Section 2.4 analyses the doctrine of margin of appreciation. Section 2.5 considers the enforcement of the Court's judgments at the national level as well as their influence beyond the parties to the dispute as well as outside the jurisdiction of the ECtHR. Section 2.6 provides a conclusion.

2.2 Research Method

The primary sources of law, namely, the Convention and the case law of the ECtHR analysed in this book have been selected from the Court's electronic database, HUDOC.[10] The selection of the case law first proceeded based on the subjective evaluation by the author, and second, on the need to define the research scope. For identifying relevant case law from HUDOC, a selection of case law was conducted with specific keywords, such as, asylum, family reunification, homosexual, and transsexual[11] in the search tool of the HUDOC database. 19 June 2024 is the last date up to which case law has been selected for doctrinal analysis. The analysis focused on certain key provisions within the Convention, including Article 3 (Prohibition of torture), Article 8 (Right to respect of family and private life), and Article 14 (Prohibition of discrimination). It is also worth noting that there is some overlap, considering that Article 14 does not appear independently. Consequently, Article 14 is only relevant in the context of one of the other substantive provisions. A selection of cases was chosen for analysis because they represent the types of complaints that are commonly brought to the attention of the Court. First, there are complaints that allege that State officials have breached rights guaranteed by the Convention, therefore, failing to meet their negative obligations under the Convention. The second type of complaints allege that State officials have failed to provide adequate safeguards against a violation of Convention rights, therefore, failing to meet their positive obligations under the Convention. Other case law and scholarly literature were also drawn upon selectively to illustrate the arguments. It is worth noting that the book does not intend to offer a comprehensive overview of the case law of the Court. The cases that are discussed in this book are considered relevant in demonstrating how the Court interprets and develops specific Convention rights.

9 ibid. See also Matilda Gillis, 'Can We Talk? The Application of the Public Law Democratic Dialogue Model to the Interactions between Domestic Legislatures and the European Courts' (2022) 23 German LJ 56, 68.

10 ECtHR case law is available at HUDOC <http://hudoc.echr.coe.int/> accessed 5 April 2024.

11 The Court and Commission have tended to use the terms 'homosexual' and 'transsexual'. Throughout this book, the term LGBT will be used as shorthand for the cases related to sexual orientation and gender identity before the Court, as well as the applicants bringing the cases.

Although a doctrinal analysis of case law has methodological and epistemological limitations, it is very rare for legal scholars to merely describe what the law is. Therefore, even the doctrinal legal scholarship typically seeks to advance a certain vision of how the law should develop.[12] Much of the doctrinal scholarship can be viewed as an undertaking to persuade the legal community to 'accept policy determinations of courts or to persuade judges to change these policy determinations'.[13] Additionally, the doctrinal legal method allows an understanding of the wide range of national processes and practices in the administration of human rights and how gender is articulated in them. Furthermore, judgments of a court are usually the only means by which the reasoning of the judges is made publicly available.[14] While the documents submitted to the Court by the parties are accessible to the public[15] and the hearings of the Court are usually conducted in public, the complex deliberation process of the judiciary of the Court is typically conducted behind closed doors.[16] This means that an analysis of case law is a key means by which it is possible to observe how the administration of human rights law at the national levels on the one hand, and by the Court on the other hand, reproduces and perpetuates contemporary gender roles and gender stereotypes.[17]

In this book, the doctrinal legal analysis is supplemented with a non-traditional approach to legal research. There is a wealth of different analytical methods and theoretical lenses through which to analyse the case law of the ECtHR.[18] The principal aim of the book is to apply a lens of intersectional feminist legal scholarship[19] to the case law of the ECtHR, thereby demonstrating how this form of analysis enables a study of case law through the recognition of patterns within it that would have otherwise been difficult to identify. Building on the work of Black feminist scholars,[20] an intersectional analysis offers an analytical frame to understand that

12 See eg Arthur Dyevre, Wessel Wijtvliet, and Nicolas Lampach, 'The Future of European Legal Scholarship: Empirical Jurisprudence' (2019) 26(3) MJ 348, 355. For an overview of doctrinal legal research method, see eg Terry Hutchinson, *Researching and Writing in Law* (2nd edn, Lawbook Co 2006); Michael McConville and Wing Hong (Eric) Chui, *Research Methods for Law* (Edinburgh UP 2017); Dawn Watkins and Mandy Burton, *Research Methods in Law* (Routledge 2013).

13 Dyevre, Wijtvliet, and Lampach (n 12) 355.

14 Paul Johnson and Silvia Falcetta, 'Human Rights Law as Social Control' (2021) 18(4) EJC 603.

15 ECHR, art 40(1)–(2).

16 Massimo Lando, 'Secret Custom or the Impact of Judicial Deliberations on the Identification of Customary International Law' (2022) CLJ 1.

17 See eg Lourdes Peroni, 'Age and gender discrimination: laudable anti-stereotyping reasoning in *Carvalho Pinto v Portugal*' (*Strasbourg Observers*, 28 September 2017) <https://strasbourgobservers.com/2017/09/28/age-and-gender-discrimination-laudable-anti-stereotyping-reasoning-in-carvalho-pinto-v-portugal/> accessed 5 April 2024.

18 including Marxist; postmodern; queer; legally pluralist; geographical; historical; political, and anthropological approaches. See eg Damian Gonzalez-Salzberg and Loveday Hodson, *Research Methods for International Human Rights Law: Beyond the Traditional Paradigm* (Routledge 2019).

19 See eg Loveday Hodson, 'A Feminist Approach to *Alyne da Silva Pimentel Teixeira (Deceased) v Brazil*' in Gonzalez-Salzberg and Hodson (n 18) 42–68.

20 See eg Patricia A Cain, 'Feminist Jurisprudence: Grounding the Theories' (1989–1990) 4 Berkeley Women's L J 191; Angela Harris, 'Race and Essentialism in Feminist Legal Theory' (1990) 42 Stan

social conditions and problems individuals face are shaped by multiple and mutually influencing factors of social division concurrently, such as, gender, sexuality, race, ethnicity, class, ability, religion, and nationality.[21] Exposing these intersecting forms of discrimination involves asking questions about the differential impact of law on women, men, non-binary people, and people whose sexual orientation or gender identity differs from the norm.[22] In this context, it is important to expose the stereotypic notions and expectations facing women and lesbian, gay, bisexual, and transgender (LGBT) persons in their everyday lives, such as, the assumption that their significance in human rights law is valued little outside of married heterosexuality and reproduction.[23] The inclusion of discrimination against the LGBT community in the scope of gendered analysis is important for various reasons. First, scholars have argued that critical to the understanding of human rights violations related to gender, gender identity, and sexual orientation is the fact that men and women experience discrimination arising from their membership to the LGBT community in different ways, depending on what other identity characteristics they may have.[24] The recognition that the scope of gendered issues is intersectional and inclusive reflects the trend of generating a wider field of legal scholarship in matters of gender, sexual orientation, and gender identity, which recognises that when a gender lens is cast upon law, it is not just women who come into view.[25] When an applicant is a gender non-conforming individual, irrespective of whether they identify as a trans individual, the circumstances of a case may cross both sexual and gender lines.[26] Even though there are frequent debates as to whether and how queer theory[27] and trans theory[28] are part of the family of feminist theories,[29] it makes no

---

L Rev 581; Marlee Kline, 'Race, Racism, and Feminist Legal Theory' (1989) 12 Harv Women's L J 115.

21 For commentary on the concept of intersectionality and intersectional discrimination in the case law of the ECtHR, see eg Shreya Atrey and Peter Dunne (eds), *Intersectionality and Human Rights Law* (Hart 2020).

22 Rosemary Grey, Kcasey McLoughlin and Louise Chappell, 'Gender and Judging at the International Criminal Court: Lessons from "Feminist Judgment Projects"' (2021) 34(1) LJIL 247, 257.

23 Diane Otto, 'Between Pleasure and Danger: Lesbian Human Rights' (2014) 19(6) EHRLR 618, 620.

24 Johanna E Bond, 'International Intersectionality: A Theoretical and Pragmatic Exploration of Women's International Human Rights Violations' (2003) 52 Emory LJ 71, 136–137.

25 See Joanne Conaghan, 'Some Reflections on Law and Gender in Modern Ireland' (2019) 27(3) Fem LS 333.

26 Alex Sharpe, 'Queering Judgment: The Case of Gender Identity Fraud' (2017) 81(5) JCL 417.

27 Sara Ahmed, 'Orientations: Towards a Queer Phenomenology' (2006) 12(4) GLQ: J Lesbian and Gay Stud 543; Kath Browne and Catherine J Nash (eds), *Queer Methods and Methodologies: Intersecting Queer Theories and Social Science Research* (Routledge 2010).

28 See eg Damian Gonzalez-Salzberg, *Sexuality and Transsexuality under the European Convention on Human Rights* (Hart 2019); Dean Spade, *Normal Life: Administrative Violence, Critical Trans Politics, and the Limits of Law* (Duke UP 2015).

29 See eg Lise Rolandsen Agustín, *Gender Equality, Intersectionality, and Diversity in Europe.* (Palgrave Macmillan 2013) (arguing that issues concerning gender are being marginalised by the increased attention to intersectionality). See also Janna Wessels, *The Concealment Controversy: Sexual Orientation, Discretion Reasoning and the Scope of Refugee Protection* (CUP 2021) (notes the existence of the debates).

logical sense to create a legal framework that protects people on paper only, but cannot take lived experience into account in a meaningful way. Gender, after all, shapes virtually everyone's identity and lived experience as it is deeply entangled in structures of power and social relational configurations.[30]

According to Conaghan, using gender as an analytical tool allows identification of the conceptual and ideological links between the unequal position of women and diasporic or minoritised groups in law and society.[31] Consequently, this book does not solely focus on the position of women, but it will also consider other minoritised or diasporic groups, such as, LGBT persons, the contemporary Black diaspora, and the contemporary Muslim diaspora in Europe who have been adversely affected by legal, social, and cultural regimes that demand conformity to traditional gender roles. In all these contexts, gender defines women's social role in relation to men, imposes strict norms of gender-conformity upon men and women, and denies the possibility of contravening gender norms.[32] Feminist and post-colonial scholars warn against making overgeneralised claims about women and women's experiences based on certain natural, biological or psychological attributes.[33] When women's experiences are generalised, there is a danger that only the problems, perspectives, and political concerns of privileged women will be represented while the experiences of non-privileged women are sidelined.[34] Although it has been acknowledged that not all privileged women are white, Western, middle-class, and heterosexual, these women are more often privileged than women who are minoritised because of their class, race, religion, ethnicity, or sexual orientation.[35]

Queer and trans theories aim to bring to the fore the experiences and perspectives of gender non-conforming people, accommodate their differences, and address their historical disadvantage.[36] A queer standpoint celebrates acts and identities that depart from the heteronormativity and opposes the idea that heterosexuality should be seen as the norm in the first place.[37] Accordingly, a queer perspective challenges the legal systems and rules that establish a binary, largely involuntary and mandatory gender model, which problematises individuals who reject being fitted into the binary categories.[38] By joining forces, feminist and queer coalitional work can counter the traditional understanding of gender founded on the biological

30 Conaghan (n 25).
31 ibid.
32 ibid.
33 See eg Ratna Kapur, 'The Tragedy of Victimisation Rhetoric: Resurrecting the "Native" Subject in International/Postcolonial Feminist Legal Politics' (2002) 15 Harv Hum Rts J 1.
34 Chandra Talpade Mohanty, 'Under Western Eyes: Feminist Scholarship and Colonial Discourses' in Chandra Talpade Mohanty, Ann Russo and Lourdes Torres (eds), *Third World Women and the Politics of Feminism* (Indiana UP 1991) 51 and 70.
35 Mohanty (n 34) 51 and 70. See also Kapur (n 33) 6.
36 Sharpe (n 26).
37 ibid. See also Damian Gonzalez-Salzberg, 'An Improved Protection for the (Mentally Ill) Trans Parent: A Queer Reading of *AP, Garçon and Nicot v France*' (2018) 81(3) MLR 526.
38 Gonzalez-Salzberg (n 37).

male-female dichotomy.[39] The construction of gender as two binary categories, which are imposed at birth following pre-established criteria and to which all individuals belong,[40] has remained largely unquestioned to date, despite the possibility to challenge binary understanding of gender based on the core human rights law principles of equality and non-discrimination.[41]

For the purposes of this book, queer and trans lenses are particularly useful in the context of case law on non-conventional parenthood (chapter 5), asylum (chapter 6), and family reunification (chapter 7). The Court has frequently received praise for its stance concerning protection of the rights of same-sex couples, especially since the Court has followed international trends to support its reasoning.[42] It also appears that LGBT rights feature prominently in legal and social science debates about court-led social change and political backlashes against judges.[43] However, it is debatable whether the Court has been as proactive as it would seem. Although research findings concerning judiciaries may often be contested, it has been argued that the judiciary, by virtue of its position, has a political and social role and greater authority in some respects than legislators.[44] Therefore, judicial expression has a potential to influence the attitudes of the public, legislators, bureaucrats, and other judges.[45] The ECtHR has been argued to have an important role in the advancement of substantive equality, considering that it is often seen to take a progressive approach towards condemning gender discrimination and further erosion of gender equality.[46] The case law in this area is discussed throughout the book, specifically in chapter 4 relating to LGBT parenting rights. Additionally, in specific chapters focusing on asylum and family reunification, reference will be made to the vulnerability theory,[47] which seeks to encourage critical reflection of the role of economic,

39 Dianne Otto, 'Queering Gender [Identity] in International Law' (2015) 33(4) Nord J Hum Rts 299, 301.

40 See eg Gonzalez-Salzberg (n 37).

41 Otto, 'Queering' (n 39) 302.

42 Jukka Viljanen, 'The European Court of Human Rights as a Developer of the General Doctrines of Human Rights Law: A Study of the Limitations Clauses of the European Convention on Human Rights' (Tampereen yliopisto 2003) 263. The change of interpretation regarding transgender rights was based partly on the international trend argumentation exemplified in *Christine Goodwin v UK* App no 28957/95 ECHR 2002-VI.

43 Laurence R Helfer and Erik Voeten, 'International Courts as Agents of Legal Change: Evidence from LGBT Rights in Europe' (2014) 68(1) Intl Org 77, 85.

44 Bruce Macdougall, *Queer Judgments: Homosexuality, Expression, and the Courts in Canada* (U Toronto Press 2000) 5 and 7.

45 ibid 5.

46 Isobel Renzulli, 'Discrimination and Gender Stereotypes in Judicial Decisions: The Jurisprudence of the European Court of Human Rights in Light of *JL v Italy*–A Retreat Into The Shadows?' (2023) 41(3) NQHR 155, 173. See also Sandra Fredman, 'Emerging from the Shadows: Substantive Equality and Article 14 of the European Convention on Human Rights' (2016) 16 HRL Rev 273.

47 See Martha Fineman, 'The Vulnerable Subject: Anchoring Equality in the Human Condition' (2008) 20(1) Yale J L & Fem 1, 9.

social, legal, and political systems in rendering some individuals and groups more vulnerable than others.[48]

2.3 Theorising the Court

The ECtHR has been of interest to legal and political science scholars alike. It has been suggested that the more light is shone on the work and output of the Court, namely its case law, the greater the degree of trust placed on it as an institution.[49] In political science scholarship, the international and national courts have been studied through various lenses concerning the limits of judicial power,[50] including the individual justice model and constitutional justice model,[51] as well as the debate focusing on the Court's apparent judicial activism and judicial restraint.[52] Voeten's seminal work from 2007 was the first one its kind to theorise the ECtHR and its work in the context of the question of how transnational judges approach alleged violations of the Convention rights.[53] The two classic approaches of intergovernmentalism and neo-functionalism represent two opposing accounts on the importance of the judiciary in the development of common human rights standards in Europe.[54] In short, neo-functionalists see transnational courts such as the ECtHR as pursuing their own agenda almost independently, whereas for intergovernmentalists the judiciary has no autonomous influence on the evolution of the general standards of human rights protection through judicial interpretation.[55] In their study of the institutional design of international courts, Dunoff and Pollack argue that the design of the court, as a whole, prioritises judicial independence and judicial transparency at the expense of judicial accountability.[56] Their argument is premised on the assumption that judges are only able to prioritise two out of the three values of independence, accountability, and transparency.[57] Consequently, if the ECtHR wanted to prioritise both accountability and independence, its transparency may be affected, for example, through the use of *per curium* decisions where individual judges are not identified through inclusion of separate concurring or

48 Aysel Küçüksu, 'Fineman in Luxembourg: Empirical lessons in asylum seeker vulnerability from the CJEU' (2022) 40(3) NQHR 290.
49 CJS Knight, 'A Court of Specialists: Judicial Behaviour on the UK Supreme Court by Chris Hanretty' (2022) 138(Oct) LQR 684.
50 Ezgi Yildiz, 'A Court with Many Faces: Judicial Characters and Modes of Norm Development in the European Court of Human Rights' (2020) 31(1) EJIL 73.
51 See eg Steven Greer and Andrew Williams, 'Human Rights in the Council of Europe and the EU: Towards "Individual", "Constitutional" or "Institutional" Justice?' (2009) 15 ELJ 462.
52 See eg Pierre Thielbörger, 'Judicial Passivism at the European Court of Human Rights' (2012) 19(3) MJ 341, 345.
53 Erik Voeten, 'The Politics of International Judicial Appointments: Evidence from the European Court of Human Rights' (2007) 61(4) Intl Org 669, 671.
54 Thomas Horsley, 'Reflections on the Role of the Court of Justice as the "Motor" of European integration: Legal Limits to Judicial Lawmaking' (2013) 50(4) CML Rev 931.
55 See eg Fabio Wasserfallen, 'The Judiciary as Legislator? How the European Court of Justice Shapes Policy-Making in the European Union' (2010) 17(8) JEPP 1128, 1131.
56 Jeffrey L Dunoff and Mark A Pollack, 'The Judicial Trilemma' (2017) 111 AJIL 225.
57 ibid 249.

dissenting opinions.[58] Whether these hypotheses are applicable to all areas of the ECtHR is questionable. Çali and Cunningham argue that the ECtHR does not consciously promote transparency because both the judicial selection to the Court and the Court's administration are decidedly non-transparent.[59]

Whereas political scientists have traditionally tried to measure judicial behaviour by generating quantitative analyses of case law to test various hypotheses about judicial decision-making and the behaviour of judges,[60] legal scholars have tried to understand the role of a judge in relation to collegial judgment-writing.[61] Although lawyers often approach statistical analysis of the case law of any court with a considerable degree of scepticism and question the value of such analysis of judicial reasoning, Hanretty has suggested that perhaps the most interesting postulation raising out of theories trying to explain judicial behaviour is the argument that knowing a particular judge's specialisation may be a useful guide to their behaviour on the bench.[62] However, there are also arguments that the specialism of a judge appears to have a strong influence only in a relatively small number of contexts, namely, who sits on the bench in each case and who writes the leading judgment.[63]

2.3.1 Individual Justice Model and Constitutional Model

The functioning of the Court has been explored in the context of two models, the individual justice model and the constitutional model. The idea behind the individual justice model[64] is that the ECtHR's primary function under Article 34 ECHR is to provide a remedy to individual complaints brought before it, regardless of the 'systemic improvements that might be simultaneously generated as a result of the process'.[65] The judgments of the Court are argued to be normative as they ensure that individuals and States act and behave in a manner that is expected of them under the Convention.[66] According to Johnson and Falcetta, this makes the ECtHR a popular destination for individuals because a favourable judgment in the Court

58 ibid 238.

59 Basak Çali and Stewart Cunningham, 'Judicial Self Government and the Sui Generis Case of the European Court of Human Rights' (2018) 19 German LJ 1977.

60 In general, see Chris Guthrie, Andrew J Wistrich and Jeffrey J Rachlinski, 'Judicial Politics and Decisionmaking: A New Approach' (2017) 70(6) Vand L Rev 2051

61 For collegiality of judges of British and Australian courts, see eg Rachel Cahill-O'Callaghan, 'Values and Judicial Difference in the High Court' in Gabrielle Appleby and Andrew Lynch (eds), *The Judge, the Judiciary and the Court: Individual, Collegial and Institutional Judicial Dynamics in Australia* (CUP 2021) 233–256; Alan Paterson, 'Creating a Group Oriented Supreme Court: Lord Neuberger's Legacy' (2021) 28(1) IJLP 107.

62 Chris Hanretty, *A Court of Specialists: Judicial Behaviour on the UK Supreme Court* (OUP 2022) 266.

63 Knight (n 49).

64 Greer and Williams (n 51) 462.

65 Yildiz (n 50) 75. See also Greer and Williams (n 51) 466.

66 Johnson and Falcetta (n 14) 607.

can have widespread effects throughout Europe and beyond. This is because all of the 46 CoE States must ensure that they address the issues that result in a violation of the Convention, with the consequence that the Court's judgments influence the lives of hundreds of millions of people.[67] The obvious downside to the individual justice model within the ECtHR system is that when individual complaints fail in the Court, existing State practices are given considerable legitimacy.[68] Given that the vast majority of complaints to the Court are declared inadmissible or struck out, and, therefore, considered unsuccessful,[69] human rights law can be seen to play an important role in maintaining the *status quo*.[70] This aspect of human rights law, which is rarely explicitly acknowledged, provides States with a powerful rhetorical resource by which to justify the actions they take against individuals or diasporic and minoritised groups.[71]

According to the constitutional model, the Court's primary responsibility is to adjudicate only the most serious human rights breaches.[72] This enables the Court to create a larger and more significant impact in the CoE States.[73] The arguments in this context include those of the right of individual petition overburdens the Court due to the sheer volume of complaints it receives.[74] This is arguably because the ECHR was not originally envisaged to deliver justice to all deserving applicants.[75] Although the CoE has rejected the idea of changing the Court's role to hearing only selected cases of high importance, some changes have been made to the admissibility of individual complaints.[76] Protocol No 14 amended Article 35 ECHR to include the new criterion of making inadmissible all applications where the individual has 'not suffered a significant disadvantage',[77] unless respect for human rights requires an examination of the case.[78] Additionally, Protocol 15 introduced a shorter time-bar on individual applications, reducing the time to four months from six months.[79]

67 ibid.
68 ibid 616.
69 Critics frequently cite as evidence the statistics published by the Court. In 2023, 82 percent of all applications decided by the Court were declared inadmissible or struck out. See eg ECtHR, 'Analysis of Statistics 2023' <https://prd-echr.coe.int/web/echr/statistical-reports> accessed 3 July 2024.
70 Johnson and Falcetta (n 14) 616.
71 ibidJohnson and Falcetta (n 14) 616.
72 Greer and Williams (n 51) 466.
73 Yildiz (n 50) 75; Greer and Williams (n 51) 462.
74 Ichim (n 7) 60.
75 Greer and Williams (n 51) 466.
76 Oddný Mjöll Arnardóttir, 'The Brighton Aftermath and the Changing Role of the European Court of Human Rights' (2018) 9(2) JIDS 223, 226.
77 Protocol No 14 to the Convention for the Protection of Human Rights and Fundamental Freedoms, amending the control system of the Convention (CETS No 194) <https://rm.coe.int/1680083711> accessed 15 August 2024.
78 See Arnardóttir (n 76) 226. See also Protocol No 15 amending the Convention for the Protection of Human Rights and Fundamental Freedoms (CETS No 213) <https://rm.coe.int/1680084831> accessed 15 August 2024.
79 Arnardóttir (n 76) 226.

2.3.2 Judicial Activism versus Judicial Restraint

Former judge of the ECtHR, Françoise Tulkens has argued that the debate on judicial activism versus judicial restraint is often presented as two contradictory and unsatisfactory alternatives between which judges must choose.[80] The judicial activism debate investigates the manner in which the ECtHR generates social and legal change, and whether the Court actively and decisively widens the scope of the Convention rights.[81] In contrast, the judicial restraint debate concerns the extent to which the Court shows deference to the national authorities.[82] This debate is often linked to a discussion about the boundaries of the Court's competence, outlined by the principles of subsidiarity and margin of appreciation.[83] In order to impose on States certain policies and laws or a certain interpretation of the Convention, the Court often emphasises that adopting a dynamic interpretive approach to the ECHR that entails a positive obligation for the State to facilitate certain progressive rights or freedoms and claims of minoritised or diasporic groups.[84] On the one hand, the Court uses the doctrine of living instrument to provide a minimum standard for the protection of human rights in Europe and to bring uniformity in existing national legislation.[85] In essence the doctrine entails that 'the concepts used by the Convention are to be understood in the sense given to them by democratic societies *today*'.[86] The need to interpret the Convention in an evolutive way,[87] considering 'the changes over time and, in particular, present-day conditions',[88] is often misinterpreted as a symbol of judicial activism by the vocal critics of the Court.[89] This frequently leads to the perception that the Court delivers judgments that unnecessarily expand the Convention rights beyond situations envisaged by the drafters of the Convention in the 1950s.[90] Van der Sloot argues that the evolutive interpretation is intended to limit State discretion to adopt national rules and interpretations of the Convention provisions in reference to specific national or cultural traditions.[91]

80 Françoise Tulkens, 'Judicial Activism v Judicial Restraint: Practical Experience of This (False) Dilemma at the European Court of Human Rights' (2022) 3(3) ECHR L Rev 293.

81 Yildiz (n 50) 75.

82 ibid.

83 For commentary on these principles, see eg Marisa Iglesias Vila, 'Subsidiarity, Margin of Appreciation and International Adjudication within a Cooperative Conception of Human Rights' (2017) 15(2) ICON 393; Róbert Spano, 'The Future of the European Court of Human Rights: Subsidiarity, Process-Based Review and the Rule of Law' (2018) 18(3) HRL Rev 473.

84 Bart van der Sloot, 'Between Fact and Fiction: An Analysis of the Case Law on Article 12 ECHR' (2014) 4 CFLQ 397; Christian H Kälin, *Citizenship and Human Rights: From Exclusive and Universal to Global Rights: A New Framework* (Hart 2024) 4.

85 See eg van der Sloot (n 84); Sanja Ivic, *European Identity and Citizenship: Between Modernity and Postmodernity* (Palgrave Macmillan 2016) 9; Kälin (n 84).

86 Tulkens (n 80) 295 (emphasis in original).

87 ibid 297.

88 *Tyrer v UK* 5856/72 (ECtHR, 25 April 1978), para 31.

89 Tulkens (n 80).

90 ibid 297–298.

91 van der Sloot (n 84).

On the other hand, the Court places a large discretion into the hands of the national authorities to interpret and apply the Convention's provisions by emphasising the States' margin of appreciation and the principle of subsidiarity, which are partly based on the respect for democracy.[92] The principle of margin of appreciation will be discussed in more detail in Section 2.4.

2.3.3 Judicial Avoidance

Frequent arguments exist that while supranational courts, such as the ECtHR, are tasked to exercise their judicial role and to resolve disputes before them, they must also be sensitive to the broader political context in which they operate.[93] The criticism against supranational courts is that they are an inappropriate venue for making decisions that have far-reaching influence on the daily life of democratic societies without the participation of the people and local communities whose lives they affect, as their judges do not act in the name of those individuals.[94] It has been argued that the ECtHR has shown itself to be sensitive and receptive to political signals from CoE States.[95] It employs selective avoidance strategies to respond to, or anticipate, State resistance against the national enforcement of its judgments.[96] On the one hand, the ECtHR may avoid ruling on highly political issues in order to prevent a negative public perception.[97] Some of the rationales for this are the aim to preserve the Court's external legitimacy, or to avoid exceeding the scope of authority delegated to it by States.[98] On the other hand, the ECtHR does not shy away from highly controversial or politically sensitive disputes, such as, cases involving the freedom to manifest one's religion under Article 9 ECHR, or due to the anticipated resistance by governments, national courts, or political parties. The ECtHR arguably uses several other avoidance strategies, including so called *ex ante* avoidance mechanisms, which prevent the Court from proceeding to the merits of the case.[99] It may also find that no dispute exists, which enables it to deal with the merits of the complaint and to show deference to the State, such as, by

92 ibid.
93 Jed Odermatt, 'Patterns of Avoidance: Political Questions Before International Courts' (2018) 14(2) Int JLC 221.
94 Spano (n 83) 476.
95 Odermatt (n 93). See also Mikael Rask Madsen, 'Rebalancing European Human Rights: Has the Brighton Declaration Engendered a New Deal on Human Rights in Europe?' (2018) 9(2) JIDS 199.
96 Odermatt (n 93).
97 ibid.
98 Normative theories of the legitimacy of human rights courts often focus on the lack of democratic legitimacy of these institutions. On the normative legitimacy of the ECtHR, see Andreas Føllesdal, 'The Legitimacy of International Human Rights Review: The Case of the European Court of Human Rights' (2009) 40 J Soc Phil 595; Jean-Raul Costa, 'On the Legitimacy of the European Court of Human Rights' Judgments' (2011) 7 EuConst 173; Kanstantsin Dzehtsiarou, *European Consensus and the Legitimacy of the European Court of Human Rights* (CUP 2015).
99 Odermatt (n 93).

modifying the depth of review.[100] According to Odermatt, the Court also uses the doctrine of the margin of appreciation as an avoidance strategy.[101]

2.4 Margin of Appreciation

The doctrine of margin of appreciation plays a role in a significant number of the ECtHR's decisions and judgments.[102] The ECtHR's legal rationale for this doctrine is based on principles relating to subsidiarity and State consensus.[103] It is a key principle adopted with the purpose of granting deference to States' judgments in protecting the Convention rights.[104] Therefore, it plays a significant role in determining whether limitations upon human rights are necessary in a democratic society.[105] Since 2021, the Preamble to the ECHR has included a reference to the doctrine of margin of appreciation and the subsidiarity principle when Article 1 of Protocol No 15 amending the Convention entered into force.[106] The ECtHR has recognised that States enjoy a margin of appreciation in assessing the necessity of their restriction to Convention rights.[107] The Court has offered various reasons justifying State deference.[108] On the one hand, it recognises that CoE States bear the greatest responsibility of human rights protection in Europe, while the ECtHR is tasked with intervening through contentious proceedings once all domestic remedies have been exhausted in accordance with Article 35 ECHR.[109] On the other hand, the Court recognises States' right to legislate in areas where no consensus exists among States, and, therefore, it often considers that national authorities have a better understanding of the prevailing social circumstances and how to handle conflicting situations.[110] Yet, it is widely acknowledged that the Court's approach to the margin of appreciation is conflicting.[111]

Fenton-Glynn convincingly argues that granting a wide margin of appreciation, especially in areas where States disagree, leads to a slow evolution of progressive understanding of human rights.[112] In her opinion, this has often meant that the

100 ibid.
101 ibid.
102 James A Sweeney, 'Margin of Appreciation in the Internal Market: Lessons from the European Court of Human Rights' (2007) 34(1) Legal Iss Econ Integ 27, 30.
103 Helga Molbæk-Steensig, 'Subsidiarity Does Not Win Cases: A Mixed Methods Study of the Relationship Between Margin of Appreciation Language and Deference at the European Court of Human Rights' (2023) 36(1) LJIL 83.
104 Iglesias Vila (n 83) 406.
105 Sweeney (n 102) 30.
106 ECtHR, 'Protocol No. 15 to the European Convention on Human Rights enters into force' (14 September 2021) <www.coe.int/en/web/podgorica/-/protocol-no-15-to-the-european-convention-on-human-rights-enters-into-force> accessed 5 April 2024.
107 Sweeney (n 102) 30.
108 Iglesias Vila (n 83) 406.
109 ibid.
110 ibid.
111 van der Sloot (n 84).
112 Claire Fenton-Glynn, *Family Formation and Parenthood* (OUP 2020).

Court has rarely been at the forefront of European human rights protection and it has advanced case law only after States have already taken the lead.[113] Radcic has criticised the Court for adopting an inconsistent definition of the term European consensus.[114] A related argument here is that the ECtHR interprets the ECHR in light of the right of each State to democratically determine what regulations meet its standards in light of its 'distinct cultural and legal background' and 'human rights principles'.[115] Similarly, it has been recognised that the ECHR is not aimed at ensuring primary protection, but this is the role of national courts.[116] Therefore, the ECtHR derives its institutional legitimacy from State Parties accepting, and appropriately implementing, its judgments.[117]

The Court has repeatedly noted that while the national legislature enjoys a wide margin of appreciation in some areas, in other areas the States' margin for appreciation is limited and it also varies according to the sensitivity of the issue.[118] Mulligan notes that a narrow margin of appreciation means that the CoE States enjoy limited discretion while acting in the area of a Convention right, meaning that the Court will tolerate only minimal interference with the right, and require a high degree of justification for such interference.[119] A broad margin of appreciation, by contrast, means that the CoE State will enjoy a broader discretion in relation to the Convention right, allowing it more scope for interference with the right and for justification of such interference.[120]

Critics have tended to point to the incoherent application of the doctrine of margin of appreciation, especially in relation to the case law concerning LGBT rights, violence against women, reproductive and sexual rights, and recognition of trans

113 ibid.

114 The legal scholarship of the doctrine of European Consensus is extensive. See eg Panos Kapotas and Vassilis P Tzevelekos, 'How (Difficult Is It) To Build Consensus on (European) Consensus?' in Panos Kapotas and Vassilis P Tzevelekos (eds), *Building Consensus on European Consensus: Judicial Interpretation of Human Rights in Europe and Beyond* (CUP 2019).

115 George (n 5) 335.

116 Eleanor Spaventa, 'A Very Fearful Court? The Protection of Fundamental Rights in the European Union after Opinion 2/13' (2015) 22 MJ 1 35, 38. For commentary between the dialogue of the ECtHR and national courts, see Johanna Rinceanu, 'Judicial Dialogue between the European Court of Human Rights and National Supreme Courts' in CD Spinellis and others (eds), 'Europe in Crisis: Crime, Criminal Justice, and the Way Forward. Essays in Honour of Nestor Courakis' (Ant N Sakkoulas 2017) 1029.

117 Peter Dunne, 'Who Is a Parent and Who Is a Child in a Same-Sex Family? Legislative and Judicial Issues for LGBT Families Post-Separation, Part I: The European Perspective' (2017) 30 Journal of the American Academy of Matrimonial Lawyers 27. More on implementing the judgments, see Dia Anagnostou, *The European Court of Human Rights: Implementing Strasbourg's Judgments on Domestic Policy* (Edinburgh UP 2013).

118 See eg *Alajos Kiss v Hungary* App no 38832/06 (ECtHR, 20 May 2010) (The Court did not accept that an absolute bar on voting by any person under partial guardianship, irrespective of his or her actual faculties, fell within an acceptable margin of appreciation).

119 Andrea Mulligan, 'Identity Rights and Sensitive Ethical Questions: The European Convention on Human Rights and the Regulation of Surrogacy Arrangements' (2018) 26(3) Med L Rev 449, 454.

120 ibid.

rights.[121] Case law has been further subject to scholarly criticism as the Court has argued to treat similar facts in a case from a different State differently.[122] The Court has been particularly criticised for using the principle of margin of appreciation for making it more difficult to generalise the legal answers of the Court, for provoking structural incoherence, and for endangering legal certainty and preventing the ECHR from consolidating a reliable system of human rights protection in Europe.[123] According to Greer, the application of the principle has been 'casuistic, uneven and largely unpredictable'.[124] This is problematic when it results in a situation that the case law does not guarantee consistent rights for individuals in the CoE as a whole. Although the ECHR contains no doctrine of binding precedent, when confronted with the same issue again in a different CoE State, the Court is expected to interpret and apply the ECHR in the same manner once it has already ruled on a particular issue.[125] One explanation for different outcomes in the Court's case law centres around arguments that it is common for the Court to reach different conclusions for similar issues in different CoE States because it makes decisions on a case-by-case basis.[126] When the Court makes its decision, it examines the conditions of each State, including the relevant legislation, societal views, and morals of the time.[127] Additionally, due to the application of the principle of margin of appreciation, the Court is extremely cautious in overstepping the State discretion.[128]

Although the Court may sometimes be faced with novel issues in its case law, it tends to favour dynamic interpretation of the Convention.[129] There are different opinions as to what extent the Court deals with novel questions of law in its jurisprudence. Although the case law of the ECtHR is vast,[130] according to the former President of the ECtHR, Róbert Spano, in many areas the case law is close to well

121 See eg Ivana Radacic, 'The Margin of Appreciations, Consensus, Morality and the Rights of Vulnerable Groups' (2010) 31 Zb Prav Fak Sveuc Rij 599, 606; Paul Johnson, *Homosexuality and the European Court of Human Rights* (Routledge 2012) 69–70; Odermatt (n 93).

122 See eg George (n 5).

123 Jeremy Letwin, 'Why Completeness and Coherence Matter for the European Court of Human Rights' (2021) 2(1) ECHR L Rev 119.

124 Steven Greer, 'The Interpretation of the European Convention on Human Rights: Universal Principle or Margin of Appreciation?' (2010) 3 UCL Hum Rts Rev 1, 3.

125 This idea reflects the principle of *res interpretata*. See Oddný Mjöll Arnardóttir, '*Res Intepretata, Erga Omnes* Effect and the Role of the Margin of Appreciation in Giving Domestic Effect to the Judgments of the European Court of Human Rights' (2017) 28 EJIL 819, 823–824.

126 George (n 5) 332.

127 Viljanen (n 42); Kristin D Brudy, '*SH v Austria*: European Court of Human Rights Holds that the Rights to Family Life and Sexism Trump Governmental Limitations on Artificial Procreation' (2011) 19 Tul J Intl & Comp L 691, 697–698.

128 George (n 5) 335; Francesca Romana Ammaturo, 'The Council of Europe and the Creation of LGBT Identities Through Language and Discourse: A Critical Analysis of Case Law and Institutional Practices' (2019) 23(4) IJHR 575, 578.

129 Henriette Jakobien Liesker, 'Caught in a Balancing Act: The European Court of Human Rights and the Road to Recognition for Sexual Minorities' (2017) 4(3) Oslo L Rev 172, 183.

130 Erik Voeten, 'Gender and Judging: Evidence from the European Court of Human Rights' (2020) JEPP 1453.

established, at least as regards the general principles.[131] Additionally, considering that from the late 1970s onwards the Court has been called on to formulate the general principles for the interpretation of almost all Convention rights,[132] in his opinion, it is relatively rare that a complaint brought to its attention confronts the judges of the ECtHR with truly novel questions of the ECHR.[133] Ichim has argued that although the Court is sometimes confronted with novel fields of law which call for an application of the guarantees within the Convention in new areas, it addressed those with the mindset that its case law evolves in line with the changes in society.[134] This indicates that some scholars are much more optimistic of the evolvement of the case law of the Court, whereas others are more critical and expect the Court to take a more proactive role.

2.5 The Reach beyond a Single Case?

Disagreement exists among scholars whether the judgments of the ECtHR are legally binding only on the parties to a particular dispute in accordance with the international law principle of *inter partes*, without being binding on other CoE States. According to Article 46(1) ECHR, the States' Parties to the Convention 'undertake to abide by the final judgment of the Court in any case to which they are parties'.[135] Therefore, the Court's case law is generally thought to be binding only on the respondent State under this provision. The argument is that the intention of the drafters of the Convention was to provide the States with discretion as to how to implement the Court's judgments in their national legal systems.[136] Because of this, the ECtHR has frequently tended to articulate interpretations only to the extent strictly necessary for the decision of a particular case.[137] Anagnostou argues that the way in which the Court confines its judgments to the specific conditions of each individual case creates an uncertainty as to how the legal norms highlighted in one case can be extended across other cases.[138] This is a challenge because it suggests that the impact of the Court's judgments is limited outside a single case. The narrow construction of a particular judgment also obscures the implications for broader and speedy legislative and policy change.[139]

131 Spano (n 83) 476.
132 ibid.
133 ibid.
134 Ichim (n 7) 53.
135 Gillis (n 9) 68.
136 Rinceanu (n 116) 1039. See also Rafaella Kunz, 'Judging International Judgments Anew? The Human Rights Courts before Domestic Courts' (2020) 30 EJIL 1129, 1133; Dzehtsiarou, 'The United Kingdom' (n 3); ECtHR, European Court of Human Rights: 'The ECHR in 50 Questions' (2014) point 38, 9 <www.echr.coe.int/Documents/50Questions_ENG.pdf> accessed 6 April 2022.
137 See Paul Mahoney, 'Judicial Activism and Judicial Self-Restraint in the European Court of Human Rights: Two Sides of the Same Coin' (1990) 11 HRLJ 87.
138 Anagnostou (n 117) 724.
139 ibid.

Other scholars argue that it has long been accepted that the ECtHR's case law reaches across all of the CoE States due to the interpretative authority of the *erga omnes partes* effects in the context of international courts.[140] There are also opinions that rather than having an *erga omnes* effect, many of the Court's rulings are intended to have such an effect.[141] This is because according to the principles of international law, State Parties to the ECHR accept the ECtHR's jurisdiction and agree to comply with specific judgments against them after ratifying the Convention.[142] The ECtHR itself has stated that although the primary purpose of the system created by the ECHR is to provide individual relief, its mission is also to determine issues on public-policy grounds in the common interest, thereby raising the general standards of human rights protection and 'extending human rights jurisprudence throughout the community of Convention States'.[143] Yet, in practice, the case law of the ECtHR has often had *erga omnes* effects, leading national legislators to proactively and voluntarily liberalise laws and policies in response to the Court's rulings against other CoE States.[144]

Due to the applicability of the *erga omnes* effects, the CoE argue that to establish standards which appear as purely voluntary at first but, in fact, 'can become effectively authoritative in ways that are similar to national decision-making'.[145] Therefore, the binding effect of the ECtHR's judgments on CoE States beyond the dispute can often be a surprise to the States.[146] This arises from the fact that by its interpretation of the Convention rights, the ECtHR often imposes more specific obligations upon the CoE States than they may have initially anticipated.[147] With the benefit of hindsight, States may sometimes feel they would not necessarily have consented to be bound by its judgments resulting from litigation in which they did not participate.[148] However, it can also be argued that this is the nature of litigation and legal interpretation, whether conducted by a supranational or national court.

In this context, scholarly commentary concerning national governments' reception of judgments of the ECtHR may be useful. Scholars have noted that the Court's case law increasingly concerns the quality of national judicial and democratic decision-making processes.[149] Therefore, the ECtHR's judgments are expected to prompt some form of response from governments. Even though the

140 See eg Arnardóttir, '*Res Interpretata*' (n 125).
141 Helfer and Voeten (n 43).
142 ibid.
143 *Karner v Austria* App no 40016/98 (ECtHR, 24 July 2003), para 26.
144 Laurence R Helfer and Clare Ryan, 'LGBT Rights as Mega-Politics: Litigating before the ECtHR' (2021) 84 LCP 59, 70.
145 Wojciech Sadurski, 'Supranational Public Reason: On Legitimacy of Supranational Norm-producing Authorities' (2015) 4 Global Constitutionalism 396, 397.
146 ibid 413.
147 ibid.
148 Helfer and Voeten (n 43); Sadurski (n 145) 413.
149 Arnardóttir, '*Res Interpretata*' (n 125) 822. See also Janneke Gerards, 'Procedural Review by the ECtHR: A Typology' in Janneke H Gerards and Eva Brems (eds), *Procedural Review in European Fundamental Rights Cases* (CUP 2017) 127.

ECHR has sometimes been described as a 'constitutional instrument of European public order',[150] the ECtHR's mandate is limited to declaring whether or not specific Convention rights have been breached.[151] Consequently, it does not have the power to declare national law inconsistent with the Convention rights or to tell the States what action they should take to rectify a breach of the Convention.[152] Nor does the Court have the direct authority to implement its judgments.[153] Consequently, the capacity of its jurisprudence to act as a mechanism whereby the Court is able to exert its control on national governments depends upon the effectiveness of the execution of its judgments at the national level.[154] The Court may be able to influence actors who have the capacity to implement its judgments, such as, national courts, executives, and international organisations.[155] In reality, this means that States have a certain level of discretion in how to implement the Court's judgments and choose the means to rectify the breaches.[156] According to Gillis, national legislatures and courts can choose to ignore or disregard the judgment and the reasoning of the ECtHR.[157] Although the Court's case law has 'a direct relevance for the courts of the signatory States',[158] it is not automatically binding on all the CoE States as each national legal system determines the extent to which international law is applicable in the legal system in question.[159] Despite this, the Court's case law has had an important influence on human rights in several CoE States.[160] Dzehtsiarou and Schwartz note that the Court does have the power to award monetary compensation for breaches of Convention rights and it can invite offending States to amend their laws accordingly.[161]

The extent to which the Court's jurisprudence truly influences State behaviour and policy change is consequently uncertain.[162] Anagnostou points out that variable implementation of general measures by national authorities in response to its judgments does not lead to reform and change in areas of law and policy, or to the expansion of protection and rights of individuals and groups whose rights the ECHR is designed to protect.[163] Consequently, individuals and groups beyond a

150 *Loizidou v Turkey* App no 15318/89 (ECtHR, 23 March 1995), para 75.

151 Greer and Williams (n 51) 464.

152 ibid.

153 Johnson and Falcetta (n 14) 607.

154 ibid.

155 Helfer and Voeten (n 43) 80.

156 Alison L Young, *Democratic Dialogue and the Constitution* (OUP 2017) 259; Dzehtsiarou, 'The United Kingdom' (n 3).

157 Gillis (n 9) 68.

158 Kerry O'Halloran, *The Politics of Adoption* (Springer 2021) 123.

159 Gillis (n 9) 68; Kunz (n 136) 1133. See also European Court of Human Rights, European Court of Human Rights: 'The ECHR in 50 Questions' (2014) point 38, 9 <www.echr.coe.int/Documents/50Questions_ENG.pdf> accessed 6 April 2022.

160 Kanstantsin Dzehtsiarou and Alex Schwartz, 'Electing Team Strasbourg: Professional Diversity on the European Court of Human Rights and Why it Matters' (2020) 21(4) German LJ 621.

161 ibid.

162 Helfer and Voeten (n 43) 85.

163 Anagnostou (n 117) 724.

particular case would not necessarily be aware of their rights. This could, at least partly, explain why it takes such a long time for the ECtHR's judgments to make a difference to the lives of hundreds of millions of people living in the CoE States. Other scholars confidently assert that it is unquestionably true that many national laws have been amended as a result of the Court's case law,[164] while others note more cautiously that some evidence suggests that issues, which have been previously excluded from the legislative agenda, may be given priority when lawmakers realise that their own laws may not survive a future challenge before the ECtHR.[165] Similarly, national courts have several options to comply with the judgment of the ECtHR. They may revisit their own case law to pre-empt future litigation before the ECtHR.[166] They can, for instance, adjust their own interpretation of the law to that of the ECtHR; reopen final domestic judicial proceedings following a judgment of the ECtHR; order the executive to implement the judgment of the Court; and disapply, or even quash, legislation that violates the Convention,[167] even though this may not happen so often in the case of the ECtHR.[168] In practice, national courts frequently take a more reticent stance, displaying the will to maintain at least a certain oversight over the effects of the rulings of the ECtHR in the national legal order.[169] In contrast, in some countries, the influence of national actors and institutions that implement the Court's judgments could be too weak to overcome local resistance to change.[170] Greer and Williams argue that surprisingly, human rights violations are persistent in some of the Western European CoE States.[171] These States have shown enormous resilience to change, considering that they were among the first States to become signatories to the Convention.[172]

In addition to having a significant impact in the CoE States, there is evidence that several courts in non-European jurisdictions, particularly many English-speaking countries, increasingly rely on the jurisprudence of the ECtHR in the context of their own judgments concerning human rights.[173] Çalý notes that the ECtHR 'enjoys authority outside Europe as evidenced by the citations and references it receives globally in legal and political practice'.[174] Although the reasons explaining why courts may choose to cite foreign judgments are varied, it has been suggested that some of the likely explanations include the long-standing democratic

164 Greer and Williams (n 51) 468.
165 Helfer and Voeten (n 43) 82.
166 ibid.
167 Kunz (n 136) 1139.
168 Elisabeth Lambert-Abdelgawad, *The Execution of Judgments of the European Court of Human Rights: No. 19 (Human Rights Files)* (2nd edn, Council of Europe 2008) 18–24.
169 Kunz (n 136) 1143.
170 Helfer and Voeten (n 43) 83.
171 Greer and Williams (n 51) 468.
172 ibid.
173 Tania Groppi and Marie-Claire Ponthoreau (eds), *The Use of Foreign Precedents by Constitutional Judges* (Hart 2013) 420.
174 Baþak Çalý, 'Does the Practice of the European Convention on Human Rights Fit the Practical Conception of Human Rights?' (2024) 24(1) HRL Rev 1, 2.

and human rights-oriented traditions of European countries, the accessibility of the ECtHR's jurisprudence due to common language and the area of human rights law, which is perceived more fertile soil for external reference.[175] Helfer and Voeten argue that citizens and elites can be swayed by the fact that a national policy is inconsistent with human rights when that information comes from a source that is perceived to have expertise that has changed laws and policies following ECtHR judgments against other countries.[176] Strikingly the explicit citations of foreign precedents by courts are generally limited to a handful of countries in the English-speaking world.[177] One reason for this could be similar cultural and legal features and the lack of linguistic and cultural barriers.[178] The acceptance of the ECtHR's judgments and reasoning outside Europe indicates that it has, in some instances, been perceived as a leading human rights court globally.

2.6 Conclusion

The perceived inadequacies in the case law of the ECtHR are at odds with the Court's seeming role at the forefront of societal changes in numerous areas, including LGBT rights, intersectional discrimination, and violence against women.[179] There is frequent criticism that the Court has been too slow to react to many societal changes, especially to do with the recognition of the rights of the LGBT community.[180] Not only do some of the Court's judgments leave a broad margin of appreciation to State authorities, but they may also leave a wide space for contestation and conflicting views as to the ways in which the recurrence of similar injustices is to be avoided in the future.[181] The fact that the judgments of the Court do not frequently lead to the issues being solved is a significant problem in some CoE States in relation to various areas, including national authorities' gender bias in cases concerning headscarf bans, racial discrimination, and violence against women (chapter 4); second parent adoption and surrogacy (chapter 5); gendered asylum (chapter 6); and family reunification (chapter 7). It has been argued that approximately 60 percent of the Court's judgments concern complaints about the same or similar violations that the Court has already condemned in the respondent State.[182] Therefore, the limited impact outside a particular case is an unfortunate downside of a human rights protection system created by the ECHR.[183]

175 Suzie Navot, 'Israel: Creating A Constitution: The Use of Foreign Precedents by the Supreme Court (1994–2010)' in Groppi and Ponthoreau (n 173) 132–133.
176 Helfer and Voeten (n 43) 82. They note, for instance, that following an ECtHR ruling against the UK's blanket ban on prisoner voting, the Irish Parliament quickly adopted legislation to allow prisoners to vote by mail.
177 Groppi and Ponthoreau (n 173) 422.
178 ibid 420.
179 Helfer and Voeten (n 43) 85.
180 ibid.
181 Anagnostou (n 117) 724.
182 Greer and Williams (n 51) 468.
183 ibid.

Additionally, as it has been pointed out that most breaches of the Convention rights never reach the ECtHR, but they are often the subject of domestic legal proceedings.[184] Consequently, it is even more important for the ECtHR to adopt a progressive interpretation of the Convention rights. There may be many more human rights violations that go undetected and never attract the attention of the authorities or courts because of the way in which human rights protection is enacted. Scholars have criticised the Court for taking an inconsistent approach to some issues it deals with. In particular, the case law has been criticised for taking an inconsistent approach towards the margin afforded to the respondent State. Indeed, the clarity and consistency in the Court's jurisprudence have been argued to be extremely important for the Court's ability to maintain its legitimacy and status as a significant promoter of common human rights standards in Europe.[185] This is of particular importance as the Court's rulings have had important effects in the development of consistent human rights standards in Europe, as CoE States with different legal systems may have varied understandings of human rights,[186] including rights that impact women and minoritised and diasporic groups.

References

Ahmed S, 'Orientations: Towards a Queer Phenomenology' (2006) 12(4) GLQ: J Lesbian and Gay Stud 543.

Ammaturo FR, 'The Council of Europe and the Creation of LGBT Identities Through Language and Discourse: A Critical Analysis of Case Law and Institutional Practices' (2019) 23(4) IJHR 575.

Anagnostou A, *The European Court of Human Rights: Implementing Strasbourg's Judgments on Domestic Policy* (Edinburgh UP 2013).

Arnardóttir OM, 'The Brighton Aftermath and the Changing Role of the European Court of Human Rights' (2018) 9(2) JIDS 223.

Arnardóttir OM, 'Cross-fertilisation, Clarity and Consistency at an Overburdened European Court of Human Rights: The Case of the Discrimination Grounds under Article 14 ECHR' (2015) 33(3) Nord J Hum Rts 220.

Arnardóttir OM, '*Res Intepretata, Erga Omnes* Effect and the Role of the Margin of Appreciation in Giving Domestic Effect to the Judgments of the European Court of Human Rights' (2017) 28 EJIL 819.

Arold N-L, 'The European Court of Human Rights as an Example of Convergence' (2007) 76(2/3) Nord J Hum Rts 305.

Atrey S and Dunne P (eds), *Intersectionality and Human Rights Law* (Hart 2020).

Blackburn R and Polakiewicz J (eds), *Fundamental Rights in Europe: The European Convention on Human Rights and its Member States, 1950-2000* (OUP 2001).

Bond JE, 'International Intersectionality: A Theoretical and Pragmatic Exploration of Women's International Human Rights Violations' (2003) 52 Emory LJ 71.

Browne K and Nash CJ (eds), *Queer Methods and Methodologies: Intersecting Queer Theories and Social Science Research* (Routledge 2010).

184 O'Halloran (n 158) 123.

185 Arnardóttir, 'Cross-fertilisation' (n 3) 221.

186 Voeten, 'The Politics' (n 53) 674; Greer and Williams (n 51) 468.

Brudy KD, '*SH v Austria*: European Court of Human Rights Holds that the Rights to Family Life and Sexism Trump Governmental Limitations on Artificial Procreation' (2011) 19 Tul J Intl & Comp L 691.
Cahill-O'Callaghan R, 'Values and Judicial Difference in the High Court' in Appleby G and Lynch A (eds), *The Judge, the Judiciary and the Court: Individual, Collegial and Institutional Judicial Dynamics in Australia* (CUP 2021).
Cain PA, 'Feminist Jurisprudence: Grounding the Theories' (1989-1990) 4 Berkeley Women's L J 191.
Çali B and Cunningham S, 'Judicial Self Government and the Sui Generis Case of the European Court of Human Rights' (2018) 19 German LJ 1977.
Çalý B, 'Does the Practice of the European Convention on Human Rights Fit the Practical Conception of Human Rights?' (2024) 24(1) HRL Rev 1.
Conaghan J, 'Some Reflections on Law and Gender in Modern Ireland' (2019) 27(3) Fem LS 333.
Costa JP, 'On the Legitimacy of the European Court of Human Rights' Judgments' (2011) 7 EuConst 173.
Dunne P, 'Who Is a Parent and Who Is a Child in a Same-Sex Family? Legislative and Judicial Issues for LGBT Families Post-Separation, Part I: The European Perspective' (2017) 30 J Am Acad Matrimonial Law 27.
Dunoff JL and Pollack MA, 'The Judicial Trilemma' (2017) 111 AJIL 225.
Dyevre A, Wijtvliet W, and Lampach N, 'The Future of European Legal Scholarship: Empirical Jurisprudence' (2019) 26(3) MJ 348.
Dzehtsiarou K, 'The United Kingdom and the European Convention on Human Rights: Together Until the End?' (2024) 5(1) ECHR L Rev 1.
Dzehtsiarou K and Schwartz A, 'Electing Team Strasbourg: Professional Diversity on the European Court of Human Rights and Why it Matters' (2020) 21(4) German LJ 621.
Dzehtsiarou K and Schwartz A, *European Consensus and the Legitimacy of the European Court of Human Rights* (CUP 2015).
Fenton-Glynn C, *Family Formation and Parenthood* (OUP 2020).
Fineman M, 'The Vulnerable Subject: Anchoring Equality in the Human Condition' (2008) 20(1) Yale J L & Fem 1.
Føllesdal A, 'The Legitimacy of International Human Rights Review: The Case of the European Court of Human Rights' (2009) 40 J Soc Phil 595.
Fredman S, 'Emerging from the Shadows: Substantive Equality and Article 14 of the European Convention on Human Rights' (2016) 16 HRL Rev 273.
George M, 'Using the European Court of Human Rights to Expand Access to In Vitro Fertilization for Straight Women and Lesbian Couples in Europe' (2021) 53(2) Geo Wash Intl L Rev 321.
Gerards J, 'Procedural Review by the ECtHR: A Typology' in Gerards JH and Brems E (eds), *Procedural Review in European Fundamental Rights Cases* (CUP 2017).
Gillis M, 'Can We Talk? The Application of the Public Law Democratic Dialogue Model to the Interactions between Domestic Legislatures and the European Courts' (2022) 23 German LJ 56.
Gonzalez-Salzberg D, 'An Improved Protection for the (Mentally Ill) Trans Parent: A Queer Reading of *AP, Garçon and Nicot v France*' (2018) 81(3) MLR 526.
Gonzalez-Salzberg D and Hodson L, *Research Methods for International Human Rights Law: Beyond the Traditional Paradigm* (Routledge 2019).
Gonzalez-Salzberg D and Hodson L, *Sexuality and Transsexuality under the European Convention on Human Rights* (Hart 2019).
Greer S, 'The Interpretation of the European Convention on Human Rights: Universal Principle or Margin of Appreciation?' (2010) 3 UCL Hum Rts Rev 1.
Greer S and Williams A, 'Human Rights in the Council of Europe and the EU: Towards 'Individual', 'Constitutional' or 'Institutional' Justice?' (2009) 15 ELJ 462.

Grey R, McLoughlin K and Chappell L, 'Gender and Judging at the International Criminal Court: Lessons from "Feminist Judgment Projects"' (2021) 34(1) LJIL 247.

Groppi T and Ponthoreau M-C (eds), *The Use of Foreign Precedents by Constitutional Judges* (Hart 2013).

Guthrie C, Wistrich AJ, and Rachlinski JJ, 'Judicial Politics and Decisionmaking: A New Approach' (2017) 70(6) Vand L Rev 2051.

Hanretty C, *A Court of Specialists: Judicial Behaviour on the UK Supreme Court* (OUP 2022).

Harris A, 'Race and Essentialism in Feminist Legal Theory' (1990) 42 Stan L Rev 581.

Helfer LR and Ryan C, 'LGBT Rights as Mega-Politics: Litigating before the ECtHR' (2021) 84 LCP 59.

Helfer LR and Voeten E, 'International Courts as Agents of Legal Change: Evidence from LGBT Rights in Europe' (2014) 68(1) Intl Org 77.

Hodson L, 'A Feminist Approach to *Alyne da Silva Pimentel Teixeira (Deceased) v Brazil*' in Gonzalez-Salzberg D and Hodson L, *Research Methods for International Human Rights Law: Beyond the Traditional Paradigm* (Routledge 2019).

Horsley T, 'Reflections on the Role of the Court of Justice as the "Motor" of European Integration: Legal limits to Judicial Lawmaking' (2013) 50(4) CML Rev 931.

Hutchinson T, *Researching and Writing in Law* (2nd edn, Lawbook Co 2006).

Ichim O, *Just Satisfaction Under the European Convention on Human Rights* (CUP 2015).

Iglesias Vila M, 'Subsidiarity, Margin of Appreciation and International Adjudication within a Cooperative Conception of Human Rights' (2017) 15(2) ICON 393.

Ivic S, *European Identity and Citizenship: Between Modernity and Postmodernity* (Palgrave Macmillan 2016).

Johnson P, *Homosexuality and the European Court of Human Rights* (Routledge 2012).

Johnson P and Falcetta S, 'Human Rights Law as Social Control' (2021) 18(4) EJC 603.

Kälin CH, *Citizenship and Human Rights: From Exclusive and Universal to Global Rights: A New Framework* (Hart 2024).

Kapotas P and Tzevelekos VP, 'How (Difficult Is It) to Build Consensus on (European) Consensus?' in Kapotas P and Tzevelekos VP (eds), *Building Consensus on European Consensus: Judicial Interpretation of Human Rights in Europe and Beyond* (CUP 2019).

Kapur R, 'The Tragedy of Victimisation Rhetoric: Resurrecting the "Native" Subject in International/Postcolonial Feminist Legal Politics' (2002) 15 Harv Hum Rts J 1.

Kline M, 'Race, Racism, and Feminist Legal Theory' (1989) 12 Harv Women's L J 115.

Knight CJS, 'A Court of Specialists: Judicial Behaviour on the UK Supreme Court by Chris Hanretty' (2022) 138(Oct) LQR 684.

Küçüksu A, 'Fineman in Luxembourg: Empirical Lessons in Asylum Seeker Vulnerability From the CJEU' (2022) 40(3) NQHR 290.

Kunz R, 'Judging International Judgments Anew? The Human Rights Courts before Domestic Courts' (2020) 30 EJIL 1129.

Lambert-Abdelgawad E, *The Execution of Judgments of the European Court of Human Rights* (2nd edn, Council of Europe Human Rights Files No. 19 2008).

Lando M, 'Secret Custom or the Impact of Judicial Deliberations on the Identification of Customary International Law' (2022) 81 CLJ 1.

Letwin J, 'Why Completeness and Coherence Matter for the European Court of Human Rights' (2021) 2(1) ECHR L Rev 119.

Liesker HJ, 'Caught in a Balancing Act: The European Court of Human Rights and the Road to Recognition for Sexual Minorities' (2017) 4(3) Oslo L Rev 172.

Macdougall B, *Queer Judgments: Homosexuality, Expression, and the Courts in Canada* (U Toronto Press 2000).

Madsen MR, 'Rebalancing European Human Rights: Has the Brighton Declaration Engendered a New Deal on Human Rights in Europe?' (2018) 9(2) JIDS 199.

Mahoney P, 'Judicial Activism and Judicial Self-Restraint in the European Court of Human Rights: Two Sides of the Same Coin' (1990) 11 HRLJ 87.
McConville M and Chui WH, *Research Methods for Law* (Edinburgh UP 2017).
Mohanty CT, 'Under Western Eyes: Feminist Scholarship and Colonial Discourses' in Mohanty CT, Russo A and Torres L (eds), *Third World Women and the Politics of Feminism* (Indiana UP 1991).
Molbæk-Steensig H, 'Subsidiarity Does Not Win Cases: A Mixed Methods Study of the Relationship Between Margin of Appreciation Language and Deference at the European Court of Human Rights' (2023) 36(1) LJIL 83.
Mulligan A, 'Identity Rights and Sensitive Ethical Questions: The European Convention on Human Rights and the Regulation of Surrogacy Arrangements' (2018) 26(3) Med L Rev 449.
Navot S, 'Israel: Creating A Constitution: The Use of Foreign Precedents by the Supreme Court (1994-2010)' in Groppi T and Ponthoreau M-C (eds), *The Use of Foreign Precedents by Constitutional Judges* (Hart 2013).
O'Halloran K, *The Politics of Adoption* (Springer 2021).
Odermatt J, 'Patterns of Avoidance: Political Questions before International Courts' (2018) 14(2) Int JLC 221.
Otto D, 'Between Pleasure and Danger: Lesbian Human Rights' (2014) 19(6) EHRLR 618.
Otto D, 'Queering Gender [Identity] in International Law' (2015) 33(4) Nord J Hum Rts 299.
Paterson A, 'Creating a Group Oriented Supreme Court: Lord Neuberger's Legacy' (2021) 28(1) IJLP 107.
Peroni L, 'Age and gender discrimination: laudable anti-stereotyping reasoning in *Carvalho Pinto v Portugal*' (*Strasbourg Observers*, 28 September 2017) <https://strasbourgobservers.com/2017/09/28/age-and-gender-discrimination-laudable-anti-stereotyping-reasoning-in-carvalho-pinto-v-portugal/> accessed 5 April 2024.
Radacic I, 'The Margin of Appreciations, Consensus, Morality and the Rights of Vulnerable Groups' (2010) 31 Zb Prav Fak Sveuc Rij 599.
Renzulli I, 'Discrimination and Gender Stereotypes in Judicial Decisions: The Jurisprudence of the European Court of Human Rights in Light of *JL v Italy*–A Retreat Into The Shadows?' (2023) 41(3) NQHR 155.
Rinceanu J, 'Judicial Dialogue between the European Court of Human Rights and National Supreme Courts' in Spinellis DC and others (eds), *Europe in Crisis: Crime, Criminal Justice, and the Way Forward. Essays in Honour of Nestor Courakis* (Ant N Sakkoulas 2017).
Rolandsen Agustín L, *Gender Equality, Intersectionality, and Diversity in Europe.* (Palgrave Macmillan 2013).
Sadurski W, 'Supranational Public Reason: On Legitimacy of Supranational Norm-producing Authorities' (2015) 4 Global Constitutionalism 396.
Sharpe A, 'Queering Judgment: The Case of Gender Identity Fraud' (2017) 81(5) JCL 417.
Spade D, *Normal Life: Administrative Violence, Critical Trans Politics, and the Limits of Law* (Duke UP 2015).
Spano R, 'The Future of the European Court of Human Rights: Subsidiarity, Process-Based Review and the Rule of Law' (2018) 18(3) HRL Rev 473.
Spaventa E, 'A Very Fearful Court? The Protection of Fundamental Rights in the European Union after Opinion 2/13' (2015) 22 MJ 1 35.
Sweeney JA, 'Margin of Appreciation in the Internal Market: Lessons from the European Court of Human Rights' (2007) 34(1) Legal Iss Econ Integ 27.
Thielbörger P, 'Judicial Passivism at the European Court of Human Rights' (2012) 19(3) MJ 341.
van der Sloot B, 'Between Fact and Fiction: An Analysis of the Case Law on Article 12 ECHR' (2014) 4 CFLQ 397.

Viljanen J, *The European Court of Human Rights as a Developer of the General Doctrines of Human Rights Law: A Study of the Limitations Clauses of the European Convention on Human Rights* (Tampereen yliopisto 2003).
Voeten E, 'Gender and Judging: Evidence from the European Court of Human Rights' (2021) 28 JEPP 1453.
Voeten E, 'The Politics of International Judicial Appointments: Evidence from the European Court of Human Rights' (2007) 61(4) Intl Org 669.
Wasserfallen F, 'The Judiciary as Legislator? How the European Court of Justice Shapes Policy-Making in the European Union' (2010) 17(8) JEPP 1128.
Watkins D and Burton M, *Research Methods in Law* (Routledge 2013).
Wessels J, *The Concealment Controversy: Sexual Orientation, Discretion Reasoning and the Scope of Refugee Protection* (CUP 2021).
Yildiz E, 'A Court with Many Faces: Judicial Characters and Modes of Norm Development in the European Court of Human Rights' (2020) 31(1) EJIL 73.
Young AL, *Democratic Dialogue and the Constitution* (OUP 2017).

3 Judicial Diversity within the ECtHR

3.1 Introduction

The idea that a court should reflect the society within which it adjudicates has gained support in the past three decades.[1] International, regional, and national courts are increasingly governed by criteria that require that their composition should reflect various forms of institutional diversity, including gender, racial, linguistic, and religious diversity.[2] Yet many such courts and tribunals continue to be under-represented by women judges.[3] Although progress has been made, the efforts to increase gender representation have enjoyed only modest success across many courts and tribunals.[4] Currently, only two out of approximately 30 of international courts and tribunals have adopted non-binding rules addressing gender imbalance within the court's composition.[5] The two exceptions are the statutory documents of the International Criminal Court and the African Court of Justice and Human Rights.[6] Hodson notes that ensuring a more representative judiciary has faced considerable institutional resistance, despite the fact that gender equality is a well-established norm of international law.[7] The former judge of the European Court of the Human Rights (ECtHR), Helen Keller, and her

1 Stéphanie Hennette Vauchez, 'More Women: But Which Women? The Rule and the Politics of Gender Balance at the European Court of Human Rights' (2015) 26(1) EJIL 195, 198.
2 ibid. See also Karen O'Connor and Alixandra B Yanus, 'Judging Alone: Reflections on the Importance of Women on the Court' (2010) 6 Politics and Gender 441.
3 Rosemary Grey, Kcasey McLoughlin and Louise Chappell, 'Gender and Judging at the International Criminal Court: Lessons from "Feminist Judgment Projects"' (2021) 34(1) LJIL 247, 248.
4 Loveday Hodson, 'Gender and the International Judge: Towards a Transformative Equality Approach' (2022) 35 LJIL 913.
5 Akua Gyekye, 'Advisory Opinion on Certain Legal Questions Concerning the Lists of Candidates Submitted with a View to the Election of Judges to the European Court of Human Rights' (2008) 47(4) ILM 518, 518. See also Andreas Føllesdal, 'How Many Women Judges are Enough on International Courts?' (2021) 52(4) Journal of Social Philosophy 436, 438; Kanstantsin Dzehtsiarou and Alex Schwartz, 'Electing Team Strasbourg: Professional Diversity on the European Court of Human Rights and Why it Matters' (2020) 21(4) German LJ 621.
6 See Rome Statute of the International Criminal Court, 2187 UNTS 90 (Rome Statute), art 36(8)(a)(iii) requires the parties to aim for a 'fair representation of female and male judges' at the Court. See also Statute of the African Court of Justice and Human Rights, arts 5-6 require the State Parties to consider equitable gender representation in the nomination and election processes.
7 Hodson (n 4).

DOI: 10.4324/9781003435099-3

colleagues make a compelling argument for diversity and gender balance as regards the ECtHR, noting 'that it would be difficult to justify an institution dedicated to protecting human rights and democratic principles, including the prohibition of discrimination on the basis of gender, without adequate respect and consideration for the representation of women'.[8] This is particularly important as through their work the judiciary and courts can be seen to reinforce and legitimise existing gender hierarchies and inequalities, thereby contributing to ongoing injustices through their case law.[9]

Gender diversity within international courts is often expressed as three broad issues. First, diversity contributes to an enhanced outcome of the court's judicial decisions because women judges contribute to more gender-sensitive case law.[10] Second, diversity contributes to judicial impartiality and legitimacy.[11] Third, diversity is part of democratic inclusion.[12] In light of this, the United Nations (UN) Convention on the Elimination of All Forms of Discrimination against Women[13] calls for State Parties to enact measures ensuring women's participation in international organisations,[14] including the courts. Ostensibly, the ECtHR's diversity is arguably reflected in the various legal families and legal traditions that the judges originate from each Contracting State to the European Convention on Human Rights[15] (ECHR), ranging from Iceland and Norway to Armenia, Azerbaijan, and Georgia.[16] Despite the assumed diversity in terms of legal traditions, the civil law jurisdictions form an overwhelming majority of the Court's judges. Yet, strikingly as a unique creation of international law, the structure of the Council of Europe (CoE) legal system arguably resembles more a common law legal system than that of a civil law system.[17] While there are distinct elements of civil law, the legal work of the ECtHR is heavily influenced by the body of existing case law.[18]

8 Helen Keller, Corina Heri, and Myriam Christ, 'Fifty Years of Women at the European Court of Human Rights: Successes and Failures of the Council of Europe's Gender Agenda' in Freya Baetens (ed), *Who Is the Judge? Identity and Diversity on the International Bench* (OUP 2020) 198. See also Føllesdal (n 5) 442.
9 Grey, McLoughlin and Chappell (n 3) 254.
10 Vauchez (n 1) 199.
11 Douglas E Edlin, *Common Law Judging: Subjectivity, Impartiality, and the Making of Law* (University of Michigan Press 2016).
12 Vauchez (n 1) 199.
13 (adopted 18 December 1979; entry into force 3 September 1981) 1249 UNTS 13, arts 4, 7 and 8.
14 Gyekye (n 5) 518; Føllesdal (n 5) 438.
15 Convention for the Protection of Human Rights and Fundamental Freedoms (European Convention on Human Rights, as amended).
16 See Andrew Drzemczewski, 'The Internal Organization of the European Court of Human Rights: The Composition of the Chambers and the Grand Chamber' (2000) 3 EHRLR 237; Erik Voeten, 'Gender and Judging: Evidence from the European Court of Human Rights' (2020) Journal of European Public Policy 1. For current membership see Council of Europe, '46 States' <www.coe.int/en/web/portal/46-members-States> accessed 4 April 2023.
17 Nina-Louisa Arold, 'The European Court of Human Rights as an Example of Convergence' (2007) 76(2/3) Nord J Intl L 305, 321.
18 ibid 321.

The ECtHR's common law elements eg the use of the doctrine of precedent,[19] the argument style, and the idea of the individual responsibility of judges expressed through the separate opinions annexed to the judgments, makes the Court look much more like a common law court than a civil law court.[20] This is remarkable, considering that the ECtHR lacks a formal *stare decisis* principle.[21] Therefore, although it does not formally abide by the doctrine of precedent, it generally follows its own rulings.[22] Pearson argues that the Court will usually not depart from a judgment of the Grand Chamber without a good reason, particularly in cases that raise politically significant implications.[23] Although the Court is open for changing its direction and frequently does so, this does not normally happen instantaneously. The Court appears to build its approach towards what it considers particularly controversial issues incrementally on its previous case law.[24] Scholars have criticised the Court for rarely being at the forefront of rights protection and advancing case law only after States have already taken the lead.[25] Some of the cases demonstrate that the Court is, indeed, forced to reconsider its previous stance due to a change to the European consensus.[26] Accordingly, the lack of consensus leads to the slow evolution of human rights within the CoE.[27] One of the unique aspects of the ECtHR is that its interpretive approach towards human rights is a result of the purposive approach (also known as the teleological, dynamic, or evolutive approach) favoured by judges from civil law jurisdictions.[28] What this approach essentially means is that the Court recognises that the ECHR should be interpreted in the light of present-day conditions.[29] It can be argued that the ECtHR can be, and has been, innovative in its decisions when it wants to be.

19 Laurence R Helfer and Erik Voeten, 'International Courts as Agents of Legal Change: Evidence from LGBT Rights in Europe' (2014) 68(1) Intl Org 77, 81.

20 Arold (n 17) 321.

21 Helfer and Voeten (n 19).

22 ibid.

23 Megan Pearson, 'What Happened to "*Vivre Ensemble*?": Developments after *SAS v France*' (2021) 10(2) OJLR 185, 185.

24 ibid. See also Helfer and Voeten (n 19).

25 Claire Fenton-Glynn, *Family Formation and Parenthood* (OUP 2020).

26 Janneke Gerards, 'Margin of Appreciation and Incrementalism in the Case Law of the European Court of Human Rights' (2018) 18 HRL Rev 495.

27 Fenton-Glynn (n 25). Tulkens argues that the Court's methods of interpretation are guided by the Vienna Convention on the Law of Treaties of 1969 (adopted 23 May 1969, entry into force 27 January 1980) 1155 UNTS 331, art 31(1) which 'gives priority to the object and purpose of treaties as a rule of interpretation'. See Françoise Tulkens, 'Judicial Activism v Judicial Restraint: Practical Experience of This (False) Dilemma at the European Court of Human Rights' (2022) 3(3) ECHR L Rev 293, 295.

28 Jens M Scherpe, 'The Right Ambit: Lady Hale and the Limitations of Article 8 ECHR' (2021) 43(3) J Soc Wel & Fam L 256, 258.

29 Henriette Jakobien Liesker, 'Caught in a Balancing Act: The European Court of Human Rights and the Road to Recognition for Sexual Minorities' (2017) 4(3) Oslo L Rev 172, 183. Sometimes this interpretive approach also referred to viewing the ECHR as a 'living instrument'.

This chapter is structured the following way: Section 3.2 analyses the role of the Court's judges. Section 3.3 examines the criteria for judgeship in the ECtHR. Section 3.4 analyses the publicly available details of the Court's judges, including their professional and educational background, age and gender. Section 3.5 explores the significance of the Court's gender composition, whereas Section 3.6 focuses on the assumed diversity within the ECtHR. Section 3.7 sets out the argument for the importance of gender and gender-sensitivity in judging. Section 3.8 provides a conclusion.

3.2 Role of the Judges

The role of judges has been identified as central to the European human rights protection system under the ECHR. The legal regime created by the Convention is *lex specialis*, 'a special regime that applies its own rules, but which sometimes refers to the general rules of responsibility or to other rules of international law whenever the judges deem it necessary to give stronger justification to the interpretation of the international norm'.[30] Existing scholarship has discussed the Court's internal working mechanisms. There are views that the ECtHR, like other international courts, is an active agent, which does more than simply apply the law to the disputes before it.[31] Indeed, international courts are argued to actively shape the law through their case law. In an international law environment, where basic treaties do not change much over time, the judgments as a pattern of precedents hold the key to understanding the law.[32] Political scientists have analysed the Court's case law using statistical analysis. Analysing judgments that contained dissenting opinions between 1960 and 2006, Voeten found that there were both liberal and conservative branches in the Court.[33] His research indicated that substantive variation existed between how the judges perceive the individual Convention rights.

Voeten's findings are in contrast with empirical interviews conducted by Arold with the Court's judiciary similarly in 2007. Arold argued that the legal culture of the judges and the other personnel working in the ECtHR makes the differences in judges' backgrounds irrelevant because they share the same fundamental approach towards human rights.[34] While there is probably some truth in both views, the judges of the Court have sometimes taken very conservative views towards equal rights in cases concerning adoption of children by single gay men and lesbian women, such as, in the 2002 judgment in *Fretté v France*[35] and the 2008 judgment in *EB v*

30 Octavian Ichim, *Just Satisfaction Under the European Convention on Human Rights* (CUP 2015) 17.

31 Karen J Alter, *The New Terrain of International Law: Courts, Politics, Rights* (Princeton UP 2014).

32 Henrik Palmer Olsen and Aysel Küçüksu, 'Finding Hidden Patterns in ECtHR's Case Law: On How Citation Network Analysis Can Improve Our Knowledge of ECtHR's Article 14 Practice' (2017) 17(1) IJDL 4.

33 Erik Voeten, 'The Politics of International Judicial Appointments: Evidence from the European Court of Human Rights' (2007) 61(4) Intl Org 669.

34 Arold (n 17) 320.

35 *Fretté v France* App no 36515/97 (ECtHR, 26 May 2002).

France.[36] The way in which judges perceive the rights and freedoms protected by the Convention has obvious implications on how the Court interprets the contents of a particular right or freedom.[37] Thus, whether a particular judge approaches a specific right or freedom from a conservative point of view means that they may see, for instance, the right to found a family under Article 12 ECHR as protecting families consisting of a married opposite-sex couple with genetic children, but excluding same-sex couples with children born through donor insemination or cross-border surrogacy. Alternatively, a judge may view the right involving a more progressive interpretation, according to which marriage is a legal contract, signifying the commitment of two individuals to build a life together.[38] The conservative interpretation has long dominated the approach taken by the Convention organs as exemplified by case law on same-sex couples, who wish to cohabit in the State of origin of one of the partners, when the other partner is a non-national and is unable to obtain a residence permit.[39] Van der Sloot suggests that the Court has adopted a more liberal stance from 2000s onwards by extending Article 12 to various groups, who were previously unable to benefit from the protection under it, including trans women and trans men, immigrants, and persons wishing to file for divorce.[40]

3.3 Criteria for Judgeship

Vauchez argues that the international courts' composition has always been the subject of close scrutiny by governing elites, who are concerned about the appointments of international judges.[41] Although the election of judges of the ECtHR has been widely discussed in legal and political science literature,[42] the diversity of judges' professional backgrounds has received less academic attention.[43] While scholarly literature in the area of appointments to the ECtHR from a gendered point

36 *EB v France* App no 43546/02 (ECtHR, 22 January 2008). For reimagined judgment in *EB v France* and commentary, see Sanna Elfving and others, '*EB v France*: Lesbian Adoption in France' in Nuno Ferreira, Senthorun Raj, and Maria Moscati (eds), *Queer Judgments Project* (Counterpress 2024).

37 See eg Bart van der Sloot, 'Between Fact and Fiction: An Analysis of the Case-Law on Article 12 of the European Convention on Human Rights' (2014) CFLQ 397.

38 ibid.

39 This topic is discussed in more detail in ch 7 concerning family reunification.

40 van der Sloot, 'Between' (n 37).

41 Vauchez (n 1) 196; See also Ruth Mackenzie and others, *Selecting International Judges: Principle, Process and Politics* (OUP 2010); Ksenia Polonskaya, 'Selecting Candidates to the Bench of the World Court: (Inevitable) Politicization and Its Consequences' (2020) LJIL 409.

42 See eg Erik Voeten, 'The Politics' (n 33); Kanstantsin Dzehtsiarou and Donal Coffey, 'Legitimacy and Independence of International Tribunals: An Analysis of the European Court of Human Rights' (2014) 37 Hastings Intl & Comp L Rev 271; Michal Bobek (ed), *Selecting Europe's Judges: A Critical Review of the Appointment Procedures to the European Courts* (OUP 2015); Helga Molbæk-Steensig, 'Judicial Independence and Impartiality: Tenure Changes at the European Court of Human Rights' (2023) 34(3) EJIL 581.

43 Dzehtsiarou and Schwartz (n 5). See also Graham Gee and Erika Rackley, *Debating Judicial Appointments in an Age of Diversity* (Routledge 2018).

of view is not extensive,[44] a substantial body of scholarly literature has focused on appointment processes and gender diversity in international and national courts in general.[45] Even less commentary is found on the sexual orientation of judges.[46] Scholars argue that while selecting more women judges to the ECtHR is an important step forward, and a priority in its own right, it is imperative for States to ensure that qualified judges with expertise in gender analysis are nominated, lobbied for, and elected.[47]

The criteria for holding judicial office in the ECtHR is specified in the ECHR, which also functions as the Court's statutory document.[48] Although the requirements for judicial appointment to the ECtHR are broadly consistent with those of other international courts and tribunals, the ECHR contains very minimalistic criteria.[49] The process of appointing judges to the ECtHR involves both the CoE States and the Parliamentary Assembly of the CoE.[50] It has been frequently argued that because the selection of judges to the ECtHR is a political process, the decisions of its judges may be politically, instead of judicially, motivated.[51] Additionally, the case law of the ECtHR impacts on the Court's prestige, especially when a dispute has important far-reaching effects.[52]

Section II of the ECHR contains the rules and procedures governing the functioning of the Court, including the composition, membership, jurisdiction, and appointments to the Court. The selection of judges is based on Articles 20–22 ECHR.[53] These provisions determine that the number of judges is equal to that of the number of CoE States (Article 20), the criteria for office (Article 21), and the election of judges by the Parliamentary Assembly on the basis of the lists of three candidates nominated by each State (Article 22).[54] According to Articles 22

44 In fact, Hodson argues that limited work exists that points to significance of judicial gender in areas beyond international criminal and human rights tribunals. See Hodson (n 4) 929. See also Vauchez (n 1); Alistair Mowbray, 'The Consideration of Gender in the Process of Appointing Judges to the European Court of Human Rights' (2008) 8(3) HRL Rev 549.

45 See eg Sally J Kenny, 'Choosing Judges: A Bumpy Road to Women's Equality and a Long Way to Go' (2012) Michigan State L Rev 1499; Sara L Kimble and Marion Röwekamp (eds), *New Perspectives on European Women's Legal History* (Routledge 2016); Başak Çalı and Stewart Cunningham, 'Judicial Self Government and the Sui Generis Case of the European Court of Human Rights' (2018) 19 German LJ 1977; Josephine J Dawuni (ed), *Gender, Judging and the Courts in Africa: Selected Studies* (Routledge 2021).

46 Leslie Moran, 'Judicial Diversity and the Challenge of Sexuality: Some Preliminary Findings' (2006) 28 Sydney L Rev 565.

47 Grey, McLoughlin and Chappell (n 3) 264.

48 Dzehtsiarou and Schwartz (n 5).

49 ibid 625.

50 Mowbray (n 44) 549.

51 Ichim (n 30) 54.

52 ibid.

53 Vauchez (n 1) 201.

54 ECHR, art 22: 'The judges shall be elected by the Parliamentary Assembly with respect to each High Contracting Party by a majority of votes cast from a list of three candidates nominated by the High Contracting Party'.

and 23(1) ECHR as well as the information provided on the Court's website,[55] the judges are elected for a non-renewable term of nine years by the Parliamentary Assembly.

According to Article 20 ECHR, there are an equal number of judges sitting in the Court as there are States that have ratified the Convention.[56] This is based on the idea that none of judges has more power over the Court's case law than any other judge. Essentially, each State that has ratified the Convention is entitled to nominate one judge to the Court.[57] Although the judges are elected in respect of a Contracting State, they hear cases as individuals, remaining independent from their respective States.[58] For this reason judges do not need to hold the nationality of the State in respect of which they sit.[59] In fact, nationality and national legal training only matter when a case is brought against a Contracting State and the national judge needs to describe the characteristics of the national legal system.[60] An elected national judge sitting in the Chamber ensures, *inter alia*, that knowledge about the national language, particularities of the case, and the significant features of the national legislation are available to the other judges.[61] Consequently, a respondent State has the privilege to have the judge nominated by it to take a seat *ex officio* in the Chamber deciding on the matter.[62] To avoid a conflict interest, however, '[w] hen sitting as a single judge, a judge shall not examine any application against the High Contracting Party in respect of which that judge has been elected'.[63] As manifestly inadmissible applications are examined by a single judge formation,[64] these cases are never decided by the judge who was elected by the respondent State.

Article 21 ECHR specifies the process of nomination. Under this provision, each State can nominate three candidates who it considers satisfy the criteria for office, namely, that candidate judges are of 'high moral character' and possess 'the qualifications required for high judicial office or be jurisconsults of recognised competence'.[65] The Parliamentary Assembly will subsequently choose one of the candidates for the seat, who is carefully scrutinised by the Court before being admitted based on Article 22 ECHR.[66] Interestingly, in comparison with other

55 ECtHR, 'Composition of the Court' <www.echr.coe.int/Pages/home.aspx?p=court/judges&c> accessed 3 July 2024.
56 ECHR, art 20: 'The Court shall consist of a number of judges equal to that of the High Contracting Parties'.
57 Bart van der Sloot, 'The *Ad Hoc* Judge: A Rehabilitation' (2022) 29(5) MJ 572.
58 ECtHR, 'Composition of the Court' (n 55).
59 Vauchez (n 1) 201.
60 Arold (n 17) 315.
61 van der Sloot, 'The *Ad Hoc*' (n 57) 573.
62 ibid 572.
63 ECHR, art 26(3).
64 ECtHR, 'Composition of the Court' (n 55).
65 ECHR, art 21 stipulates only two necessary requirements: 'judges shall be of high moral character and must either possess the qualifications required for appointment to high judicial office or be jurisconsults of recognized competence'. See eg Dzehtsiarou and Schwartz (n 5) 625.
66 van der Sloot, 'The *Ad Hoc*' (n 57).

international courts and tribunals, Article 21 ECHR does not require the appointees to be independent or impartial or to be recognised specialists in human rights law. Since their initial formulation in 1959, the Rules of the Court merely stress that: 'A judge may not exercise his functions while he is a member of a Government or while he holds a post or exercises a profession which is likely to affect confidence in his independence. In case of need the Court shall decide'.[67] Further, the judges 'cannot engage in any activity that would be incompatible with their duty of independence and impartiality'.[68]

Article 21 ECHR is also silent about whether a nominee should be a person appointable to high judicial office at the national level and whether judicial experience is a pre-condition for appointment.[69] The reason why the ECHR makes only two stipulations about the individual judges' suitability for judicial appointment has not been fully explored in legal scholarship. While the ECHR provides a foundation for appointing a more gender-balanced bench, without provisions mandating that judges demonstrate sensitivity to gender norms and hierarchies, the actors within and outside the Court must take the lead in diversifying the Court and in ensuring gender-sensitive judging in the Court.

3.4 Judges of the Court

The Court's website lists the name, date, and place of birth, position, country they represent, and educational and professional background of each of the Court's 46 judges.[70] Most of its judges appear to be white, able-bodied males in their 50s. It is impossible to say whether there are any members of minoritised groups among the judges as their backgrounds do not include any additional information. As of 2 July 2024, out of 46 judges just over one-third were women (17) and two-thirds were men (29). Consequently, women constitute a minoritised group in the Court. In terms of age, 21 of the Court's 46 judges are between 50–59 years old (14 men and eight women), whereas 12 judges are between the ages 60 and 69 (eight men and four women), and 13 judges are between the ages 40 and 49 (eight men and five women). Judge Saadet Yüksel (Türkiye) is the youngest of all the judges at 41 years of age. Remarkably, she joined the Court when she was in her mid-30s. The oldest judges are Gabriele Kucsko-Stadlmayer (Austria) and Branko Lubarda (Serbia) at 68 years.

The elected judges of the ECtHR have strong formal powers with regard to the daily functioning of the Court because the Court itself creates, adopts, and amends the Rules of Court.[71] Judges are also responsible for the election of their peers to the positions of President and one or two Vice-Presidents of both the Courts and

67 ECtHR, Rules of Court, rule 4. <www.echr.coe.int/documents/d/echr/rules_court_eng> accessed 9 April 2024.
68 ECtHR, 'Composition of the Court' (n 55).
69 Dzehtsiarou and Schwartz (n 5) 624.
70 ECtHR, 'Composition of the Court' (n 55).
71 Çalı and Cunningham (n 45) 1988.

the Sections within the Court.[72] The election of judges to these positions is undertaken by the full Plenary Court by way of secret ballot.[73] According to Article 25(a) ECHR, the President and Vice-Presidents are elected for a renewable period of three years, meaning that they may be re-elected by the Court.[74] The Plenary Court also elects the Registrar and one or more Deputy Registrars.[75] The functions and organisation of the Registry are laid down in the Rules of Court.[76] Under Rules 48–50 of the Rules of Court, the Court works in Sections and the President of the Section designates a judge to act as Judge Rapporteur in a case.[77] Under Rule 49(3) , the Rapporteur can decide the number of judges considering a particular complaint. The options under the Rules of Court include consideration by a single judge, a Committee, or a Chamber.

Male judges have traditionally held many of the senior roles within the Court, including the role of the President of the Court. In September 2022, the ECtHR historically elected its first female president, Judge Síofra O'Leary (Ireland). However, after her mandate ended in July 2024, the Presidency returned to the hands of male judges as Judge Marko Bošnjak (Slovenia) was subsequently chosen as the President of the Court. The Vice-Presidency is jointly held by Judges Gabriele Kucsko-Stadlmayer (Austria) and Arnfinn Bårdsen (Norway). The five Sections of the Court from which Chambers are formed, are largely male dominated. Although Rule 25 on the composition of Sections stipulates that: '[t]he composition of the Sections shall be geographically and gender balanced and shall reflect the different legal systems among the Contracting Parties',[78] this is clearly aspirational in terms of gender balance as currently, two of the five Section President roles are held by women judges: Ivana Jelić (Montenegro) and Gabriele Kucsko-Stadlmayer. The Court's website explains that a Section is an administrative entity, and a Chamber is a judicial formation of the Court within a given Section.[79] On average, the Sections have three women judges each. Considering that there are nine to ten judges in each Section, the fact that there are three women per Section means that women never form a majority in any of the Sections. Although there are no Sections without women in them, it is difficult to say what the gender balance of the Chambers looks like since the composition of the Chambers is not publicly available on the Court's website. Consequently, the Court could well have Chambers where no women are present.[80] The Grand Chamber essentially consists of 17 judges,

72 ibid.

73 ECtHR, Rules of Court, rule 8 <www.echr.coe.int/Documents/Rules_Court_ENG.pdf> accessed 9 April 2024. See also Çali and Cunningham (n 45) 1988.

74 ECHR, art 25(a).

75 ibid, art 25(e).

76 ibid, art 24(1).

77 Ichim (n 30) 54.

78 Drzemczewski (n 16).

79 ECtHR, 'Composition of the Court' (n 55).

80 The Court's Chambers may consist of either five, seven or 17 members. See ECHR, art 26(1): 'To consider cases brought before it, the Court shall sit in a single-judge formation, in committees of three judges, in Chambers of seven judges, and in a Grand Chamber of seventeen judges'.

including the Court's President and Vice-Presidents, the Section Presidents, and the national judge, together with other judges selected by the drawing of lots[81] from all the sections of the Court.[82] According to Article 26(2) ECHR, at the request of the Plenary Court, the Committee of Ministers may reduce the number of judges in each Chambers to five for a fixed period, provided that it takes its decision unanimously.

The current women judges have similar experiences as the nominees in Vauchez's 2015 study where she analysed the backgrounds of all women included in the list of nominees until then. Vauchez has argued that the list of nominees elected to the Court has consistently included highly internationalised profiles.[83] Although analysing all the recent nominations is outside the scope of the chapter, it is useful to examine the experience of current judges. Therefore, the ideal nominee has not changed considerably. It is perhaps notable that fewer women judges have previous experience of working for their governments or even previous judicial experience. Out of 17 women judges, only five have worked for their governments and ten have previous judicial experience, whereas 13 hold doctoral degrees[84] and ten have also held academic positions at national universities and some visiting scholar positions abroad. Most of the current female judges also have experience of working in some capacity for international organisations, including the institutions of the European Union (EU), the UN or the CoE (11 out of 17). Particularly one woman judge stands out in terms of her experience at international organisations: Ivana Jelić (Montenegro) has previous expertise at the International Committee of the Red Cross, various committees, and working groups within the CoE and the UN Human Rights Committee. In comparison to the observations Vauchez made about the candidates' studies abroad, especially in the US, only one or two of the current women judges have completed either a doctoral degree or master's degree in the US.

The credentials of the Court's male judges are similar to those of its women judges. Out of 29 current male judges, 19 have previous experience of working as a national judge or *ad hoc* judge for the ECtHR before becoming a judge at the Court. In contrast, 12 male judges have no previous judicial experience before becoming a judge of the ECtHR. These judges, however, usually have previous international and academic experience instead. Fewer current male judges have worked exclusively in judicial and governmental positions, possibly as a government lawyer, with a few exceptions. Thirteen male judges have previous experience working for their national government, whereas 25 have previously worked in academia. Similarly, 19 current male judges have previous experience of working

81 ECtHR, 'Composition of the Court' (n 55).
82 Voeten, 'The Politics' (n 33) 673.
83 Including that of Françoise Tulkens (listed by Belgium and elected in 1998) and Helen Keller (listed by Switzerland and elected in 2010). See Vauchez (n 1) 216.
84 Many women judges hold PhDs from the universities of their respective countries, whereas only one judge (Anja Seibert-Fohr, Germany) holds a Doctor of Juridical Science from George Washington University, the United States.

for international organisations, which means that ten have no previous international experience of any kind. Whereas most current male judges, who have gained international experience, have held various roles within the CoE, the EU Fundamental Rights Agency, the European Committee for the Prevention of Torture and Inhuman or Degrading Treatment or Punishment, the International Labour Organisation, the International Committee of the Red Cross, the Organisation for American States, or the World Bank. Nineteen male judges have completed a PhD, although only a few of them have completed postgraduate degrees at a higher education institution abroad. A minority of male judges have completed their LLM degrees abroad; two have LLM degrees from universities in the United States and some have completed their LLM degrees in the UK. Strikingly, one male judge (Georgios Serghides, Cyprus) has been awarded several higher degrees in three different countries, including France, the UK, and Greece. Overall, rather remarkably, nearly one-third of current judges (both male and female) have no previous international experience, although the requirement for highly internationalised profiles has been often imposed on candidates included on the list of nominees elected to the international courts.[85] Therefore, the male judges' profiles are very similar when compared to those of the female judges, with a couple of notable exceptions.

3.5 Significance of the Gender Composition

One obvious place to begin an examination of the ECtHR from a wider equality perspective is to examine the gender representation or gender balance and wider diversity within the Court. The Parliamentary Assembly has adopted several Recommendations to improve the quality of candidates nominated for the Court. Although Resolution 1366 (2004)[86] has been seen first and foremost the recommendation that promotes the gender balance of the Court, it elaborated on several other criteria based on which the Parliamentary Assembly would not consider candidates with the aim of preventing the States from nominating unsuitable candidates for judicial office. The criteria included the rejection of candidates who appear to have limited competence, have insufficient knowledge of at least one of the two official languages of the Court, and those who lack the stature to meet the criteria in Article 21(1) ECHR.[87] Although the Resolutions are not legally binding, they are argued to carry significant political weight as the expression of the views of the peoples of Europe.[88] Resolution 1366 (2004), indeed, also stated that the lists of nominees

85 Vauchez (n 1).

86 CoE, Parliamentary Assembly, Resolution 1366 (2004), Candidates for the European Court of Human Rights, 30 January 2004, 8th Sitting (Res 1366 (2004) <https://assembly.coe.int/nw/xml/XRef/Xref-XML2HTML-en.asp?fileid=17194&lang=en> accessed 8 August 2024.

87 ibid.

88 Iakovos Iakovidis and Paul McDonough, 'The *Molla Sali* Case: How the European Court of Human Rights Escaped a Legal Labyrinth While Holding the Thread of Human Rights' (2019) 8(2) OJLR 427.

that did not contain at least one woman and at least one man would be rejected.[89] It further suggested that in case of two equally qualified nominees, 'a candidate of the sex under-represented at the Court' would be appointed.[90] Other documents adopted by the Parliamentary Assembly specify that the nominees should have 'knowledge and awareness of European Convention jurisprudence' among other attributes,[91] and that they should have experience in the field of human rights.[92]

The minimal obligation to include at least one woman and one man on the list of candidates in 2004 raised a strong opposition within both the Parliamentary Assembly and the Committee of Ministers.[93] As a consequence, in 2008, the ECtHR deliberated in its first ever Advisory Opinion[94] whether the Parliamentary Assembly and the Committee of Ministers were competent to develop interpretations of the Article 21 criteria for judicial office.[95] In its Advisory Opinion, the Grand Chamber unanimously decided that the rejection of a list of all male candidates nominated for the Court would be incompatible with the ECHR.[96] This indicated that States could essentially keep submitting all male lists for the consideration of the Parliamentary Assembly without any consequences. The Advisory Opinion has, therefore, been criticised as a backward step in the jurisprudence concerning gender mainstreaming and gender equality.[97] Others have been less critical noting that although the Parliamentary Assembly could still decide to consider an all-male shortlist, it would need to elaborate on the reasons as to why this was important.[98] As a result of the Advisory Opinion, the selection to the Court now requires that 'Lists of candidates should as a general rule contain at least one candidate of each sex, unless the sex of the candidates on the list is under-represented on the Court (under 40 per cent of judges) or if exceptional circumstances exist to

89 Res 1366 (2004), pt 2.

90 ibid pt 3: 'in the case of equal merit, preference should be given to a candidate of the sex under-represented at the Court'.

91 See the explanatory report to European Parliamentary Assembly, Res 1366, Candidates for the European Court of Human Rights (2004); European Parliamentary Assembly, Rep. on Candidates for the European Court of Human Rights, Doc No 9963 (2003) <http://assembly.coe.int/nw/xml/XRef/X2H-Xref-ViewHTML.asp?FileID=10348&lang=EN> accessed 7 April 2024.

92 European Parliamentary Assembly, Rec 1649, Candidates for the European Court of Human Rights (2004), para 19.2. See also Dzehtsiarou and Schwartz (n 5) 625.

93 Vauchez (n 1) 201.

94 The Court has competence to deliver advisory opinions conferred by ECHR, art 47(1) and Protocol 2. See Advisory Opinion on Certain Legal Questions Concerning the Lists of Candidates Submitted with a View to the Election of Judges to the European Court of Human Rights (12 February 2008) (Advisory Opinion).

95 ECtHR, Advisory Opinion on Certain Legal Questions Concerning the Lists of Candidates Submitted with a View to the Election of Judges to the ECtHR (Election of Judges), GC, No 1, ECtHR, para 47 (12 February 2008) <http://hudoc.echr.coe.int/eng?i=003-2268009-2419060> accessed 8 April 2024. For a commentary, see Mowbray (n 44).

96 Gyekye (n 5) 518; Vauchez (n 1) 201.

97 ibid.

98 Mowbray (n 44) 559.

derogate from this rule'.[99] Critics have argued that as there are no guarantees that more women will be selected to the Court, 'listing diverse candidates is a weak attempt to improve the gender balance within the ECtHR'.[100]

One of the main arguments raised by those who oppose diversity measures to defend the *status quo* is the argument according to which diversity will increase due to natural evolution.[101] However, critics argue that the attempts to increase the gender balance at the ECtHR has by no means been natural.[102] While some scholars support at least the 'token representation' of one candidate for a judge being a woman, others argue there needs to be a critical mass of women and men judges in order for changes to occur.[103] In the context of the ECtHR, achieving a critical mass would mean 40–60 percent of women judges in order to result in a change in the group dynamics, to ensure that women do not simply make decisions the same way as men, and to encourage more men to make decisions like women.[104] Stronger forms of affirmative action would involve solutions that are specifically designed to solve the issues related to the under-representation of women and minoritised groups quicker, such as, gender quotas and preferences.[105] Thornton has argued that proactive strategies designed to promote institutional diversity include measures encouraging women and members of minoritised or diasporic groups to apply.[106] As a minimum, these strategies would ensure shortlisting of women as well as individuals who belong to minoritised and diasporic groups.[107] Therefore, including one woman on the list of nominees is only a starting point for diversifying the ECtHR and not a particularly strong one. Despite the sustained efforts of the Parliamentary Assembly, States still privilege a minimalist understanding of gender balance objectives at the ECtHR.[108] If the Parliamentary Assembly does not reject all-male lists, nothing changes as States keep selecting male nominees to the Court.[109]

99 Guidelines of the Committee of Ministers on the Selection of Candidates for the Post of Judge at the European Court of Human Rights (Guidelines on the Selection of Candidates), Resolution CM (2012) 40 final (29 March 2012) <https://rm.coe.int/16805cb1ac> accessed 8 August 2024.
100 Vauchez (n 1) 201.
101 It has been widely used in debates over gender parity in Parliaments and judiciaries. See Vauchez (n 1) 201.
102 Vauchez (n 1) 221.
103 Føllesdal (n 5) 438.
104 ibid 439.
105 Margaret Thornton, 'Otherness on the Bench: How Merit Is Gendered' (2007) 29 Sydney L Rev 406.
106 ibid.
107 ibid. Thornton calls these measures as 'a weak form of affirmative action'.
108 Vauchez (n 1) 221.
109 ibid.

3.6 Diversity within the ECtHR

As it was noted in Section 3.1, just because the judges of the ECtHR are appointed by 46 different States, this does not mean that the ECtHR is a genuinely diverse institution. Although the judges of the Court undoubtedly bring together rich experiences and outlooks shaped by different legal traditions, education, professional backgrounds, personal experiences, and different historical-political contexts,[110] the reality is that the majority of judges of the Court are still men. As far it is possible to tell, there is very little racial, ethnic, or religious diversity within the ECtHR. Evidence suggests that judges, both at the international and domestic levels, are generally part of a middle- or upper-class professional elite, which is principally composed of members of dominant gender, racial, and socio-cultural groups.[111] Similarly, the ECtHR's judiciary is principally composed of well-educated and upper middle-class men and women of a certain age, of European ethnicity, and culturally Christian.[112] Additionally, the ECtHR judgeships are high-profile and well-paying positions which tend to be the type of positions where women are under-represented.[113] Therefore, the ECtHR is essentially an elite institution.

Traditionally, the ECtHR judges have included former national judges, professors, attorneys, ambassadors, or other public officials.[114] This is because most judges often have extensive prior work experience and will have spent longer in practice, academia or the government than on the bench.[115] The prioritisation of these particular qualities have led to the presence, at the ECtHR, of judges who have the required legal expertise and have also served governmental interests in various capacities.[116] This stems from the fact that legal careers as an attorney, judge, or law professor are characteristically complemented by a position as a jurisconsult at the Foreign Office or as a member of a national delegation to an international organisation, or by a political position, such as a member of parliament or of government.[117] However, due to the similarity of judges' backgrounds, it is

110 Arold (n 17) 307; Dzehtsiarou and Schwartz (n 5).

111 See eg Josephine J Dawuni, 'African Women Judges on International Courts: Symbolic or Substantive Gains' (2018) 47 U Baltimore L Rev 199; Nienke Grossman, 'Achieving Sex-Representative International Court Benches' (2016) 110(1) AJIL 82. See also Nienke Grossman, 'Sex on the Bench: Do Women Judges Matter to the Legitimacy of International Courts?' (2012) 12 Chicago J Intl L 647.

112 For similar arguments concerning international organisations in general, see Vauchez (n 1).

113 Voeten, 'Gender' (n 16).

114 Arold (n 17) 312.

115 CJS Knight, 'A Court of Specialists: Judicial Behaviour on the UK Supreme Court by Chris Hanretty' (2022) 138(Oct) LQR 684, 687.

116 Mikael Madsen, 'From Cold War Instrument to Supreme European Court: The European Court of Human Rights at the Crossroads of International and National Law and Politics' (2007) 32 Law and Social Inquiry 137.

117 Vauchez (n 1) 216.

likely that women judges within the ECtHR have more in common with their male counterparts.[118]

Despite Arold's persuasive findings during her empirical interviews with judges of the Court discussed in Section 3.2,[119] the diversity of judiciary raises a question about women judges which might be important in the context of the ECtHR, namely, whether women's complaints before the ECtHR are more likely to be successful if there are more women on the bench.[120] The implied question here is generally about whether access to justice is gendered.[121] This has been argued to have implications for the type of complaints that are brought to the attention of the ECtHR.[122] The next section considers the need to appoint gender-sensitive judges to international and regional courts, as opposed to appointing equal number of men and women judges.[123]

3.7 Gender and Judging

Judicial decision-making has been frequently discussed in legal scholarship.[124] While some scholars suggest that women incorporate their gendered experiences to judging, others maintain that gender difference is absent in the judicial process because the daily work and professional role of judges makes gender irrelevant.[125] Despite varied research findings, judicial decision-making is subject to implicit influences associated with individual judges' life experiences and other demographic variables, including gender.[126] Three theoretical perspectives have emerged in existing scholarly literature on gender and judging.[127] First, international judges

118 For a commentary on the judging at the CJEU, see Jessica Guth and Sanna Elfving, *Gender and Court of Justice of the European Union* (Routledge 2018); Konstantinos Alexandris Polomarkakis, 'United in Diversity? Gender and Judging at the Court of Justice of the European Union (CJEU)' (2019) 34 Conn J Intl L 336.

119 Arold (n 17).

120 For similar deliberation concerning international courts, see Grey, McLoughlin and Chappell (n 3) 249.

121 ibid 249.

122 For publications which are aimed at educating judges about the issues faced by women, see eg Elisabeth Duban and Ivana Radacic, *Training Manual for Judges and Prosecutors on Ensuring Women's Access to Justice* (Partnership for Good Governance 2017).

123 Grey, McLoughlin and Chappell (n 3) 249.

124 Anqi Shen, 'Women Judges Who Judge Women Offenders: A Chinese Case Study on Gender and Judging' (2020) 27(1) IJLP 63. See also Rachel Cahill-O'Callaghan and Bernadette Richards, 'Policy, Principle and Values: An Exploration of Judicial Decision Making' (2018) 79(2) Louisiana L Rev 397.

125 Revital Ludewig and Juan LaLlave, 'Professional Stress, Discrimination and Coping Strategies: Similarities and Differences Between Female and Male Judges in Switzerland' in Ulrike Schultz and Gisela Shaw (eds), *Gender and Judging* (Hart 2013).

126 See eg Rachel Cahill-O'Callaghan, 'Reframing the Judicial Diversity Debate: Personal Values and Tacit Diversity' (2015) 35(1) LS 1.

127 See eg Kate Malleson, 'Gender Quotas for the Judiciary in England and Wales' in Schultz and Shaw (n 124); Hilary Sommerlad, 'Let History Judge? Gender, Race, Class and Performative Identity: A Study of Women Judges in England and Wales' in Schultz and Shaw (n 124).

operate within highly gendered contexts, 'in which structural exclusions, discrimination, and oppression are rendered invisible'.[128] In the past, the courts have seemingly aimed at being neutral arbitrators, although this has changed in recent decades. Indeed, one of the fundamental ideals that still permeates the image of the judiciary and courts is the traditional, predominant ideal of the judges as neutral arbiters of justice that suggests that rationality and reason are the primary features of the task of judging.[129] Former judge of the ECtHR, Françoise Tulkens, has also criticised the way in which the Court has solved conflicts between women's rights, standards of non-discrimination, and freedom of religion in mid-2000s, without hearing the views of the Muslim women.[130] Many of the so-called headscarf cases before the ECtHR concern national law prohibiting students, teachers, and other employees from wearing headscarves at educational establishments and other workplaces in order to preserve the secular nature of State institutions. While the ECtHR has frequently upheld the bans, this has sparked criticism among scholars.[131]

Second, it is unclear whether the gender of the individual bringing the complaint has any effect on judging in the ECtHR.[132] Voeten notes that although no evidence exists to support such an argument, it is frequently suggested that women judges may be more receptive to human rights cases filed by women, particularly those concerning discrimination, possibly due to similar or common experiences.[133] This is indeed a familiar argument often made in scholarly literature. The suggestion that women judges may be more receptive to allegations concerning gender discrimination seems plausible, given that many women judges are likely to have experienced sex-based discrimination during their careers and are thus more sympathetic towards discrimination claims by women. It has been suggested that one reason why differences in judicial outcomes are most visible in gender discrimination cases is that although women's legal training and interpretation of the law may vary, they have shared life experiences that may inform their legal reasoning.[134]

What the current debates are lacking, however, is the discussion of women judges' expertise and the operation of gender outside of the contexts of international courts dealing with cases concerning sexual violence and gender discrimination, such as, the International Criminal Court.[135] Although women judges have been identified to be potentially more effective at adjudicating cases involving gen-

128 Hodson (n 4) 914.

129 Moa Bladini, Sara Uhnoo and Åsa Wettergren, 'It Sounds Like Lived Experience: On Empathy in Rape Trials' (2013) 72 IJLCJ doi:10.1016/j.ijlcj.2023.100575. See also Grey, McLoughlin and Chappell (n 3) 254.

130 In her dissenting opinion in *Leyla Şahin v Turkey*, Judge Tulkens noted that Ms Şahin, a 25-year-old university student wore the headscarf of her own free will. See *Leyla Şahin v Turkey* App no 44774/98 (ECtHR, 10 November 2005) dissenting opinion of Judge Tulkens, para 12.

131 See ch 4.

132 For argument in the international context, see Freya Baetens, *Identity and Diversity on the International Bench: Who Is the Judge?* (OUP 2020).

133 Erik Voeten, 'Gender' (n 16).

134 See O'Connor and Yanus (n 2).

135 Hodson (n 4) 926.

der discrimination and violence against women,[136] these are not the only situations in which gender-sensitivity on the bench is likely to be an asset.[137] This implies that a gender-sensitive approach should be applied beyond disputes involving violence against women.

Third, the presence of women judges in the individual Chambers and the ECtHR overall may enhance perceptions of the Court's social legitimacy, inclusiveness and procedural fairness, which may in turn encourage more women to defend their rights in the first place, ultimately leading into filing a complaint to the Court or to seek a career in legal profession or even as a judge.[138] Existing research suggests when women serve with other women, they decide cases differently. Collins and his colleagues have noted that when there are other women present in the room making decisions with them, the collegiality may make a difference.[139] Similarly, Føllesdal suggests that women judges' participation may change the nature of collegial deliberation,[140] despite the fact that there are arguments that the institutional and normative constraints on both men and women judges and judging are considerable.[141] Perhaps rather optimistically, Føllesdal notes that because women judges engage colleagues in arguments that raise issues of equality in deliberation, the Court may be expected to issue somewhat different judgments and interpretations both in contents and in form.[142]

The question, therefore, arises that if there were more women judges in the ECtHR, would they bring a more gender-aware voice to the Court and would this be reflected in the judgments and decisions of the Court. There are views that the diversity in experience might make for an overall better judiciary.[143] The need to have judges who have a gender-sensitive approach to adjudication is equally important. Gender-sensitivity of a Chamber or Bench means that judges who adopt this approach are willing to interpret and apply the Convention in a gender-sensitive way, which considers the ways in which privilege and discrimination operate in different contexts, depending on the gender of an individual.[144] However, it is insufficient that only the judiciary takes a gender-sensitive approach. There is a

136 Grey, McLoughlin and Chappell (n 3) 248. See also Joseph Powderly, *Judges and the Making of International Criminal Law* (Brill 2020).

137 Grey, McLoughlin and Chappell (n 3) 250.

138 Bobek (n 42) 226.

139 Paul M Collins Jr, Kenneth L Manning, and Robert A Carp, 'Gender, Critical Mass, and Judicial Decision Making' (2010) 32(2) Law and Policy 260, 275. See also Rosemary Hunter, 'More Than Just a Different Face? Judicial Diversity and Decision-making' (2015) CLP 1.

140 Føllesdal (n 5) 441.

141 Hodson (n 4) 927; Fionnuala Ní Aoláin, 'More Women: But Which Women? A Reply to Stéphanie Hennette Vauchez' (2015) 26(1) EJIL 229.

142 Føllesdal (n 5) 441.

143 Claire L'Heureux-Dubé, 'Outsiders on the Bench: The Continuing Struggle for Equality' 16 Wisconsin Women's L J (2001) 15; Collins, Manning and Carp (n 138); Erika Rackley, *Women, Judging and the Judiciary: From Difference to Diversity* (Routledge 2013).

144 For similar arguments in the context of international courts, see Grey, McLoughlin and Chappell (n 3) 248.

need for a more comprehensive shift in the way of thinking at the societal level. Both legislators and lawyers, regardless of gender, should understand that the intersection of gender, age, ability, race, and class can limit access to justice.[145] This requires commitment to empower women and minoritised and diasporic groups through the interpretation and application of law.[146]

3.8 Conclusion

In the absence of the strong commitment to improve institutional diversity within the ECtHR, diversity remains incidental.[147] Women continue to be significantly under-represented on the bench, which reflects a wider pattern of exclusion throughout international organisations.[148] When just over one-third of the Court's judges are women, attention still needs to be paid to gender in the judicial selection processes of the ECtHR.[149] In addition to gender balance, one obvious potential source of institutional diversity for the ECtHR is the professional background of judges.[150] Although the lack of previous judicial experience in human rights law has not been argued to be as critical for the judgeship in the ECtHR as it may be for the International Criminal Court,[151] considering that the Court specialises in human rights law, it would seem critical that its judges not only have significant working knowledge of human rights law,[152] but also are familiar with case law under the Convention's main discrimination provision Article 14 ECHR.

As a critical mass of women judges have been identified as important, gender quotas would help in electing equal numbers of women and men judges to the Court.[153] As a complementary measure, the CoE States should support candidates with expertise in gender issues, and support judges who bring intersectional and a feminist approach to their work.[154] Based on Hunter's suggestion as to the qualities a feminist judge, this chapter argues that a gender-aware judge, once appointed, should be able to, *inter alia*, identify the relevance of gender in the dispute; recognise and challenge biased narratives laid before the judiciary; identify with the interests of women and minoritised and diasporic groups; draw from the applicants' lived experiences; and promote substantive equality.[155] Gender-competency of a judge should, therefore, be incorporated as one of the requirements concerning

145 ibid 255.
146 ibid.
147 Dzehtsiarou and Schwartz (n 5) 643.
148 Hodson (n 4) 914.
149 Vauchez (n 1) 221.
150 See Dzehtsiarou and Schwartz (n 5).
151 ibid 624.
152 Matilda Gillis, 'Can We Talk? The Application of the Public Law Democratic Dialogue Model to the Interactions between Domestic Legislatures and the European Courts' (2022) 23 German LJ 56, 68.
153 See eg Føllesdal (n 5) 439; Thornton (n 104) 406.
154 Grey, McLoughlin and Chappell (n 3) 257.
155 Rosemary Hunter, 'Can Feminist Judges Make A Difference?' (2008) 15(1–2) IJLP 7.

professional expertise.[156] Specialist legal expertise in gender issues could include appointing judges with legal expertise in not only gender discrimination but discrimination on the basis of sexual orientation, gender identity, religious beliefs, and disability.

Although several jurisdictions recommend that judges undergo some forms of judicial training, the requirement that judges undergo training to understand the importance of interpreting the law in a gender-sensitive way or receive guidance on how to address issues relating to discrimination or violence against women is unlikely to have been included in standard training so far.[157] In order for gender-aware judging to become normalised at the ECtHR, support is needed outside the Court, in particular, State Parties must show leadership in this regard.[158] Making gender and ethnic diversity a priority should inform the working methods of the panels selecting and interviewing the nominees, as well as the policymakers reforming the system of the selection of judges.[159]

The ECtHR selection system can be revised in several ways. First, the CoE should actively encourage States to submit a list of nominees of diverse backgrounds by making equality, diversity, and inclusion strategies an integral part of the nomination process. A more diverse judiciary, which extends beyond representation of nationality of each CoE State, may help counteract the under-representation of women judges and of judges from minoritised and diasporic groups.[160] Judges drawn from a variety of cultural and social backgrounds are likely to bring diverse perspectives to bear on critical legal issues, thus adding quality to judicial deliberation and improving the integrity of judging, and by adding perspectives and reasons that are typically missing in discussions among the judiciary who may not attach enough significance to the perspectives of diasporic groups or structurally minoritised groups.[161] Second, as an important complementary measure, the CoE should adjust its own procedures to reflect the need for judicial diversity. The Committee on the Election of Judges to the Court, which interviews candidates and publishes suggestions, should commission studies to determine the backgrounds that are under-represented or over-represented on the bench.[162] Finally, a

156 Grey, McLoughlin and Chappell (n 3) 257.

157 Except for Duban and Radacic (n 122).

158 Grey, McLoughlin and Chappell (n 3) 264.

159 For similar suggestions in the context of diversifying judges' professional backgrounds, see Dzehtsiarou and Schwartz (n 5) 643.

160 Neus Torbisco-Casals, 'The Legitimacy of International Courts: The Challenge of Diversity' (2021) 52(4) Journal of Social Philosophy 491.

161 ibid.

162 A permanent Committee on the Election of Judges to the Court within Parliamentary Assembly was established in 2015. The Committee is composed of 20 parliamentarians, and it scrutinises the lists of nominees to the Court and interviews the candidates. See Parliamentary Assembly, 'Committee on the Election of Judges to the European Court of Human Rights' <https://pace.coe.int/en/pages/committee-30/committee-on-the-election-of-judges-to-the-european-court-of-human-rights> accessed 5 August 2024.

representative of the Court should participate in an observatory capacity during the interviews and express the preferences of the Court to the Committee.

References

Alter KJ, *The New Terrain of International Law: Courts, Politics, Rights* (Princeton UP 2014).

Arold NL, 'The European Court of Human Rights as an Example of Convergence' (2007) 76(2/3) Nord J Intl L 305.

Baetens F, *Identity and Diversity on the International Bench: Who Is the Judge?* (OUP 2020).

Bladini M, Uhnoo S and Wettergren Å, 'It Sounds Like Lived Experience': On Empathy in Rape Trials (2013) 72 IJLCJ doi:10.1016/j.ijlcj.2023.100575.

Bobek B (ed), *Selecting Europe's Judges: A Critical Review of the Appointment Procedures to the European Courts* (OUP 2015).

Cahill-O'Callaghan R, 'Reframing the Judicial Diversity Debate: Personal Values and Tacit Diversity' (2015) 35(1) LS 1.

Cahill-O'Callaghan R and Richards B, 'Policy, Principle and Values: An Exploration of Judicial Decision Making' (2018) 79(2) Louisiana L Rev 397.

Çalı B and Cunningham S, 'Judicial Self Government and the Sui Generis Case of the European Court of Human Rights' (2018) 19(7) German LJ 1977.

Collins PM Jr, Manning KL, and Carp RA, 'Gender, Critical Mass, and Judicial Decision Making' (2010) 32(2) Law and Policy 260.

Dawuni JJ, 'African Women Judges on International Courts: Symbolic or Substantive Gains' (2018) 47 U Baltimore L Rev 199.

Dawuni JJ (ed), *Gender, Judging and the Courts in Africa: Selected Studies* (Routledge 2021).

Drzemczewski A, 'The Internal Organization of the European Court of Human Rights: The Composition of the Chambers and the Grand Chamber' (2000) 3 EHRLR 237.

Duban E and Radacic I, *Training Manual for Judges and Prosecutors on Ensuring Women's Access to Justice* (Partnership for Good Governance 2017).

Dzehtsiarou K and Coffey D, 'Legitimacy and Independence of International Tribunals: An Analysis of the European Court of Human Rights' (2014) 37 Hastings Intl & Comp L Rev 271.

Dzehtsiarou K and Schwartz A, 'Electing Team Strasbourg: Professional Diversity on the European Court of Human Rights and Why it Matters' (2020) 21(4) German LJ 621.

Edlin DE, *Common Law Judging: Subjectivity, Impartiality, and the Making of Law* (U Michigan Press 2016).

Elfving S and others, '*EB v France*: Lesbian Adoption in France' in Ferreira N, Raj S, and Moscati M (eds), *Queer Judgments* (Counterpress 2024).

Fenton-Glynn C, *Family Formation and Parenthood* (OUP 2020).

Føllesdal A, 'How Many Women Judges are Enough on International Courts?' (2021) 52(4) J Social Philosophy 436.

Gee G and Rackley E, *Debating Judicial Appointments in an Age of Diversity* (Routledge 2018).

Gerards J, 'Margin of Appreciation and Incrementalism in the Case Law of the European Court of Human Rights' (2018) 18 HRL Rev 495.

Gillis M, 'Can We Talk? The Application of the Public Law Democratic Dialogue Model to the Interactions between Domestic Legislatures and the European Courts' (2022) 23 German LJ 56.

Grey R, McLoughlin K and Chappell L, 'Gender and Judging at the International Criminal Court: Lessons from "Feminist Judgment Projects"' (2021) 34(1) LJIL 247.

Grossman N, 'Achieving Sex-Representative International Court Benches' (2016) 110(1) AJIL 82.

Grossman N, 'Sex on the Bench: Do Women Judges Matter to the Legitimacy of International Courts?' (2012) 12 Chicago J Intl L 647.

Guth J and Elfving S, *Gender and Court of Justice of the European Union* (Routledge 2018).

Gyekye A, 'Advisory Opinion on Certain Legal Questions Concerning the Lists of Candidates Submitted with a View to the Election of Judges to the European Court of Human Rights' (2008) 47(4) ILM 518.

Helfer LR and Ryan C, 'LGBT Rights as Mega-Politics: Litigating before the ECtHR' (2021) 84 LCP 59.

Helfer LR and Voeten E, 'International Courts as Agents of Legal Change: Evidence from LGBT Rights in Europe' (2014) 68(1) Intl Org 77.

Hodson L, 'Gender and the International Judge: Towards a Transformative Equality Approach' (2022) 35 LJIL 913.

Hunter R, 'Can Feminist Judges Make A Difference?' (2008) 15(1–2) IJLP 7.

Hunter R, 'More Than Just a Different Face? Judicial Diversity and Decision-making' (2015) 68 CLP 1.

Iakovidis I and McDonough P, 'The Molla Sali Case: How the European Court of Human Rights Escaped a Legal Labyrinth While Holding the Thread of Human Rights' (2019) 8(2) OJLR 427.

Ichim O, *Just Satisfaction Under the European Convention on Human Rights* (CUP 2015).

Keller K, Heri C, and Christ M, 'Fifty Years of Women at the European Court of Human Rights: Successes and Failures of the Council of Europe's Gender Agenda' in Baetens F (ed), *Who Is the Judge? Identity and Diversity on the International Bench* (OUP 2020).

Kenny SJ, 'Choosing Judges: A Bumpy Road to Women's Equality and a Long Way to Go' (2012) 2012 Michigan State L Rev 1499.

Kimble SL and Röwekamp M (eds), *New Perspectives on European Women's Legal History* (Routledge 2016).

Knight CJS, 'A Court of Specialists: Judicial Behaviour on the UK Supreme Court by Chris Hanretty' (2022) 138(Oct) LQR 684.

L'Heureux-Dubé C, 'Outsiders on the Bench: The Continuing Struggle for Equality' (2001) 16 Wisconsin Women's L J 15.

Liesker HJ, 'Caught in a Balancing Act: The European Court of Human Rights and the Road to Recognition for Sexual Minorities' (2017) 4(3) Oslo L Rev 172.

Ludewig R and LaLlave J, 'Professional Stress, Discrimination and Coping Strategies: Similarities and Differences Between Female and Male Judges in Switzerland' in Schultz and Shaw (eds), *Gender and Judging* (Hart 2013).

Mackenzie R and others, *Selecting International Judges: Principle, Process and Politics* (OUP 2010).

Madsen M, 'From Cold War Instrument to Supreme European Court: The European Court of Human Rights at the Crossroads of International and National Law and Politics' (2007) 32 Law and Social Inquiry 137.

Malleson K, 'Gender Quotas for the Judiciary in England and Wales' in Schultz U and Shaw G (eds), *Gender and Judging* (Bloomsbury 2013).

Molbæk-Steensig H, 'Judicial Independence and Impartiality: Tenure Changes at the European Court of Human Rights' (2023) 34(3) EJIL 581.

Moran L, 'Judicial Diversity and the Challenge of Sexuality: Some Preliminary Findings' (2006) 28 Sydney L Rev 565.

Mowbray A, 'The Consideration of Gender in the Process of Appointing Judges to the European Court of Human Rights' (2008) 8(3) HRL Rev 549.

Ní Aoláin F, 'More Women: But Which Women? A Reply to Stéphanie Hennette Vauchez' (2015) 26(1) EJIL 229.

O'Connor K and Yanus AB, 'Judging Alone: Reflections on the Importance of Women on the Court' (2010) 6 Politics and Gender 441.

Olsen HP and Kücüksu A, 'Finding Hidden Patterns in ECtHR's Case Law: On How Citation Network Analysis Can Improve Our Knowledge of ECtHR's Article 14 Practice' (2017) 17(1) IJDL 4.
Pearson M, 'What Happened to '*Vivre Ensemble*?': Developments after *SAS v France*' (2021) 10(2) OJLR 185.
Polomarkakis KA, 'United in Diversity? Gender and Judging at the Court of Justice of the European Union (CJEU)' (2019) 34 Conn J Intl L 336.
Polonskaya K, 'Selecting Candidates to the Bench of the World Court: (Inevitable) Politicization and Its Consequences' (2020) 33 LJIL 409.
Powderly J, *Judges and the Making of International Criminal Law* (Brill 2020).
Rackley E, *Women, Judging and the Judiciary: From Difference to Diversity* (Routledge 2013).
Scherpe JM, 'The Right Ambit: Lady Hale and the Limitations of Article 8 ECHR' (2021) 43(3) J Soc Wel & Fam L 256.
Shen A, 'Women Judges Who Judge Women Offenders: A Chinese Case Study on Gender and Judging' (2020) 27(1) IJLP 63.
Sommerlad H, 'Let History Judge? Gender, Race, Class and Performative Identity: A Study of Women Judges in England and Wales' in Schultz U and Shaw G (eds), *Gender and Judging* (Bloomsbury 2013).
Thornton M, 'Otherness on the Bench: How Merit Is Gendered' (2007) 29 Sydney L Rev 406.
Torbisco-Casals N, 'The Legitimacy of International Courts: The Challenge of Diversity' (2021) 52(4) J Social Philosophy 491.
Tulkens F, 'Judicial Activism v Judicial Restraint: Practical Experience of This (False) Dilemma at the European Court of Human Rights' (2022) 3(3) ECHR L Rev 293.
van der Sloot B, 'The *Ad Hoc* Judge: A Rehabilitation' (2022) 29(5) MJ 572.
van der Sloot B, 'Between Fact and Fiction: An Analysis of the Case-Law on Article 12 of the European Convention on Human Rights' (2014) 4 CFLQ 397.
Vauchez SH, 'More Women: But Which Women? The Rule and the Politics of Gender Balance at the European Court of Human Rights' (2015) 26(1) EJIL 195.
Voeten E, 'Gender and Judging: Evidence from the European Court of Human Rights' (2021) 28 JEPP 1453.
Voeten E, 'The Politics of International Judicial Appointments: Evidence from the European Court of Human Rights' (2007) 61(4) Intl Org 669.

4 Gender Equality Case Law

4.1 Introduction

This chapter focuses on case law of the European Court of Human Rights (ECtHR) concerning the main non-discrimination provision in the European Convention on Human Rights[1] (ECHR). The scope of the ECHR to deal with structural discrimination against women has been thought to be limited in non-State environments, such as, workplaces where gender discrimination frequently occurs.[2] This is largely because the Convention has been typically viewed to govern only violations by State actors.[3] Yet, complaints invoking Article 14 ECHR have produced most gender equality case law within the ECtHR.[4] Although the Court has considered case law concerning gender equality most often by applying Article 14 in conjunction with the substantive provisions of the Convention, individuals do not always allege discrimination when complaining a violation of their rights.[5] Additionally, even where they do so, the Court does not always rule on the violation of Article 14, with the result that sometimes it overlooks discrimination in cases that allege violation of this provision. For instance, although the Court has recognised that the lack of legal recognition of the change of gender of post-operative trans individuals is central to complaints under Article 14, it has consistently avoided examining these issues under this provision on the grounds that it has found of a violation of Article 8 (Right to private life).[6]

In her seminal work, Radacic argued in 2008 that the Court's gender equality jurisprudence has been largely ineffectual in challenging gender discrimination and

1 Convention for the Protection of Human Rights and Fundamental Freedoms (European Convention on Human Rights, as amended) (ECHR).

2 Lisa McIntosh Sundstrom, Valerie Sperling and Melike Sayoglu, *Courting Gender Justice: Russia, Turkey and the European Court of Human Rights* (OUP 2019) 137.

3 ibid.

4 See eg Ivana Radacic, 'Gender Equality Jurisprudence of the European Court of Human Rights' (2008) 19(4) EJIL 841, 842; McIntosh Sundstrom and others (n 2) 136.

5 See eg Svitlana Karvatska, Ivan Toronchuk, and Alyona Manyk, 'Gender Equality Principle: Application in ECtHR's Practice' (2021) 9 Logos Universality Mentality Education Novelty Section Law 83, 86.

6 See eg *Christine Goodwin v UK* App no 28957/95 (ECtHR, 11 July 2002), para 108.

DOI: 10.4324/9781003435099-4

achieving equality between women and men.[7] She argues that owing to the formalistic interpretation of equality, the Court has addressed only a limited number of problems, and at times the Court's jurisprudence may have diminished the importance of gender equality, rather than promote it.[8] It is, therefore, vital to examine advances made in this regard since 2008. If some of the past cases were decided today, the outcome may well be different as societies have changed considerably in the past two to three decades.[9] Yet, pending and future complaints are likely to highlight lingering problems in the protection of human rights at a transnational level. In some contexts, the Court is willing to uphold concepts that are consistent with gender equality in line with significant legal instruments, such as, the United Nations Convention on the Elimination of All Forms of Discrimination against Women[10] (CEDAW) and the Council of Europe (CoE) Istanbul Convention.[11] However, there is still scope for improvement as it has been argued that the ECtHR could reference the work of the CEDAW Committee in its reasoning.[12]

This chapter is structured in the following way: Section 4.2 examines what is meant by differential treatment of women and men in the context of Article 14. The next three sections evaluate specific areas of case law where discrimination against women is most visible, namely intersectional discrimination of women on grounds of age, race or ethnicity, and religious beliefs (Section 4.3); violence against women (Section 4.4), and discrimination against trans individuals (Section 4.5). Section 4.6 provides a conclusion.

4.2 Differential Treatment between Women and Men

The Court has repeatedly stated that the advancement of gender equality is a major goal in the CoE States,[13] and that significant reasons must exist for a difference in treatment to be compatible with the Convention.[14] Considering that the book's principal aim is to analyse case law through the lens of intersectional feminist legal

7 Radacic (n 4) 842.

8 ibid.

9 Claire Fenton-Glynn, *Family Formation and Parenthood* (OUP 2020).

10 (adopted 18 December 1979; entry into force 3 September 1981) 1249 UNTS 13.

11 Convention on preventing and combating violence against women and domestic violence (adopted 11 May 2011) CETS No 210. For commentary, see Lourdes Peroni, 'Violence Against Migrant Women: The Istanbul Convention Through a Postcolonial Feminist Lens' (2016) 24 Fem LS 49.

12 Isobel Renzulli, 'Discrimination and Gender Stereotypes in Judicial Decisions: The Jurisprudence of the European Court of Human Rights in Light of *JL v Italy*–A Retreat Into The Shadows?' (2023) 41(3) NQHR 155, 157. See eg CEDAW Committee, General Recommendation No 33 'Women's Access to Justice' (2015).

13 See eg *Konstantin Markin v Russia* App no 30078/06 (ECtHR, 22 March 2012), para 127. See also Natalie Alkiviadou and Andrea Manoli, 'The European Court of Human Rights Through the Looking Glass of Gender: An Evaluation' (2021) 11(1) Goettingen J Intl L 191.

14 *Abdulaziz, Cabales, and Balkandali v UK* App nos 9214/80, 9473/81, and 9474/81 (ECtHR, 28 May 1985), para 78.

scholarship,[15] it is noteworthy that the Court has repeatedly held that, just like differences based on sex, difference in treatment based on sexual orientation require 'particularly convincing and weighty reasons' by way of justification.[16] The ECtHR has similarly established that where a difference in treatment is based on race or ethnicity, the notion of objective and reasonable justification for the differential treatment must be interpreted as strictly as possible.[17] No difference in treatment, which is based exclusively, or to a decisive extent, on a person's ethnic origin, can be objectively justified in a contemporary democratic society built on the principles of pluralism and respect for different cultures.[18] In certain circumstances, racial discrimination can amount to degrading treatment within the meaning of Article 3 ECHR (Prohibition of torture).[19] Additionally, discrimination on account of a person's actual or perceived ethnic origin is a form of racial discrimination.[20] Consequently, the State's margin of appreciation in these areas is narrow.

The Court has on several occasions found that differential treatment on the grounds of gender amounts to discrimination against women falling within the scope of Article 14. It has found a violation of this provision in various areas, including family reunification;[21] violence against women;[22] ability of women to keep their surnames after marriage;[23] registration of children after their father's surname;[24] and marital status.[25] Voeten notes that existing gendered analysis of

15 See eg Charlotte Helen Skeet, 'Intersectionality as Theory and Method: Human Rights Adjudication by the European Court of Human Rights' in Naomi Creutzfeldr, Marc Mason, and Kirsten McConnachie (eds), *The Routledge Handbook of Socio-Legal Theory and Method* (Routledge 2019).

16 See eg *Vallianatos and Others v Greece* App nos 29381/09 and 32684/09 (ECtHR, 7 November 2013), para 77 (violation of art 14).

17 See eg *DH and Others v Czech Republic* App no 57325/00 (ECtHR, 7 February 2006), para 196 (placement of Roma children in a school for mentally disabled children).

18 ibid para 176.

19 *East African Asians v UK* App nos 4403/70 and Others (Commission Decision, 14 December 1973); *Abdu v Bulgaria* App np 26827/08 (ECtHR, 11 March 2014), para 23 (The authorities' failure to investigate a possible racist motive for the violence perpetrated against two Sudanese men was a violation of art 3 in conjunction of art 14).

20 *Timishev v Russia* App nos 55762/00 and 55974/00 (ECtHR, 30 March 2004), para 55 (A violation of art 14 taken in conjunction with art 2 of Protocol No 4 in respect of a Russian national who was denied permanent residence in Russia due to being an ethnic Chechen).

21 *Abdulaziz* (n 14).

22 *Opuz v Turkey* App no 33401/02 (ECtHR, 9 September 2009); *Volodina v Russia* App no 41261/17 (ECtHR, 9 July 2019). See also McIntosh Sundstrom and others (n 2).

23 See eg *Burghartz v Switzerland* App no 16213/90 (ECtHR, 22 February 1994), para 27 (Swiss authorities' refusal to correctly record wife's surname as a married couple's joint surname violated art 14); *Ünal Tekeli v Turkey* App no 29865/96 (ECtHR, 16 November 2004) (Turkish Law preventing married women from keeping their own surname violated art 14).

24 *Cusan and Fazzo v Italy* App no 77/07 (ECtHR, 7 January 2014) (the authorities' decision to register children under her father's surname violated art 14 in conjunction with art 8). See also *León Madrid v Spain* App no 30306/13 (ECtHR, 26 October 2021).

25 *Nurcan Bayraktar v Türkiye* App no 27094/20 (ECtHR, 27 June 2023) (The refusal of the Turkish authorities to grant an exemption to the obligation imposed on divorced women to wait for 300 days

the Court's case law has often focused on gender discrimination,[26] reproductive rights,[27] and family issues, whereas there is less analysis of economic rights such as access to property, parental leave and other allowances,[28] survivor's pensions,[29] employment,[30] and inheritance rights.[31] While these are important areas to analyse, there are still relatively few cases concerning economic rights.

The types of discrimination that fall within the scope of Article 14, of course, extend beyond gender[32] as the provision explicitly prohibits 'discrimination on any ground such as sex, race, colour, language, religion, political or other opinion, national or social origin, association with a national minority, property, birth or other status'.[33] The list is considered non-exhaustive, which allows the Court to extend and include grounds that are not expressly mentioned.[34] Therefore, Article 14 requires the Court to interpret the possible grounds of discrimination in an extensive manner.[35] However, not all differences in treatment constitute discrimination.[36] For an issue to arise under Article 14, it must be determined that other persons in an analogous or relevantly similar situation enjoy preferential treatment.[37] Consequently, the distinction is discriminatory, unless there is an objective and

---

before remarrying, unless they provide a medical certificate attesting that they are not pregnant, constituted a violation of art 14).

26 See eg Alexandra Timmer, 'Toward an Anti-Stereotyping Approach for the European Court of Human Rights' (2011) 11(4) HRL Rev 707.

27 See eg Liiri Oja and Alicia Ely Yamin, '"Woman" in the European Human Rights System: How is the Reproductive Rights Jurisprudence of the European Court of Human Rights Constructing Narratives of Women's Citizenship?' (2016) 32(1) Colum J Gender & L 62.

28 *Markin* (n 13) (The Court rejected the stereotypical portrayal of women as primary child-carers and men as breadwinners); *Gruba and Others v Russia* App nos 66180/09 and others (ECtHR, 6 July 2021).

29 *Willis v UK* App no 36042/97 (ECtHR 11 June 2002) (The difference in treatment between men and women as regards entitlement to the widow's payment and widowed mother's allowance violation of art 14 taken in conjunction with art 1 of protocol no 1); *Beeler v Switzerland* App no 78630/12 (ECtHR, 11 October 2022).

30 *Emel Boyraz v Turkey* App no 61960/08 (ECtHR, 2 December 2014) (Ms Emel Boyraz's dismissal from her job as a security officer after several years on the grounds that the job involved nighttime work in rural areas and carrying and using firearms and physical force without an objective reason violated art 14 taken in conjunction with art 8).

31 Erik Voeten, 'Gender and Judging: Evidence from the European Court of Human Rights' (2020) 28(9) JEPP 1453.

32 Loveday Hodson, 'Sexual Orientation and the European Convention on Human Rights: What of the "L" in LGBT?' (2019) 23(3) J Lesbian Stud 383.

33 ECHR, art 14.

34 Oddný Mjöll Arnardóttir, 'Cross-fertilisation, Clarity and Consistency at an Overburdened European Court of Human Rights: The Case of the Discrimination Grounds under Article 14 ECHR' (2015) 33(3) Nord J Hum Rts 220, 225.

35 ibid.

36 ECtHR, 'Guide on Article 14 of the European Convention on Human Rights and on Article 1 of Protocol No 12 to the Convention: Prohibition of discrimination' (29 February 2024) 16 <https://ks.echr.coe.int/web/echr-ks/article-14> accessed 25 May 2024.

37 See eg *Tekeli* (n 23) para 49.

reasonable justification for the difference in treatment.[38] The argument that the distinction pursues a legitimate aim is not acceptable on its own, but there must be a 'reasonable relationship of proportionality between the means employed and the aim sought'.[39] In the context of gender discrimination, references to justifications, such as, traditional distribution of gender roles, gender stereotypes, or prevailing social attitudes in the State are insufficient.[40]

4.3 Intersectional Discrimination

The way in which Article 14 is relevant in finding differential treatment between women and men in neutrally seeming legislation and practice is illustrated in the case law analysis. Scholars have suggested that because individuals have multiple protected identity characteristics, the Court should take an intersectional approach when adjudicating cases under Article 14.[41] According to scholars, discrimination on more than one ground listed in Article 14 often affects women in particular, although multiple or intersectional discrimination is not exclusively limited to women.[42] To make wider equality policies fully effective for all disadvantaged applicants, the Court should consider the nature of situations where discrimination occurs on the basis of multiple grounds operating separately or interacting with each other all at once.[43] There has been much emphasis on multiple, accumulative, or intersectional discrimination in equality law. The most well-known conceptualisation may be Crenshaw's 1989 theory of intersectionality,[44] which expresses the idea that Black women are disadvantaged by the interaction of their race and gender. Scholars have built on this theory, extending intersectional discrimination, for instance, to the spheres of gender and religious beliefs and gender and sexual orientation. While law confers protection upon individuals it seemingly benefits, it can also uphold patterns of difference that maintain existing inequalities.[45] One more

38 ECtHR, 'Guide on Article 14' (n 36).

39 See eg *Petrovic v Austria* App no 20458/92 (ECtHR, 27 March 1998), para 30 (The Court found no violation of art 14 due to the Austrian authorities' refusal to grant parental leave allowance to a father, on the ground that allowance was only available to mothers). See also ECtHR, 'Guide on Article 14' (n 36) 18.

40 See eg *Semenya v Switzerland* App no 10934/212023 (ECtHR, 11 July 2023) (The Court found a violation of art 14 taken in conjunction with art 8 on account of the limited institutional and judicial review of the grounds relied upon to justify the non-State regulations or of the side-effects of the hormonal treatment on a professional athlete, Ms Mokgadi Caster Semenya, who was required to lower her natural testosterone levels to compete in the women's category in international competitions).

41 Issues of intersectional or multiple discrimination can be addressed under Article 14. See Arnardóttir (n 34) 225.

42 Karvatska, Toronchuk, and Manyk (n 5) 92.

43 ECtHR, 'Guide on Article 14' (n 36) 14.

44 Kimberlé Crenshaw, 'Demarginalizing the Intersection of Race and Sex: A Black Feminist Critique of Antidiscrimination Doctrine, Feminist Theory, and Antiracist Politics' (1989) U Chicago L Forum 139.

45 Alison Diduck and William Wilson, 'Prostitutes and Persons' (1997) 24(4) J L & Society 504.

recent extension of the intersectional theory is so-called mixed intersectionality, which Malleson characterises as a situation where individuals have a blend of multiple competing privileged and disadvantaged identity characteristics, which may privilege them in one way but discriminate or disadvantage them in other ways.[46]

Even though the Court has acknowledged that multiple disadvantaged identities exist, it does not expressly use the term intersectionality.[47] As both Article 14 and Article 1 of Protocol No 12 prohibit discrimination on multiple grounds, making a claim on more than one ground is theoretically possible.[48] Although Yoshida suggested in 2013 that the Court may be open to intersectional considerations,[49] its engagement with the term in the past decade has been relatively limited.[50] The Court has been criticised for being insufficiently sensitive to intersectional discrimination, particularly in its case law concerning headscarves worn by Muslim women.[51] Before looking at specific case law examples of discrimination arising from the intersection of gender and race or ethnic origin[52] and gender and religious beliefs, the next subsection considers a sole case involving the intersection of age and gender.

4.3.1 Gender and Age

In the 2017 judgment in *Carvalho Pinto de Sousa Morais v Portugal*,[53] the Court recognised the combined effect of the age and gender. The case concerned a decision of the Portuguese court to reduce the amount of non-pecuniary damage awarded to Ms Maria Ivone Carvalho Pinto de Sousa Morais due to medical negligence, which resulted in her inability to have sexual relations. To justify the reduction, the national court relied on the fact that Ms Carvalho was 50 years old at the time of the surgery. It considered that at 50, sexuality was not as important as in younger years and that its significance diminished with age. The ECtHR found significant that, in two previous sets of medical malpractice proceedings brought by two male patients

46 Kate Malleson, 'Equality Law and the Protected Characteristics' (2018) 81 MLR 598.

47 Keina Yoshida, 'Towards Intersectionality in the European Court of Human Rights: The Case of *BS v Spain*' (2013) 21 Fem LS 195. The term was explicitly used in the dissenting opinion of Judge Pinto de Albuquerque in a dispute concerning inability of a single mother relying on social benefits to access moderate-cost rented housing due to minimum income requirements. See *Garib v Netherlands* App no 43494/09 (ECtHR, 6 November 2017), dissenting opinion of Judge Pinto de Albuquerque joined by Judge Vehabović.

48 ECtHR, 'Guide on Article 14' (n 36) 14.

49 Yoshida (n 47).

50 See eg Sarah Ganty 'Poverty as Misrecognition: What Role for Antidiscrimination Law in Europe?' (2021) 21(4) HRL Rev 962.

51 Radacic (n 4)

52 According to the Court, ethnic origin and race are related and overlapping concepts. See *Biao v Denmark* [2017] 64 EHRR 1, para 94: 'No difference in treatment based exclusively or to a decisive extent on a person's ethnic origin is capable of being justified in a contemporary democratic society. Discrimination on account of, *inter alia*, a person's ethnic origin is a form of racial discrimination'.

53 *Carvalho Pinto de Sousa Morais v Portugal* App no 17484/15 (ECtHR, 3 October 2017).

in their 50s, the national court considered that the fact that the men could no longer have normal sexual relations resulted in a shock, without seeing the age of the male applicants as relevant. It noted that the question in the case was not considerations of age or sex as such, but rather the stereotypical assumption that sexuality was unimportant for a middle-aged woman. The assumption reflected the idea of female sexuality as being linked to child-bearing purposes.[54] Finding a breach of Article 14 in conjunction with Article 8, the ECtHR concluded that Ms Carvalho's age and gender were decisive factors in the national court's final decision, introducing a difference of treatment based on those grounds. Renzulli has criticised the Court for not going far enough. According to her, while the judgment is a step forward in the Court's gender anti-stereotyping case law, it is a modest advancement in terms of challenging deep-seated structures underlying gender discrimination.[55] Time will tell whether the Court will decide other similar cases that clearly rule out discrimination against women on the combined grounds of age and gender.

4.3.2 Gender and Race or Ethnic Origin

After the Second World War, Europe has become home to several diasporic groups.[56] The specific cases where gender and race or ethnic origin have been an issue involve discrimination of spouses in immigration law, forced sterilisation of Roma women in Slovakia,[57] and racial violence impacting Black women.[58] The analysis demonstrates that States engage in what Becker terms as othering based on religion, race, and ethnic origin[59] as the States distinguish between citizens and diasporic and minoritised groups. Although fewer cases have concerned women, the Court has built extensive case law concerning racially motivated discrimination and violence against Roma men,[60] Black men,[61] and men observing a non-Christian faith,[62] which may be insightful in future cases concerning discrimination of women on grounds of race and ethnicity.

54 *Carvalho* (n 53) para 52. See also ECtHR, 'Guide on Article 14' (n 36) 15.
55 Renzulli (n 12) 165.
56 Elizabeth Becker, 'Theorizing "new ethnicities" in diasporic Europe: Jews, Muslims and Stuart Hall' (2024) 47(9) Ethnic and Racial Stud 1858.
57 See eg *NB v Slovakia* App no 29518/10 (ECtHR, 12 June 2012). See also Ruth Rubio-Marín and Mathias Möschel, 'Anti-Discrimination Exceptionalism: Racist Violence before the ECtHR and the Holocaust Prism' (2015) 26(4) EJIL 881.
58 *BS v Spain* App no 47159/08 (ECtHR, 24 July 2012).
59 Becker (n 56).
60 See eg *Nachova and Others v Bulgaria* App nos 43577/98 and 43579/98 (ECtHR, 6 July 2005) (A violation of art 14 taken in conjunction with art 2 due to the authorities' failure to investigate possible racist motives behind the fatal shooting of two Bulgarian men of Roma origin).
61 For cases where the Court found a violation of art 14 taken in conjunction with art 8 in relation to identity checks based on racial profiling, see *Basu v Germany* App no 215/19 (ECtHR, 18 October 2022); *Wa Baile v Switzerland* App nos 43868/18 and 25883/21 (ECtHR, 20 February 2024).
62 See *Sejdić and Finci v Bosnia and Herzegovina* App nos 27996/06 and 34836/06 (ECtHR, 22 December 2009) (A violation of art 14 taken in conjunction with art 3 of protocol no 1 after two

One of the first cases alleging racial discrimination by women is the ECtHR's 1985 landmark judgment in *Abdulaziz, Cabales, and Balkandali v UK*.[63] The applicants were three women of non-British origin, residing lawfully in the UK, namely Ms Nargis Abdulaziz, a citizen of Malawi; Ms Arcely Cabales, a citizen of the Philippines; and Ms Sohair Balkandali, a citizen of the UK and Colonies. They complained that the UK immigration rules denied legal residence to their husbands. They consequently alleged a violation of their right to family life (Article 8) as well as discrimination on the grounds of sex, race, and birth (Article 14). According to the women, UK immigration rules had a disproportionate impact on racialised individuals, and the legislative history disclosed that their purpose was to limit the number of non-white immigrants from the former British colonies in Asia and Africa.[64] The ECtHR found violation of Article 14 on the grounds of sex discrimination, holding that the UK could not favour wives over husbands for family reunification.[65] Yet, it found no discrimination on the grounds of race or birth. It reiterated the Commission's earlier finding[66] that giving priority to nationals of countries with which the State had the closest links did not constitute racial discrimination.[67] De Vries and Spijkerboer argue that the British immigration legislation did, in fact, limit the numbers of the citizens of its former colonies admitted to the UK territory, because admission was available only for individuals who were born in the UK or were descendants of a parent born in the UK.[68] Although the immigration legislation did not openly differentiate between individuals on the grounds of race or ethnicity, white Commonwealth citizens were considered nationals, and everyone else were viewed as immigrants.[69] The case demonstrates the States' focus on gender, in a reverse way, as States expect the family members seeking family reunification to be wives joining their husbands, rather than the other way round.[70]

The Court changed its approach only decades after when examining the lawfulness of the Danish family reunification legislation in the 2017 judgment in *Biao v Denmark*.[71] It stated that the difference in treatment between persons born with the Danish nationality and naturalised Danish citizens was inconsistent with Article 14. The case concerned the Danish authorities' rejection of a family reunification

citizens of Bosnia and Herzegovina were denied a right to stand for election to the House of Peoples under the Constitution due to their ethnic origin).

63 *Abdulaziz* (n 14).

64 ibid para 84.

65 Karin de Vries and Thomas Spijkerboer, 'Race and the Regulation of International Migration: The Ongoing Impact of Colonialism in the Case Law of the European Court of Human Rights' (2021) 39(4) NQHR 291. 301.

66 *X v UK* App no 9088/80 (Commission Decision, 6 March 1982); *X, Y and Z v UK* App no 9285/81 (Commission Decision, 6 July 1982).

67 *Abdulaziz* (n 14) paras 84–85.

68 De Vries and Spijkerboer (n 65) 299.

69 ibid 301.

70 ibid.

71 *Biao* (n 52).

request by the Ghanaian woman, Ms Asia Adamo-Biao, who was married to Mr Ousmane Biao, a naturalised Danish citizen of Togolese origin. The couple complained before the ECtHR that the Danish migration rules amounted to indirect discrimination on the basis of race and ethnic origin between Danish-born citizens, and naturalised Danish citizens, whom in the majority of cases would have different ethnic and national origins.[72] They argued that the refusal amounted to a violation of Article 8 in combination with Article 14 because it was impossible for the couple to live in Denmark before 2030.[73] This was because Mr Biao had only been a Danish national for two years, and the authorities considered that their combined attachment to Ghana was stronger than their attachment to Denmark.[74] As a result, the couple moved to Sweden, while Mr Biao commuted to Denmark for work.[75] The Court agreed and held that the requirement for Mr Biao to have lived in Denmark for 28 years before family reunification was possible created a difference in treatment between Danish citizens, which amounted to indirect discrimination on grounds of race or ethnic origin.[76] It further noted that as no other country distinguished between nationals from birth and naturalised persons in their family reunification policy, such a rule had a disproportionately prejudicial effect on naturalised Danish citizens.[77]

In a series of complaints against Slovakia concerning forced sterilisation of married Roma women at a public hospital at the time of their second caesarean section, the Court found that the sterilisation of a mentally competent woman without her full and informed consent, when there was no immediate threat to her life, amounted to ill-treatment contrary to Article 3.[78] Forced sterilisation is a violation of an individual's physical integrity. Additionally, each of the women alleged discrimination on the grounds of gender and ethnic origin or race.[79] They also alleged that their infertility led into a breakdown of their marital relationships and ostracisation by the Roma community.[80] However, the Court did not consider the claims of ethnic

72 ibid para 68.

73 Sergio Carrera Nuñez, 'The ECtHR's Judgment in *Biao v Denmark*: Non-Discrimination Among Nationals and Family Reunification as Converging European Standards: ECtHR, *Biao v Denmark*, Judgment of 24 May 2016, Application No 38590/10' (2016) 23(5) MJ 865.

74 *Biao* (n 51) paras 10–31. Matilda Gillis, 'Can We Talk? The Application of the Public Law Democratic Dialogue Model to the Interactions between Domestic Legislatures and the European Courts' (2022) 23 German LJ 56, 70.

75 *Biao* (n 52).

76 ibid para 96.

77 Gillis (n 74) 70.

78 See *VC v Slovakia* App no 18968/07 (ECtHR 8 November 2011); *NB v Slovakia* App no 29518/10 (ECtHR, 12 June 2012); *IG and Others v Slovakia* App no 15966/04 (ECtHR, 13 November 2012). Additionally, the Istanbul Convention (art 39) prohibits forced sterilisation.

79 *NB* (n 78) paras 6 and 118 (The Court found a violation of arts 3 and 8 on account Ms NB's sterilisation during the delivery of her second child via Caesarean section. She alleged particularly that her race or ethnic origin had played a determining role in her sterilisation and that in that respect she had been discriminated because of her gender).

80 ibid para 18.

discrimination in any of these cases.[81] Instead, it decided to focus on violation of Article 8, without the need to investigate whether Article 14 was violated. In all cases the Court concluded that there was insufficient evidence to demonstrate in a convincing manner that the practice was 'part of an organised policy', 'the hospital staff's conduct was intentionally racially motivated', or that 'the doctors acted in bad faith, with the intention of ill-treating the applicant'.[82] This was despite the fact that it had dealt with three similar complaints against Slovakia at the time, while there could have well been many more women in the same position.

The Court's understanding of issues relating to women's reproductive health has seemingly improved throughout the years. In its 2022 judgment in *YP v Russia*,[83] the Court reflected back on the Slovakian cases, stating that sterilisation without informed consent called for serious criticism, considering the fact that the Roma women were a vulnerable minoritised population group; they were young women at an early stage of their reproductive life; there was an absence of imminent medical necessity; and the sterilisation procedure was associated with serious medical and psychological after-effects .[84] Yet, this does not help the Roma women who underwent forced sterilisation over a decade before the judgment in *YP*. The problem with judgments like these is that it is impossible to restore the damage endured by the individuals.[85]

Another example of intersectional discrimination on grounds of gender and race is the 2012 judgment in *BS v Spain*.[86] In this case, Ms BS, a Black migrant woman of Nigerian origin, who was legally a resident in Spain, alleged that the Spanish police abused her physically and verbally due to her race, gender, and profession as a sex worker. She was stopped on multiple occasions by the police, who asked her for her identification papers purely because she was Black, made racist and degrading remarks at her, and struck her with a truncheon on her wrists and thigh.[87] Ms BS especially claimed that she was singled out from the Caucasian sex workers operating in the same area near Palma de Mallorca. She alleged a violation of Article 3 under its procedural limb, on account of Spain's failure to sufficiently and effectively investigate her allegations concerning Article 3. She also alleged a violation of Article 14 taken in conjunction with Article 3. The ECtHR unanimously held that there was a violation of Article 3 under its procedural limb, and a violation of Article 14 taken in conjunction with Article 3 because the Spanish authorities failed to investigate the potentially racist attitudes of the officers.[88] Of most importance for this research is the attention the ECtHR gave to

81 ibid para 123: 'In these circumstances, the Court does not find it necessary to separately determine whether the facts of the case also gave rise to a breach of Article 14'.

82 See eg *VC* (n 78) para 177.

83 *YP v Russia* App no 43399/13 (ECtHR, 20 September 2022), para 34.

84 ibid.

85 Octavian Ichim, *Just Satisfaction Under the European Convention on Human Rights* (CUP 2015) 16.

86 *BS* (n 58).

87 ibid para 8.

88 *BS* (n 58) para 62.

the intersections of Ms BS's identity when it noted that the Spanish courts failed to take account of the particular vulnerability of Ms BS 'inherent in her position as an African woman working as a prostitute'.[89] *BS* can be argued to mark a significant moment for the ECtHR in recognising intersectional discrimination against Black women. The Court not only recognised Ms BS's intersectional identity as a minoritised woman, but it also explicitly stated that intersections in her identity resulted in her vulnerability that deserved heightened protection under the Convention.[90] Despite this, the Court is yet to explicitly identify the existence of intersectional discrimination in its case law.

4.3.3 Gender and Religious Beliefs

The gendered dimension of religious manifestation has culminated in the French and Belgian legislation banning full-face coverings in public. The bans illustrate how women's clothing has become the site of political battles focusing on gender, religion, and identity.[91] They have also sparked scholars to argue that some European States have adopted oppressive policies against Muslim women. The French and Belgian bans cover the *niqab*, a garment which entirely conceals the face apart from the eyes and the *burqa*, a full body covering including a mesh over the face.[92] Because of its judgments concerning Europe's diasporic Muslims, the Court has been accused of not supporting religious freedom.[93] The Court has approached its jurisprudence on Article 9 ECHR (Freedom of thought, conscience, and religion) in terms of the 'freedom of others to remain unaffected from the beliefs of others' within the meaning of Article 9(2).[94] Under this provision, the freedom of religion is a qualified right that can be subject to limitations prescribed by law which pursue legitimate aims. Under Article 9(2), legitimate aims are the interests of public safety, the protection of public order, health or morals, or the protection of the rights and freedoms of others.

A review of the Court's case law reveals that most cases on Muslim women's right to manifest their religious beliefs have focused on bans on headscarves covering the hair and neck while leaving the face uncovered (*hijab*), particularly at educational establishments and workplaces in various CoE States. Teachers, academic staff, pupils, university students, and social workers wearing a headscarf are often

89 ibid.
90 Yoshida (n 47).
91 Pablo Castillo-Ortiz, Amal Ali and Navajyoti Samanta, 'Gender, Intersectionality, and Religious Manifestation Before the European Court of Human Rights' (2019) 18(1) J Hum Rts 76.
92 Malak Benslama-Dabdoub, 'Epistemic Violence and Colonial Legacies in the Representation of Refugee Women: Contesting Narratives of Vulnerability and Victimhood' (2024) 20(1) Intl JLC 54.
93 Stijn Smet, 'Conscientious Objection Under the European Convention on Human Rights: The Ugly Duckling of a Flightless Jurisprudence' in Jeroen Temperman, Jeremy Gunn and Malcolm Evans (eds) *The European Court of Human Rights and the Freedom of Religion or Belief: The 25 Years Since Kokkinakis* (Brill 2019) 282.
94 ECHR, art 9(2). See also *Dahlab v Switzerland* App no 42393/98 (ECtHR, 15 February 2001).

portrayed as women who defy the authority by knowingly and willingly refusing to remove their headscarves, even if they could face disciplinary proceedings, dismissal from their jobs, suspension from studies, or the risk their employment contract not being renewed. The damage that the headscarf bans inflict on women's careers and career aspirations is profound. Despite such a disruption to their lives, the Court has not found a violation of Article 9 taken alone and in conjunction with Article 14 in any of the cases considering wearing a headscarf in the context education or employment.

The first case in the area is the 2001 inadmissible decision in *Dahlab v Switzerland*.[95] In this case, Ms Lucia Dahlab, a newly qualified primary-school teacher, converted to Islam and began wearing a headscarf after marrying an Algerian man. After she returned to work from her second maternity leave, the primary-education department issued a ban on Muslim employees wearing headscarves, on the ground that by doing so teachers were breaking the law and that imposing a visible sign of identity on pupils was unacceptable in a public, secular education system. The case was declared inadmissible under Article 14 on the grounds that the ban was not imposed because of Ms Dahlab's gender, but it pursued the legitimate aim of ensuring the neutrality of State primary education. According to the Court, it would hardly be compatible with values, such as, tolerance, equality, and the rights of others that a primary school teacher could potentially impose her religious beliefs on her students. Yet, the same values were not extended to Ms Dahlab.

In its 2006 inadmissible decision in *Kurtulmuş v Turkey*,[96] Istanbul University prohibited its staff from wearing the Islamic headscarf in the exercise of their functions. Ms Sevgi Kurtulmuş, an Associate Professor at the Faculty of Economics, complained that she was dismissed from her job at the age of 40 on the grounds that she wilfully failed to comply with the headscarf ban. The Court did not consider that her rights under Article 9 were violated because this provision did not confer on individuals, who chose to behave in a certain way due to their religious beliefs, the right to disregard rules, which were shown to be justified, and that principle applied also to civil servants. It ruled that Ms Kurtulmuş's complaint under Article 14 was inadmissible, noting that the impugned rules were not based on her religion or gender.

Several inadmissible decisions have concerned the prohibition of pupils to wear a headscarf in State schools in Türkiye and France. In its 2006 decision in *Köse v Turkey*,[97] girls were prohibited from entering school when wearing a headscarf on the grounds that wearing one in a State-funded religious school was prohibited by law. The Court noted that although the right to education guaranteed everyone a right of access to educational institutions, that right could be subject to restrictions.

95 *Dahlab* (n 94).
96 *Kurtulmuş v Turkey* App no 65500/01 (ECtHR, 24 January 2006).
97 *Köse and Others v Turkey* App no 26625/02 (ECtHR, 24 January 2006).

The 2008 decision in *Kervanci v France*[98] concerned an expulsion of girls from a State school for refusing to remove headscarves during physical education and sports lessons. The Court found no violation of Article 9. In its 2009 decision *Dogru v France*,[99] the Court similarly upheld a French ban of headscarves worn by girls at school. According to the decision, the French ban was rooted in the high priority of secularism in the French constitution.

The alleged negative influential power inherent in the wearing of religious symbols was also at stake in the Court's 2007 judgment in *Leyla Şahin v Turkey* where a 25-year-old medical student, Ms Leyla Şahin, was barred from taking an exam because she ignored the headscarf ban imposed by the Faculty of Medicine at Istanbul University. The following year, the Dean of the Faculty suspended Ms Şahin from the university for a semester.[100] The Court did not find a violation of either Article 9 or Article 14, but accepted Türkiye's argument that the university had taken measures aimed at reducing the influence that fundamental religious groups could exert on non-religious students. In such a situation, the ban on religious symbols was considered to pursue the goal of peaceful co-existence between students of diverse beliefs. The impact that the disruption caused to her studies prompted Ms Şahin to abandon her studies at Istanbul University altogether and she subsequently enrolled as a student at the University of Vienna, Austria.[101]

The 2013 judgment in *Eweida and others v UK*[102] illustrates how a necklace featuring a cross is seen more acceptable than a headscarf. Ms Nadia Eweida was a Christian woman who had emigrated from Egypt to the UK at the age of 18.[103] She complained that as a check-in staff for British Airways, she was required to cover her necklace featuring a cross with her uniform.[104] The Court considered that, while her employer's wish to project a certain corporate image was indisputably legitimate, as no evidence indicated that British Airways' brand or image was not negatively affected by the fact that other employees had been previously authorised to wear other items of religious clothing, such as *hijabs* and turbans.[105] Essentially, the Court pitted Muslim and Sikh workers against Ms Eweida. It concluded that penalising Ms Eweida for wearing a discreet cross that could be hidden out of sight, if needed to be,[106] the UK authorities failed sufficiently to protect her right to manifest her religion, in breach of the positive obligation under Article 9, taken alone and in conjunction with Article 14.[107]

98 *Kervanci v France* App no 31645/04 (ECtHR, 4 December 2008).
99 *Dogru v France* (2009) 49 EHRR 8.
100 *Leyla Şahin v Turkey* App no 44774/98 (ECtHR, 10 November 2005), para 24.
101 *Şahin* (n 100) para 28.
102 *Eweida and Others v UK* App nos 48420/10 and others (ECtHR, 15 January 2013) (The Court found no violation of art 9 in respect to the three other applicants).
103 ibid para 9.
104 ibid para 10.
105 ibid para 94.
106 ibid.
107 ibid.

One of the most controversial cases before the ECtHR concerning the intersection of gender and religion is the 2014 judgment in *SAS v France*[108] which concerned the French ban on *niqab* in public places. In its third party intervener's submission, Amnesty International pointed out that the French law banning *niqab* risked Muslim women experiencing a distinct form of discrimination due to the intersection of gender with religion.[109] It also noted that the assumption that Muslim women wore a *niqab* only under coercion was an expression of gender- and religion-based stereotyping.[110] *SAS* has attracted considerable commentary,[111] and it has been criticised as inconsistent and confusing because the Court acknowledged that by prohibiting everyone from wearing a covering designed to conceal the face in public places, French law had specific negative effects on the situation of Muslim women who wished to wear a *niqab* in public for religious reasons.[112]

The 2015 judgment in *Ebrahimian v France*[113] concerned a complaint by 49-year-old Ms Christine Ebrahimian that the refusal of the psychiatric unit of a Parisian hospital to renew her two fixed-term contracts was motivated by her religious beliefs. She was recruited to work as a social worker on two successive fixed-term contracts covering a period of 15 months.[114] Ms Ebrahimian was subsequently informed that her contract would not be renewed following complaints by patients that she refused to remove her headscarf while on duty.[115] Additionally, disciplinary proceedings were brought against her. Unhelpfully, the Court concluded that Ms Ebrahimian was aware of the requirement not to wear a headscarf during her working hours and she consequently rendered herself liable to the disciplinary proceedings.[116] The Court considered that France did not exceed its margin of appreciation in finding that it was impossible to reconcile Ms Ebrahimian's religious beliefs and the obligation not to manifest them.[117] As in *Dahlab*, the Court found that it was imperative to restrict the rights of one woman in the name of placing 'greater emphasis on the rights of others, equal treatment for patients and the proper functioning of the [health care] service' in the French legislation.[118] In conclusion, there was no discrimination on the grounds of Article 9.

In two parallel judgments from 2017 in *Dakir v Belgium*[119] and *Belcacemi and Oussar v Belgium*,[120] the Court considered the impact of municipal and national

108 *SAS v France* App no 43835/11 (ECtHR, 1 July 2014).
109 ibid para 90.
110 ibid para 91.
111 See eg Megan Pearson, 'What Happened to '*Vivre Ensemble*?: Developments after *SAS v France*' (2021) 10(2) OJLR 185; Eva Brems, '*SAS v France*: A Reality Check' (2016) 25 Nott L J 58.
112 *SAS* (n 108) para 161. See also ECtHR, 'Guide on Article 14' (n 36) 11.
113 *Ebrahimian v France* App no 64846/11 (ECtHR, 26 November 2015).
114 ibid para 6.
115 ibid para 7.
116 *Ebrahimian* (n 113) para 70.
117 ibid.
118 ibid para 71.
119 *Dakir v Belgium* App no 4619/12 (ECtHR, 11 July 2017).
120 *Belcacemi and Oussar v Belgium* App no 37798/13 (ECtHR, 11 July 2017).

bans on the *niqab* on Muslim women. The three applicants, Ms Fouzia Dakir, Ms Samia Belcacemi and Ms Yamina Oussar, argued that despite the fact that Belgian by-laws were expressed in general terms, the ban and the penalties provided impacted Muslim women.[121] The Belgian government relied on arguments that were similar to those relied on by the French government in *SAS*, including the unsuccessful arguments that wearing the *niqab* undermined gender equality and dignity as well as the need for the citizens to live together.[122] It also argued that wearing a full face covering, including covering one's face with a *niqab*, in public places was inconsistent with democratic values.[123] The government argued that the bans were not discriminatory as they were not based on religion and they applied to any item concealing the face in public, regardless of the gender of the person and purpose of the item.[124] However, despite the denial that the bans specifically targeted the *niqab*, in practice only the *niqab* was included as the bans permitted numerous exemptions, such as, where face coverings were necessary for safety in employment, and when the clothing was worn as part of artistic and traditional events or festivities.[125] It cannot be a coincidence that the Belgian legislation allowed face coverings in the context of Catholic religious processions, carnivals, or rituals, but no exception was made for Muslim women.[126]

The Belgian government's additional arguments in *Dakir* resonate with the arguments raised by populist political parties against cultural diversity. It argued that the more multicultural a society became, the notion of living together meant that more extensive prohibitions of what it considered ostensible manifestations of religious beliefs and cultural traditions were necessary.[127] Therefore, the legislation should protect widely shared social norms, such as, seeing each other's faces in public. Disappointingly, the Court considered that in both cases the bans on face coverings had an objective and reasonable justification, namely, pursuing the aims of public safety and of respect for the minimum set of values of an open and democratic society.[128] Consequently, it found no violation of Article 14 in conjunction with Article 9 in either case. This is disappointing because the Court previously has held that ethnic and cultural diversity should be perceived as a source of enrichment, rather than a threat to the society.[129] Yet, the *niqab* is perceived as a threat to democracy and European values.

The Court's more recent case law has adopted a different approach. The 2018 judgment in *Lachiri v Belgium*[130] involved a refusal to permit the entry to a courtroom

121 *Dakir* (n 119) 63.
122 Pearson (n 111) 196.
123 *SAS* (n 108) para 31.
124 Pearson (n 111) 187.
125 *Dakir* (n 119) 64. See also Pearson (n 111) 187.
126 Pearson (n 111) 187.
127 *Dakir* (n 119) para 31.
128 *SAS* (n 108) paras 160–162.
129 *Nachova* (n 60) para 145.
130 *Lachiri v Belgium* App no 3413/09 (ECtHR, 18 September 2018).

while wearing a headscarf.[131] The Court found that refusing Ms Hagar Lachiri to attend a criminal trial involving the unlawful killing of her brother because she was wearing a *hijab* amounted to a restriction on the exercise of Article 9. Although the Court found that the restriction pursued the legitimate aim of protecting public order, with a view to preventing conduct that was disrespectful towards the judiciary or disruptive of the proper conduct of a hearing, Ms Lachiri's conduct on entering the courtroom was not disrespectful and did not constitute a threat to the proper conduct of the hearing. Therefore, the need for the restriction was not established and the infringement of Ms Lachiri's right to freedom to manifest her religion was unjustified in a democratic society.[132]

Although the Court arguably demonstrates increasing awareness and sensitivity to religious discrimination in *Lachiri*, the case law concerning the headscarf bans in educational establishments and work environment remains problematic, particularly because the Court's case law concerning Article 9 has consistently highlighted the need of a healthy democratic society to value diversity and pluralism.[133] Yet, it fails to recognise that equality and tolerance of pluralism and diversity do not mean that Muslim women should suffer discrimination because of a particular piece of clothing. Although the Court is focused on weighing the interest of an individual against the interests of a wider community, employer, or the public, the fact that a woman's clothing bears negative connotations of trying to impose one's religious beliefs on others is highly problematic.

In this regard it is valid to ask a question regarding whether the Court's approach towards Muslim women risks endangering the concept of equality in the European societies. Many of the headscarf cases have undertones of ageism, misogyny, and othering based on religious beliefs, race or ethnic origin that serve to set Muslim girls and women apart from Christian and secular populations. The Court has repeatedly justified its stance on the grounds that Article 9 does not allow women to impose their religious beliefs on others. Becker notes that although Muslims have not traditionally been considered as a unified ethnic group,[134] discrimination on the grounds of race, ethnic origin, and religion are not always indistinguishable. Therefore, the Court's jurisprudence on *hijabs* and *niqabs* lacks the acknowledgment that discrimination in these cases is intersectional as it arises from both gender and religious beliefs. Considering that significant Muslim populations live in major European urban areas,[135] courts and legislatures must show the way forward to a European multicultural landscape which can be established through reciprocal tolerance, equality, and respect for diversity.[136]

131 Pearson (n 111) 196.
132 ibid.
133 ibid 186. See also *Eweida* (n 102) para 94.
134 Becker (n 56).
135 ibid.
136 Iakovos Iakovidis and Paul McDonough, 'The *Molla Sali* Case: How the European Court of Human Rights Escaped a Legal Labyrinth While Holding the Thread of Human Rights' (2019) 8(2) OJLR 427.

4.4 Violence against Women

One particular area concerning explicit discrimination on the grounds of gender is violence against women (VAW). The Court has built extensive case law in this area under Articles 2 and 3 ECHR taken in conjunction with Article 14 ECHR, confirming that various forms of VAW are committed by State and non-State actors alike.[137] It has addressed complaints concerning various forms of violence, such as, physical violence perpetrated against women by unknown individuals,[138] rape and sexual abuse,[139] ill-treatment in detention,[140] police violence,[141] acid attacks,[142] and trafficking in human beings.[143] However, most cases in this area have concerned prolonged and serious physical VAW committed by opposite-sex partners or spouses.[144] Although concerted efforts have been taken at the international and regional levels over several decades to eradicate VAW,[145] it is widely acknowledged that women are significantly more likely to experience violence in a range of familial contexts.[146] Previous research highlights the attempts by male partners and husbands to coerce, control, and dominate their wives and female partners.[147] There is also consistent evidence demonstrating a strong association

137 See eg Jelena Ristik, 'Protection from Gender-Based Violence before the European Court of Human Rights' (2020) 6(2) Journal of Liberty and International Affairs 71; Ronagh JA McQuigg, '*Tkhelidze v Georgia*: Domestic Abuse and the European Court of Human Rights' (2022) 11(2) Hum Rts L Rev.

138 See eg *Sandra Janković v Croatia* App no 38478/05 (ECtHR, 5 March 2009); *Irina Smirnova v Ukraine* App no 1870/05 (ECtHR, 13 October 2016).

139 Many of the Court's judgments concerning rape and sexual abuse have focused on young girls and adolescents. See eg *X and Y v Netherlands* App no 8978/80 (ECtHR, 26 March 1985); *IG v Moldova* App No 53519/07 (ECtHR, 15 May 2012); *Söderman v Sweden* App no 5786/08 (ECtHR, 12 November 2013); *O'Keeffe v Ireland* App no 35810/09 (ECtHR, 28 January 2014); *MGC v Romania* App no 61495/11 (ECtHR, 15 March 2016); *IC v Romania* App no 36934/08 (ECtHR, 24 May 2016); *Loste v France* App no 59227/12 (ECtHR, 3 November 2022).

140 *Juhnke v Turkey* App no 52515/99 (ECtHR, 13 May 2008) (The gynaecological examination imposed on Ms Eva Juhnke during her detention violated her rights under art 8). The Court found a violation of art 3 in all the following detention cases: *Aydin v Turkey* App no 23178/94 (ECtHR, 25 September 1997); *BS* (n 58); *Afet Süreyya Eren v Turkey* App no 36617/07 (ECtHR, 20 October 2015); *Dilek Aslan v Turkey* App no 34364/08 (ECtHR, 20 October 2015).

141 See eg *Ebru Dinçer v Turkey* App no 43347/09 (ECtHR, 29 January 2019) (Violation of rights of Ms Dinçer under art 3 after she suffered serious injury in a fire caused by the police to stop a riot in a women's prison).

142 *Tërshana v Albania* App no 48756/14 (ECtHR, 4 August 2020).

143 For cases concerning trafficking in human beings and international protection, see *LR v UK* App no 49113/09 (ECtHR, 14 June 2011); *VF v France* App no 7196/10 (29 November 2011); *FA v UK* App no 20658/11 (ECtHR, 10 September 2013); *OGO v UK* App no 13950/12 (ECtHR, 18 February 2014).

144 often referred to as domestic violence.

145 See Joanne Conaghan, 'Some Reflections on Law and Gender in Modern Ireland' (2019) 27(3) Fem LS 333.

146 Catherine Briddick, 'Resisting Domestic Violence' (2024) IJRL 1.

147 ibid.

between coercive and controlling behaviours and intimate partner femicide.[148] This section focuses principally on cases concerning physical violence during and after the end of an intimate partner relationship.

In 2009, the Court accepted for the first time that VAW, and particularly violence in the context of intimate partner relationships, constitutes discrimination against women.[149] The case law demonstrates that domestic authorities have often failed to adequately investigate reports of intimate partner violence. In some cases, the applicants have unsuccessfully tried to institute civil proceedings.[150] In this regard, the failure of State authorities to investigate alleged crimes and protect applicants in an effective manner breaches women's right to equal protection of the law.[151] Additionally, the Court has noted that the authorities' failure to conduct sufficient investigation does not need to be intentional.[152]

Legislative efforts in Europe culminated in the adoption of the 2011 CoE Istanbul Convention , which defines the term VAW as any violence that disproportionately affects women or violence that is directed at women because of their gender.[153] The term comprises 'all acts of gender-based violence that result in, or are likely to result in, physical, sexual, psychological or economic harm or suffering to women, including threats of such acts, coercion or arbitrary deprivation of liberty, whether occurring in public or in private life'.[154] Additionally, various forms of violence are explicitly prohibited by the Convention, including psychological and sexual violence.[155] Although huge steps forward have been made in relation to legal codification to combat VAW in the past decade in the context of the Istanbul Convention, it would be optimistic to think that women and girls in even the most gender-equal societies do not experience violence in intimate partner relationships.[156] Many of the difficulties with the operation of law derive from deeply engrained, often 'unconsciously held social attitudes regarding (hetero)sexual behaviour'.[157] Scholars argue that rape and sexual violence stem from 'a social construct of overarching social attitudes and perceptions of how women and men should look like and behave in

148 Claire Ferguson and Freya McLachlan, 'Continuing Coercive Control After Intimate Partner Femicide: The Role of Detection Avoidance and Concealment' (2023) 18(4) Feminist Criminology 353.

149 *Opuz* (n 22) paras 184–191, 200; *Talpis v Italy* App no 41237/14 (ECtHR, 2 March 2017); *Volodina* (n 22); *Tkhelidze v Georgia* App no 33056/17 (ECtHR, 8 July 2021); *AE v Bulgaria* App no 53891/20 (ECtHR, 23 May 2023). See also ECtHR, 'Guide on Article 14' (n 36) 24.

150 *Valiulienė v Lithuania* App no 33234/07 (ECtHR, 26 June 2013).

151 This issue may constitute breach of arts 2, 3, 8 and 14 ECHR. See eg McQuigg (n 137).

152 *Opuz* (n 22) para 191.

153 Istanbul Convention, art 3(d).

154 ibid art 3(a).

155 ibid arts 33 and 36.

156 Conaghan (n 145).

157 Susan Leahy, 'Sexual Offences Law in Ireland: Countering Gendered Stereotypes in Adjudications of Consent in Rape Trials' in Lynsey Black and Peter Dunne (eds), *Law and Gender in Modern Ireland* (Hart 2019) 17–18.

society'.[158] Therefore, societal attitudes and the entire structures underpinning societies, not just the law, must change in order for violence against women and lesbian, gay, bisexual and transgender (LGBT) persons to be eliminated.[159]

Additionally, Juraz and Barker note the problems with inadequate recognition of online forms of VAW in the CoE.[160] Even though the ECtHR has decided a handful of cases concerning violence in this context, including image-based sexual abuse,[161] legislative frameworks both at the regional and national level are insufficient because of inadequate attention to violence targeted at women in online environments. Consequently, much of the Court's case law is largely limited to physical violence experienced by women in the hands of their former or current intimate partners.[162]

One of the earliest cases concerning intimate partner violence is the Court's 1979 judgment in *Airey v Ireland*.[163] Dembour has praised the Court as being specifically gender-aware when deciding the case. According to her, it is a rare example in the Court's jurisprudence where the judges adopted a progressive interpretation of the Convention to relieve a situation of a married mother of four who was unable to obtain a decree of judicial separation from her husband who was convicted of her assault.[164] In the absence of legal aid provision in Ireland, she was unable to engage a lawyer to represent her before the national court.[165] The case demonstrates that the lack of financial independence impacts women, who may be forced to endure physical violence and controlling and coercive behaviour within their marriages, which in turn impacts on their ability to leave abusive relationships.[166] The ECtHR found that the high costs of seeking a separation order before the Irish courts violated Ms Airey's right to access court under Article 6 ECHR. It also found that her inability to obtain a judicial separation from her husband constituted a violation of Article 8. The Court's main point was that it was insufficient to claim that Ms Airey could not afford court proceedings.[167] Accordingly, the access to judicial remedies should be

158 Carlotta Rigotti, 'A Long Way to End Rape in the European Union: Assessing the Commission's Proposal to Harmonise Rape Law, Through A Feminist Lens' (2022) 13(2) NJECL 153, 160.

159 Conaghan (n 145).

160 Olga Jurasz and Kim Barker, 'Sexual Violence in the Digital Age: A Criminal Law Conundrum?' (2021) 22 German LJ 784, 786.

161 *Volodina v Russia* (no 2) App no 40419/19 (ECtHR, 14 September 2021). See also Roisin A Costello, '*Volodina v Russia (no 2)*: Intimate Images, Domestic Violence and the Positive Obligations of Member States under Article 8 ECHR' (2021) 7 European Data Protection Law Rev 614. See also *Buturugă v Romania* App no 56867/15 (ECtHR, 11 June 2020) (Ms Buturugă's ex-husband accessed her email and social media accounts and copied her private conversations, documents, and photographs. This constituted a breach of digital privacy and was considered an aspect of a broader pattern of intimate partner violence).

162 See eg *Opuz* (n 22); *Valiulienė* (n 150); *Volodina* (n 22).

163 *Airey v Ireland* App no 6289/73 (ECtHR, 9 October 1979).

164 Marie-Bénédicte Dembour, *Who Believes in Human Rights?: Reflections on the European Convention* (CUP 2006) 215. See also *Airey* (n 162) para 8.

165 *Airey* (n 162) para 11.

166 Ristik (n 137) 77.

167 Linda Hart, 'Relational Subjects: Family Relations, Law and Gender in the European Court of Human Rights' (Ph.D. thesis, University of Helsinki 2016) 112.

modified so that everyone, regardless of their financial means, had access to a court in civil matters.[168] The unavailability of proceedings to end the marital relationship violated Article 8,[169] as the delay in obtaining divorce meant that Ms Airey remained in a legal relationship against her will.

It is significant to note also that the ECtHR was long argued to be reluctant to find State officials guilty of gender discrimination based on unwritten patterns of behaviour, which is where discrimination is more likely to occur.[170] The 2009 judgment in *Opuz v Turkey*[171] presents a breakthrough in the jurisprudence in this area because the Court finally accepted that VAW cannot be viewed as a private issue.[172] The ECtHR rejected the Turkish government's argument that national authorities' interference violate the victim's rights under protection of private life (Article 8).[173] The case concerned prolonged violence and threats against Ms Nahide Opuz by her ex-husband during and after their marriage, culminating in her mother's murder. The ECtHR confirmed that physical violence and psychological pressure in the context of intimate partner relationships amounts to ill-treatment within the meaning of Article 3 ECHR.[174] It also considered that Turkish law did not make an explicit distinction between men and women in the enjoyment of rights and freedoms or in access to justice.[175] Thus, although the discrimination was not based on the legislation *per se*, it resulted from the authorities' general attitude, such as, the manner in which women were treated at police stations when they reported violence and judicial passivity in providing effective protection to victims.[176] Despite the reforms carried out by the Turkish government, the overall unresponsiveness of the judicial system and impunity enjoyed by the perpetrators indicated that the Turkish authorities' commitment to take appropriate action to address violence targeted at women was insufficient.[177]

The ECtHR has made similar pronouncements about insufficiency of State protection in its subsequent case law.[178] In its 2013 judgment in *Valiulienė v Lithuania*,[179] the Court found a violation of Article 3 as the circumstances of Ms Loreta Valiulienė's case were never established by a competent criminal court even though she reported her co-habiting Belgian partner, Mr JHL, to the police for repeatedly inflicting physical violence against her.[180] Consequently, the ECtHR

168 ibid 112.
169 ibid.
170 McIntosh Sundstrom and others (n 2) 137.
171 *Opuz* (n 22).
172 McIntosh Sundstrom and others (n 2).
173 *Opuz* (n 22) para 144.
174 ibid para 200.
175 ECtHR, 'Guide on Article 14' (n 36) 11.
176 *Opuz* (n 22) para 191.
177 ibid para 200.
178 Lyra Jakulevičienė and Laurynas Biekša, 'Trends in the Qualification of Asylum Claims Related to Gender-Based Violence Under International and European Law' (2021) 26(5) IJHR 833.
179 *Valiulienė* (n 150).
180 ibid para 7.

found that Lithuania failed to provide Ms Valiulienė with adequate protection from her partner as criminal proceedings against him ended because of the flaws in the authorities' actions during the investigation.[181] When the prosecution became time-barred, the public prosecutor discontinued the investigation.[182]

Despite several judgments condemning VAW, European societies have not become less violent. Two judgments against Georgia demonstrate that the ECtHR frequently considers cases involving femicide. In its 2021 judgment in *Tkhelidze v Georgia*,[183] the Court dealt with a complaint by the father of a 33-year-old English language professor, Ms MT, who was murdered by a man she briefly dated. Her father complained that the Georgian authorities failed to prevent prolonged serious violence perpetrated against her, even though she reported her former partner to the police. Ms MT's former partner physically and verbally abused, stalked, and threatened her for the period of at least six months. The Court concluded that the authorities should conduct a meaningful inquiry into the gender-based discrimination and bias underlying the police inaction.[184] The shortcomings in the police investigations amounted to a breach of Georgia's procedural positive obligations under Article 2 read in conjunction with Article 14.[185]

The 2022 judgment in *A and B v Georgia*[186] dealt with a similar issue. The Court found a violation of Georgia's positive obligations under Article 2 taken together with Article 14 for its failure to prevent systematic physical and psychological violence and eventual murder of Ms C by her former partner, Mr D, who was a police officer.[187] Ms C was still underage when 22-year-old Mr D was claimed to have forced her to live with him. Ms C became pregnant during the couple's cohabitation.[188] When Ms C moved out after six months, Mr D stalked his ex-partner and shot her in broad daylight, pointing the gun at himself afterwards. The Court noted that the passive and even accommodating attitudes of law-enforcement were likely to proliferate 'violence against victims merely because they are women'.[189] This was the first time the Court explicitly used the wordings in the Istanbul Convention, albeit not explicitly referring to it. This seemed like a clumsy first attempt to condemn VAW in the context of a Convention the CoE itself has adopted.

4.5 Trans Women and Trans Men

Although the Court has set several international benchmarks for gay rights in its case law concerning sexual orientation and gender identity, the struggle for LGBT

181 Jakulevičienė and Biekša (n 178).
182 *Valiulienė* (n 149) paras 85-86. See also Jakulevičienė and Biekša (n 178).
183 *Tkhelidze* (n 149).
184 ibid para 60.
185 ibid.
186 *A and B v Georgia* App no 73975/16 (ECtHR, 10 February 2022).
187 ibid para 17.
188 ibid para 6.
189 ibid para 49.

rights in Europe is ongoing.[190] Up until relatively recently, the Court has granted considerable freedom to States to require trans individuals to adhere to a set of complicated administrative requirements in order to legally change their identity on official documents.[191] Although self-declaratory gender recognition systems, which allow individuals to self-identify, operate in a growing number of jurisdictions, many national regimes have been criticised for their bureaucratic and pathologising requirements, such as, a diagnosis of gender dysphoria and compulsory gender reassignment surgery.[192] As scholarly commentary focusing on the Court's case law concerning gender non-conforming persons have largely concentrated on the rights of trans women, for the interest of balance, it is useful to look at the issues arising in cases concerning the rights of trans men in more detail.

Although the Court seemingly takes a progressive approach towards post-operative trans persons, who find themselves in the grey zone between two genders even after their gender reassignment surgery,[193] there is room for the Court to approach cases concerning gender non-conforming persons in a way which does not diminish or render inauthentic their gender experiences.[194] Scholars have criticised the Court for stubbornly adhering to binary gender categories and its insistence to address the applicants in the gender that they are still officially registered,[195] rather than their self-identified gender identity.[196] The building blocks for more inclusive judicial decision-making can already be found in existing case law on Article 8, which protects the personal sphere of each individual, including the right to establish details of their identity as individual human beings.[197] Article 8 is applicable to the question of the legal recognition of the gender identity of post-operative trans individuals,[198] the conditions for access to surgery,[199] and the legal recognition of the gender identity of pre-operative trans individuals, who are yet to undergo, or do not wish to undergo, gender reassignment surgery or other treatment.[200]

190 Hodson (n 32) 383.

191 ECtHR, 'Guide on Article 8 of the Convention: Right to respect for private and family life' (31 August 23) 64 <https://ks.echr.coe.int/web/echr-ks/article-8> accessed 24 May 2024.

192 See eg Pieter Cannoot, 'The Pathologisation of Trans* Persons in the ECtHR's Case Law on Legal Gender Recognition' (2019) 37(1) NQHR 14; Alex Sharpe, 'Will Gender Self-Declaration Undermine Women's Rights and Lead to an Increase in Harms?' (2020) 83(3) MLR 539.

193 *Goodwin* (n 6) para 90; *Grant v UK* App no 32570/03 (ECtHR, 23 May 2006), para 40; *L v Lithuania* App no 27527/03 (ECtHR 11 September 2007), para 59.

194 Alex Sharpe, 'Queering Judgment: The Case of Gender Identity Fraud' (2017) 81(5) J Crim L 417.

195 This is obvious also in recent judgments, including *Savinovskikh and Others v Russia* App no 16206/19 (ECtHR, 9 July 2024).

196 Cannoot (n 192) 24.

197 *Goodwin* (n 6) para 90.

198 *Hämäläinen v Finland* App no 37359/09 (ECtHR, 16 July 2014), para 68.

199 *L* (n 193) paras 56–57 (Delay in accessing gender reassignment surgery was violation of art 8); *Schlumpf v Switzerland* App no 29002/06 (ECtHR, 8 January 2009), para 107; *YY v Turkey* App no 14793/08 (ECtHR, 10 March 2015), paras 65–66.

200 *AP, Garçon and Nicot v France* App nos 79885/12 and others (ECtHR, 6 April 2017), paras 95–96. See also Peter Dunne, 'Legal Gender Recognition in Europe: Sterilisation, Diagnosis and Medical Examination Requirements' (2017) 39 (4) J Soc Wel & Fam 497.

The unwillingness to recognise the rights of pre-operative trans individuals can partly be explained by the fact that the vast majority of the Court's early case law focuses on post-operative trans individuals who have completed their gender reassignment surgery.[201] The authority in this area is *Christine Goodwin v UK*,[202] which confirmed that the UK had failed to comply with its positive obligation to respect Ms Goodwin's private life in the absence of legal recognition of her 1990s gender reassignment surgery. The Court emphasised the fact that treatment for so-called gender dysphoria was provided from public funds, but Ms Goodwin was unable to obtain legal recognition of her new gender.[203] This permeated every aspect of her life.[204] As there were no significant factors of public interest to weigh against her interest in obtaining legal recognition of her new gender, the UK violated Article 8.[205]

4.5.1 Pre-Operative Trans Men

On the surface it seems that trans women and trans men face similar barriers relating to the delays in their ability to access gender reassignment surgery or new identity documents; conditions of sterility imposed on accessing gender reassignment surgery, and requirements to complete gender reassignment surgery before obtaining legal recognition. Yet, many cases regarding trans men have concerned applicants who are yet to have surgery. Additionally, complaints concerning pre-operative trans men have been brought before the Court earlier than many complaints concerning pre-operative trans women. This is significant, considering that case law concerning the latter is often seen as the landmark cases. Additionally, the case law analysis reveals that some issues touch only on pre-operative trans men, such as, the ability to give birth.[206] As requirements for trans individuals to undergo gender confirmation surgery, sterilisation, or a combination of the two are no longer acceptable, not all trans individuals have commenced hormone therapy or undergone any surgeries at the time of the dispute. As gender reassignment surgery inevitably leads to an irreversible loss of reproductive potential, the legitimacy and indispensability of these types of requirements to gain legal recognition of a person's gender identity have been contested before the Court.[207]

201 See eg *Rees v UK* App no 9532/81 (ECtHR, 17 October 1986); *Cossey v UK* App no 10843/84 (ECtHR, 27 September 1990); *X, Y and Z v UK* (ECtHR, 22 April 1997); *I v UK* App no 25680/94 (ECtHR, 11 July 2002).
202 *Goodwin* (n 6).
203 Hart (n 167) 118–119.
204 The case touched upon several issues where gender mattered, including the possibility to marry; identity documents; social security contributions; State pensions; and the requirement to reveal one's identity in the context of employment. See *Goodwin* (n 6) paras 15–19. See also Hart (n 167) 118–119; ECtHR, 'Guide on Article 8 of the Convention' (n 191) 64.
205 *Goodwin* (n 6) para 93.
206 These cases are discussed in ch 5. See also Alice Margaria, 'Trans Men Giving Birth and Reflections on Fatherhood: What to Expect?' (2020) 34(3) IJLPF 225, 228.
207 ibid 228.

Considering that in *Goodwin* the Court has established that the inability to legally register one's gender causes considerable disruption to an individual, the 2007 judgment in *L v Lithuania*[208] deserves more attention. *L* is significant because the absence of relevant national legislation regulating gender reassignment surgery and the subsequent inability to obtain amended documentation attesting Mr L's new gender left him in the intermediate position where legally he was considered a woman when he was required to prove his identity, such as when he wished to travel abroad or when he sought for work.[209] Mr L complained that accessing his new identity documents was conditional on the completion of gender reassignment surgery. He unsuccesfully requested the amendment of his identity papers in 1999. However, he was told that his personal code on his new birth certificate, passport, and university diploma could not be amended until he underwent the full surgery. Although he underwent partial reassignment surgery involving breast removal in 2000, his full surgery could not be completed in the absence of national legislation governing the appropriate conditions and procedure enabling gender reassignment surgery. The ECtHR found a violation of Article 8 because of the authorities' persistent failure to adopt the relevant legislation, even though the 2000 Civil Code provided for a right to legal gender recognition based on gender reassignment. Indeed, the legislative gap left Mr L in a situation of distressing uncertainty regarding his private life, whereas the budgetary restraints in the public-health service relied on by Lithuania did not justify a delay of over four years.[210]

The Court returned to the issue in its 2015 judgment in *YY v Turkey*.[211] At the time of his application for authorisation to undergo surgery, Mr YY was recognised as female. His application was refused on the grounds that he did not satisfy the prior requirement of permanent inability to procreate.[212] *YY* is significant as the Court found that in denying Mr YY the possibility of undergoing gender reassignment surgery for many years, Türkiye had breached his right to respect for his private life.[213] Additionally, the Court specifically held that the requirement of sterilisation to have access to gender reassignment therapy violated Article 8. This is significant as it was the first time when the Court considered that the national requirement of permanent infertility as a condition for gender reassignment surgery violated Article 8.

However, the judgment in *YY* seems to have been buried somewhere under the findings made in the 2017 judgment in *AP, Garçon and Nicot v France*,[214] which is often presented as a significant change for individuals, who do not wish to undergo gender reassignment surgery or hormone therapy.[215] *AP* concerned a complaint by

208 *L* (n 193).
209 ibid para 57.
210 *L* (n 193) para 59.
211 *YY* (n 199).
212 ibid para 44.
213 ibid paras 121–122.
214 *AP* (n 200).
215 See eg Cannoot (n 192).

three trans women, Ms AP, Ms Émile Garçon and Ms Stéphane Nicot, who alleged that the condition of undergoing *de facto* sterilisation before the recognition of new legal gender was inconsistent with Article 8.[216] While the judgment is no doubt significant as it resulted in a legislative change in France,[217] the Court essentially confirmed what had already been established two years earlier in *YY*.[218] It recognised that even absence of European consensus on the requirements for individuals to become sterile in order to legally change their gender, a trend had emerged in Europe with regard to abandoning the criterion of sterility.[219] However, the Court found that due to the wide margin of appreciation, France could still require a prior diagnosis of gender dysphoria syndrome[220] and a medical examination confirming gender reassignment.[221] Therefore, *AP* does not enforce a view that trans individuals should be able to self-identify.[222]

Two more recent judgments concerning trans men have revolved around the lack of legal recognition of new gender or names on the birth certificates before undergoing gender reassignment surgery. In its 2019 judgment in *X v Macedonia*[223] Mr X, a preoperative trans man, complained that Macedonia violated Article 8 due to the lack of a regulatory framework for legal recognition and the requirement that such recognition was conditional on the completion of gender reassignment surgery. The Court ruled that the lack of transparent, accessible, and speedy procedures for changing one's registered sex on a birth certificate resulted in a violation of Article 8.[224] Consequently, Macedonia failed to comply with its positive obligation to create an effective and accessible procedure, with clearly defined conditions securing Mr X's right to respect for his private life.

The 2020 judgment in *YT v Bulgaria*[225] concerned the lack of recognition of the new gender in circumstances where Mr YT's physical appearance and social and family identity had been altered for an extended period of time. He sought to change his gender from female to male in the civil-status register as he was using his male forename and surname. In 2010, his co-habiting female partner gave birth to a child via donor insemination. Mr YT and the child considered each other as father and son. The Court held that the refusal to record Mr YT's new legal gender in the civil-status register, when his physical appearance and social and family identity had been altered for a long time, constituted a violation of his right to private life. In particular, the domestic courts failed to provide relevant and

216 *AP* (n 199).
217 Before *AP* French law required that individuals presented proof irreversible of transformation of bodily appearance. See Cannoot (n 192) 21.
218 *YY* (n 199).
219 ECtHR, 'Guide on Article 8 of the Convention' (n 192) 64.
220 *AP* (n 200) paras 139–143.
221 ibid paras 150–154.
222 See eg *SV v Italy* App no 55216/08 (ECtHR, 11 October 2018), paras 54–55. See also Cannoot (n 192) 18.
223 *X v Macedonia* App no 29683/16 (ECtHR, 17 January 2019).
224 ibid para 70.
225 *YT v Bulgaria* App no 41701/16 (ECtHR, 9 July 2020).

sufficient reasons for the refusal.[226] These judgments demonstrate an accommodating attitude towards trans men, which is a welcome development. The Court found a violation of the applicant's rights in each case due to the refusal of the national authorities to recognise their gender identities.

4.6 Conclusion

It has been argued that women are often discriminated against on multiple grounds listed in Article 14.[227] This chapter has considered three specific areas of the Court's case law where discrimination against women and gender non-confirming persons is most visible, namely intersectional discrimination, VAW, and discrimination against trans individuals. Although the Court may be open to considering intersectional discrimination, it rarely expressly addresses intersectional considerations[228] and there are only a handful cases where the Court recognises the individual's intersectional identities, especially in the context of family migration, police violence, and discrimination of women due to age. The case law analysis demonstrates that women and diasporic and minoritised individuals continue to be penalised for behaviours that violate certain gender stereotypes and cultural beliefs, prescribing acceptable behaviours for women and men.[229] Yet there are so few cases in this area that drawing definitive conclusions about the way in which the Court approaches intersectional discrimination is likely to develop.

In one promising judgment from 2024, the ECtHR recognised the failure of the French authorities to prosecute a perpetrator of hate crimes involving misogyny and anti-Semitism aimed at a Jewish woman, constituted discrimination. In *Allouche v France*,[230] the Court found a violation of Article 8 taken in conjunction with Article 14 due to the French authorities' failure to provide effective and appropriate protection for Ms Myriam Allouche. She was subjected to a barrage of anti-Semitic emails by a man, Mr B, a bartender, who had served her at a bar. After she declined his romantic advances, Ms Allouche received, in a matter of few days, 26 emails from Mr B accompanied with threats of violence, rape, and death, and anti-Semitic remarks. This case is an important one, considering that even though the Court has built an extensive case law concerning discrimination and violence against men on grounds of race, ethnicity or religious beliefs,[231] only a handful of cases have concerned women.

Additionally, many of the cases concerning wearing headscarves at schools, universities, and other workplaces have certain undertones of ageism, misogyny,

226 ibid para 74.

227 Karvatska, Toronchuk, and Manyk (n 5) 92.

228 Yoshida (n 47). See also ECtHR, 'Guide on Article 14' (n 36) 14.

229 Tamar Kricheli-Katz, 'Gender Inequalities in Markets' (2021) 17 Annual Rev L & Social Science 109, 114; Rigotti (n 158) 160.

230 *Allouche v France* App no 81249/17 (ECtHR, 11 April 2024).

231 For cases concerning ethnic and racial violence and discrimination, and discrimination on grounds of religious beliefs, see s 3.2.

and othering based on religion, race or ethinic origin.[232] Muslim women are frequently portrayed as individuals who knowingly and willingly defy the authorities by refusing to remove their headscarves even when facing disciplinary proceedings, dismissal from their jobs, or suspension from their studies. Despite a profound disruption to their lives, the Court has rarely found a violation of Article 9 taken alone and in conjunction with Article 14 in these cases. It is difficult to even comprehend how wearing a particular piece of clothing by women can invite so much criticism from the public.

Although the Court has accumulated extensive case law condemning VAW, discrimination and VAW remain recurrent problems in all CoE States. It appears that many of the difficulties with the operation of law in the context of VAW derive from deeply engrained social attitudes regarding heterosexual behaviour.[233] Although the Court has accepted that VAW is a form of gender discrimination, national authorities often fail to adequately investigate crimes committed against women which violates women's right to equal protection of the law.[234]

Although many countries have relaxed the requirement of sterilisation as a precondition for gender reassignment surgery, this is a relatively recent development, with the Court first ruling on the issue in 2015. Changes in the applicants' appearance, the incompatibility of compulsory requirement of sterilisation with Article 8,[235] and emerging European consensus[236] have forced the Court to consider its stance on the rights and freedoms of pre-operative trans individuals. It is noticeable that cases concerning trans men have been less often cited in academic literature as those involving trans women, exposing an important oversight in scholarly analysis. The case law is not perfect, but there has been some improvement. The cases where the Court has found discrimination on grounds of Article 14 will be marking definitive turning points for the ECtHR in the years to come.

References

Alkiviadou N and Manoli A, 'The European Court of Human Rights Through the Looking Glass of Gender: An Evaluation' (2021) 11(1) Goettingen J Intl L 191.

Arnardóttir OM, 'Cross-fertilisation, Clarity and Consistency at an Overburdened European Court of Human Rights: The Case of the Discrimination Grounds under Article 14 ECHR' (2015) 33(3) Nord J Hum Rts 220.

Becker E, 'Theorizing "New Ethnicities" in Diasporic Europe: Jews, Muslims and Stuart Hall' (2024) 47(9) Ethnic and Racial Stud 1858.

Benslama-Dabdoub M, 'Epistemic Violence and Colonial Legacies in the Representation of Refugee Women: Contesting Narratives of Vulnerability and Victimhood' (2024) 20(1) Intl JLC 54.

232 Becker (n 56).

233 Leahy (n 157) 17–18.

234 *Opuz* (n 22). See also McQuigg (n 137).

235 *YY* (n 199).

236 *AP* (n 200).

Brems E, '*SAS v France*: A Reality Check' (2016) 25 Nott L J 58.
Briddick C, 'Resisting Domestic Violence' (2024) 36 IJRL 1.
Cannoot P, 'The Pathologisation of Trans* Persons in the ECtHR's Case Law on Legal Gender Recognition' (2019) 37(1) NQHR 14.
Carrera Nuñez S, 'The ECtHR's Judgment in *Biao v Denmark*: Non-Discrimination Among Nationals and Family Reunification as Converging European Standards: ECtHR, *Biao v Denmark*, Judgment of 24 May 2016, Application No 38590/10' (2016) 23(5) MJ 865.
Castillo-Ortiz P, Ali A, and Samanta N, 'Gender, Intersectionality, and Religious Manifestation Before the European Court of Human Rights' (2019) 18(1) J Hum Rts 76.
Conaghan J, 'Some Reflections on Law and Gender in Modern Ireland' (2019) 27(3) Fem LS 333.
Crenshaw K, 'Demarginalizing the Intersection of Race and Sex: A Black Feminist Critique of Antidiscrimination Doctrine, Feminist Theory, and Antiracist Politics' (1989) 1989 U Chicago L F 139.
de Vries K and Thomas Spijkerboer T, 'Race and the Regulation of International Migration: The Ongoing Impact of Colonialism in the Case Law of the European Court of Human Rights' (2021) 39(4) NQHR 291.
Dembour MB, *Who Believes in Human Rights?: Reflections on the European Convention* (CUP 2006).
Diduck A and Wilson W, 'Prostitutes and Persons' (1997) 24(4) J L & Society 504.
Dunne P, 'Legal Gender Recognition in Europe: Sterilisation, Diagnosis and Medical Examination Requirements' (2017) 39 (4) J Soc Wel & Fam L 497.
Fenton-Glynn C, *Family Formation and Parenthood* (OUP 2020).
Ferguson C and McLachlan F, 'Continuing Coercive Control After Intimate Partner Femicide: The Role of Detection Avoidance and Concealment' (2023) 18(4) Fem Criminology 353.
Ganty S, 'Poverty as Misrecognition: What Role for Antidiscrimination Law in Europe?' (2021) 21(4) HRL Rev 962.
Gillis M, 'Can We Talk? The Application of the Public Law Democratic Dialogue Model to the Interactions between Domestic Legislatures and the European Courts' (2022) 23 German LJ 56.
Hart L, 'Relational Subjects: Family Relations, Law and Gender in the European Court of Human Rights' (PhD Thesis, University of Helsinki 2016).
Hodson L, 'Sexual Orientation and the European Convention on Human Rights: What of the "L" in LGBT?' (2019) 23(3) J Lesbian S 383.
Iakovidis I and l McDonough P, 'The Molla Sali Case: How the European Court of Human Rights Escaped a Legal Labyrinth While Holding the Thread of Human Rights' (2019) 8(2) OJLR 427.
Ichim O, *Just Satisfaction Under the European Convention on Human Rights* (CUP 2015).
Jakulevičienė L and Biekša L, 'Trends in the Qualification of Asylum Claims Related to Gender-Based Violence under International and European Law' (2021) 26(5) IJHR 833.
Jurasz O and Barker K, 'Sexual Violence in the Digital Age: A Criminal Law Conundrum?' (2021) 22 German LJ 784.
Karvatska S, Toronchuk I, and Manyk A, 'Gender Equality Principle: Application in ECtHR's Practice' (2021) 9 Logos Universality Mentality Education Novelty Section Law 83.
Kricheli-Katz T, 'Gender Inequalities in Markets' (2021) 17 Annual Rev L & Social Science 109.
Leahy S, 'Sexual Offences Law in Ireland: Countering Gendered Stereotypes in Adjudications of Consent in Rape Trials' in Black L and Dunne P (eds), *Law and Gender in Modern Ireland* (Hart 2019).
Malleson K, 'Equality Law and the Protected Characteristics' (2018) 81 MLR 598.

Margaria A, 'Trans Men Giving Birth and Reflections on Fatherhood: What to Expect?' (2020) 34(3) IJLPF 225.

McIntosh Sundstrom L, Sperling V, and Sayoglu M, *Courting Gender Justice: Russia, Turkey and the European Court of Human Rights* (OUP 2019).

McQuigg RJA, '*Tkhelidze v Georgia*: Domestic Abuse and the European Court of Human Rights' (2022) 11(2) Intl Hum Rts L Rev 138.

Oja L and Yamin AE, '"Woman" in the European Human Rights System: How is the Reproductive Rights Jurisprudence of the European Court of Human Rights Constructing Narratives of Women's Citizenship?' (2016) 32(1) Colum J Gender & L 62.

Pearson M, 'What Happened to '*Vivre Ensemble*?': Developments after *SAS v France*' (2021) 10(2) OJLR 185.

Peroni L, 'Violence Against Migrant Women: The Istanbul Convention Through a Postcolonial Feminist Lens' (2016) 24 Fem LS 49.

Radacic I, 'Gender Equality Jurisprudence of the European Court of Human Rights' (2008) 19(4) EJIL 841.

Renzulli I, 'Discrimination and Gender Stereotypes in Judicial Decisions: The Jurisprudence of the European Court of Human Rights in Light of *JL v Italy*–A Retreat Into The Shadows?' (2023) 41(3) NQHR 155.

Rigotti C, 'A Long Way to End Rape in the European Union: Assessing the Commission's Proposal to Harmonise Rape Law, Through A Feminist Lens' (2022) 13(2) NJECL 153.

Ristik J, 'Protection from Gender-Based Violence before the European Court of Human Rights' (2020) 6(2) J Liberty and International Affairs 71.

Sharpe A, 'Queering Judgment: The Case of Gender Identity Fraud' (2017) 81(5) J Crim L 417.

Sharpe A, 'Will Gender Self-Declaration Undermine Women's Rights and Lead to an Increase in Harms?' (2020) 83(3) MLR 539.

Skeet CH, 'Intersectionality as Theory and Method: Human Rights Adjudication by the European Court of Human Rights' in Creutzfeldr N, Mason M, and McConnachie K (eds), *The Routledge Handbook of Socio-Legal Theory and Method* (Routledge 2019).

Smet S, 'Conscientious Objection Under the European Convention on Human Rights: The Ugly Duckling of a Flightless Jurisprudence', in Temperman J, Gunn J, and Evans M (eds), *The European Court of Human Rights and the Freedom of Religion or Belief: The 25 Years Since Kokkinakis* (Brill 2019).

Voeten E, 'Gender and Judging: Evidence from the European Court of Human Rights' (2020) 28(9) JEPP 1453.

Yoshida Y, 'Towards Intersectionality in the European Court of Human Rights: The Case of *BS v Spain*' (2013) 21 Fem LS 195.

5 Gendered Parenthood

5.1 Introduction

This chapter critically examines the case law of the European Court of Human Rights (ECtHR) on legal recognition of non-conventional[1] parent-child relationships through a critical perspective using an intersectional feminist lens. Although women's concerns continue to warrant attention, feminist scholars increasingly examine the issues of sexuality and gender identity. It is widely accepted that understanding that women and men's experiences of exclusion are different is critical to a richer understanding of violations of the rights in the European Convention on Human Rights[2] (ECHR) because the intersectional discrimination on the grounds of gender, gender identity, and sexual orientation may produce distinctive forms of disadvantage.[3] It has also been argued that sexual orientation, civil status, and access to assisted reproductive technologies (ART) are closely linked.[4] The ECtHR is considered to have the lengthiest history of engagement with the rights of the lesbian, gay, bisexual, and transgender (LGBT) community globally.[5] There are arguments that courts are a crucial part of any movement towards equal treatment for the LGBT community, and the judicial decisions and attitudes have a potential to make significant difference for the recognition of parental rights of the LGBT community.[6] Despite this, the ECtHR's case law on parenting rights of LGBT applicants under Article 8 (The right to respect for private and family life)

1 The family structure in cross-border surrogacy cases is still considered non-conventional as the child is carried by a surrogate. See Lydia Bracken, 'Accommodations of Private and Family Life and Non-Traditional Families: The Limits of Deference in Cases of Cross-Border Surrogacy before the European Court of Human Rights' (2024) 32(2) Med L Rev 141.

2 Convention for the Protection of Human Rights and Fundamental Freedoms (European Convention on Human Rights, as amended).

3 See eg Diane Otto, 'Between Pleasure and Danger: Lesbian Human Rights' (2014) 6 EHRLR 618, 620.

4 Melanie Levy, 'Surrogacy and Parenthood: A European Saga of Genetic Essentialism and Gender Discrimination' (2022) 29 Mich J Gender and L 121, 123.

5 Loveday Hodson, 'Sexual Orientation and the European Convention on Human Rights: What of the "L" in LGBT?' (2019) 23(3) J Lesbian Studies 383; Paul Johnson, 'UK Withdrawal from the European Convention on Human Rights: A Disaster for LGBT People' (2024) ECHR L Rev 83.

6 Bruce Macdougall, *Queer Judgments: Homosexuality, Expression, and the Courts in Canada* (University of Toronto Press 2000) 5 and 7.

DOI: 10.4324/9781003435099-5

has attracted significant criticism on the grounds that it displays varying degrees of incoherence.[7] One explanation for this in the scholarly literature is the argument that the Court's reasoning is influenced by which country is the respondent State.[8] Many of the Court's judgments cite the lack of consensus amongst the member States of the Council of Europe (CoE) on related issues, ranging from the recognition of same-sex relationships and adoption rights for single men and women, to access to ART, including cross-border surrogacy.[9] It has been noted, however, that how the Court applies the concept of European consensus in practice is not always straightforward as the Court has adopted changeable criteria to establish what constitutes consensus.[10] For instance, sometimes it refers to the evolution of social attitudes as an indication of an emerging consensus.[11] The resulting variability is characteristic of, *inter alia*, the case law on trans rights.[12]

The concept of European consensus is a key interpretive tool prioritising a particular solution in cases where that solution is supported by most CoE States.[13] Consensus has a decisive role in the way that the ECtHR determines the States' margin of appreciation.[14] Therefore, establishing the existence of European consensus has a significant role in the Court's case law.[15] While examining whether a consensus exists, the Court makes a comparison amongst the legal solutions and practices adopted by the CoE States.[16] Additionally, it may also consider international developments and trends.[17] The differences among CoE States concerning parenthood have led to inevitable tensions among the States as the ECtHR lays down benchmarks for standards to be upheld by all the signatory States to the ECHR.[18]

7 See eg Lydia Bracken, 'Strasbourg's Response to Gay and Lesbian Parenting: Progress, then Plateau' (2016) 24 Intl J Child Rts 358, 358–359; Mareena George, 'Using the European Court of Human Rights to Expand Access to *In Vitro* Fertilization for Straight Women and Lesbian Couples in Europe' (2021) 53(2) Geo Wash Intl L Rev 321; Henriette Jakobien Liesker, 'Caught in a Balancing Act: The European Court of Human Rights and the Road to Recognition for Sexual Minorities' (2017) 4(3) Oslo L Rev 172.

8 See George (n 7).

9 ibid 342.

10 See eg Petra Minnerop, 'European Consensus As Integrative Doctrine of Treaty Interpretation: Joining Climate Science and International Law under the European Convention on Human Rights' (2023) 40(2) Berk J Intl L 206, 219.

11 See Ivana Radacic, 'The Margin of Appreciations, Consensus, Morality and the Rights of Vulnerable Groups' (2010) 31 Zb Prav Fak Sveuc Rij 599, 606.

12 Damian Gonzalez-Salzberg, *Sexuality and Transsexuality under the European Convention on Human Rights: A Queer Reading of Human Rights Law* (Hart 2019) 194.

13 See eg Kanstantsin Dzehtsiarou, *European Consensus and The Legitimacy of the European Court of Human Rights* (CUP 2015).

14 George (n 7) 343.

15 See, eg, George (n 7); Dzehtsiarou (n 13).

16 Jukka Viljanen, *The Role of the ECtHR as a Developer of International Human Rights Law* (Tampereen Yliopisto 2003) 251. See also Radacic (n 11) 606.

17 ibid.

18 Kerry O'Halloran, *The Politics of Adoption* (Springer 2021) 123.

Another reason for different outcomes in the case law is the way in which national law on parental rights is drafted. For instance, in many countries the birth mother is often considered to be the child's legal mother, even in cases of gestational surrogacy.[19] Therefore, family law continues to privilege opposite-sex couples in the context of family life.[20] There are two major reasons for this. First, the national legislation on parental rights lack coherence.[21] Newer legislation may be using a gender-neutral term parent, whereas older legislation has not been amended to recognise the diversity of families and the reality that trans men may be able to become pregnant and give birth to their own genetic children. Second, there is a lack of consensus among CoE States on LGBT parenting rights. National legislation governing access to ART, in particular, often provides inadequate parental rights for single women and men, same-sex couples, and unmarried fathers.[22] This could be for instance as customarily the man, who is married to the woman giving birth, has been recognised automatically as the child's father in some legal systems.[23] As family law in Europe still reflects the view that a child should always have one mother and one father,[24] the law is 'gendered and (hetero)sexualised'.[25] These types of laws do not take into account the fact that not all individuals wishing to become parents are married, civil partnered, cohabiting, or have any plans to do so as individuals may also wish to become parents using ART such as *in vitro* fertilisation (IVF) treatment and surrogacy. Yet, the concept of LGBT parenthood appears to be at odds with the ideal position in which to raise children, namely a married opposite-sex couple with genetic children.[26] Some CoE States have in the past few decades even adopted anti-LGBT laws and enacted constitutional bans on same-sex marriage in order to enforce traditional heteronormative family values.[27]

The analysis reveals that the Court's case law concerning parenthood reinforces the heteronormative two-parent family as it is very much focused on biologically

19 See eg *AM v Norway* App no 30254/18 (ECtHR, 24 March 2022); *H v UK* App no 32185/20 (ECtHR, 23 June 2022); *KK and Others v Denmark* App no 25212/21 (ECtHR, 6 December 2022).

20 Atina Krajewska and Rachel Cahill-O'Callaghan, 'When a Single Man Wants to be A Father: Revealing the Invisible Subjects in the Law Regulating Fertility Treatment' (2020) 29(1) Social & L Stud 85, 89.

21 Alan Brown, 'Trans (Legal) Parenthood and The Gender of Legal Parenthood' (2024) 44(1) LS 168.

22 Brian Tobin, 'The (D)evolving Nature of Guardianship Rights for Unmarried Fathers under Irish Law' (2020) 32(3) CFLQ 285. See also Krajewska and Cahill-O'Callaghan (n 20) 90.

23 See *Boeckel and Gessner-Boeckel v Germany* App no 8017/11 (ECtHR, 7 May 2013).

24 See eg Anna Lorenzetti, 'The European Courts and Transsexuals: The Binary Distinction and the Pattern of Family' in Maribel Pascual and Aida Torres Pérez (eds), *The Right to Family Life in the European Union* (Routledge 2017); O'Halloran (n 18); Marie Digoix, 'Introduction: LGBT Questions and the Family' in Elwood D Carlson, Stuart Gietel-Basten, and Marie Digoix, *Same-Sex Families and Legal Recognition in Europe* (Springer 2020); Brown, 'Trans (Legal)' (n 21).

25 Gonzalez-Salzberg (n 12) 155.

26 Alice Margaria, 'Trans Men Giving Birth and Reflections on Fatherhood: What to Expect?' (2020) 34(3) IJLPF 225, 234.

27 Peter Dunne, 'Who Is a Parent and Who Is a Child in a Same-Sex Family? Legislative and Judicial Issues for LGBT Families Post-Separation, Part I: The European Perspective' (2017) 30 J Am Acad Matrimonial Lawyers 27.

grounded maternity and paternity.[28] As usually only one of the parents in a same-sex couple is genetically related to the child, lesbian and gay couples are disadvantaged as their situation is often compared to that of a married opposite-sex couple where both parents are genetically related to the child. It is also frequent in the case of opposite-sex parents, who conclude a surrogacy agreement, that the intended mother is not genetically related to the child, even if the couple may have used the gametes of the intended father.[29] Consequently, direct genetic links are central particularly in two specific areas of the Court's case law, namely second parent adoption[30] and the recognition of filiation in cases of cross-border surrogacy.[31] The case law concerning the parental rights of lesbian women deserves more prominence as the ECtHR has dealt with cases concerning single person adoption and second parent adoption. Hodson argues that the experiences of lesbian women are frequently marginalised in the Court's case law.[32] For instance, French legislation has long refused lesbian partners the right to adopt their partner's biological child, whereas only married spouses have been able to apply for second parent adoption.[33] Even though France has seemingly adopted new mechanisms to address the situation, the solutions do not appear particularly effective.[34] Despite continued disadvantages in terms of parental rights, the Court has not recognised that lesbian women experience discrimination on the grounds of their sexual orientation when they are prevented from equal parenting rights. The case law also demonstrates that when the parents' relationship ends, regardless of whether the couple is a same-sex couple or an opposite-sex couple, it is almost impossible for the non-genetic parent to obtain legal recognition of the parent-child relationship due to the way law on adoption is formulated. For instance, if the genetic parent, who has the parental responsibilities in respect of the child, refuses to acknowledge the parenthood of the non-genetic parent, the latter is left without recognition of their parental relationship with the child.[35] Additionally, a growing body of case law involves parental rights of trans men and trans women.

The absence of adequate parental rights underlines the need for the national legislation to reflect the evolving nature of families and the move to a more inclusive

28 Linda Hart, Relational Subjects: Family Relations, Law and Gender in the European Court of Human Rights (PhD thesis, University of Helsinki 2016); Hodson (n 5). For a comprehensive study to inquire into gender equality before the ECtHR from the perspective of fathers, see Alice Margaria, *The Construction of Fatherhood: The Jurisprudence of the European Court of Human Rights* (CUP 2019).

29 Levy (n 4) 124–125.

30 *Gas and Dubois v France* App no 25951/07 (ECtHR, 15 March 2012); *CE and Others v France* App nos 29775/18 and 29693/19 (ECtHR, 24 March 2022).

31 See s 6.

32 Hodson (n 5). On the invisibility of lesbian women in international law more generally, see, eg, Diane Otto, 'Lesbians? Not in My Country' (1995) 20 Alt LJ 288.

33 Giulia Dondoli, 'An Overnight Success A Decade in The Making: Indirect Discrimination on the Grounds of Sexual Orientation' (2018) 18(1) IJDL 5.

34 *CE* (n 30).

35 See eg *AM* (n 19).

understanding of the concepts of family and parenthood.[36] As the boundaries of family overlap with other areas of social life, the recognition of parental rights; same-sex unions; and accessibility of ART, such as, egg, sperm, or embryo donation, donor insemination, IVF, or cross-border surrogacy have created social realities of families that do not fit into the restrictive national legal frameworks.[37] Although there are arguments that only a small percentage of children are born through surrogacy or that only economically privileged individuals can afford to use ART,[38] there is ample case law in this area. This is because national authorities frequently refuse to recognise legal parenthood established by birth certificates issued in States outside Europe, regardless of whether the intended or social[39] parents are a same-sex or opposite-sex couple.

This chapter is structured as follows: The second section focuses on access to ART. The third section aims to give prominence to cases touching upon intercountry adoption. Section 5.4 outlines the developments in the Court's case law regarding single parent adoption and second parent adoption. Section 5.5 analyses the case law on the parental rights of trans persons. Section 5.6 discusses the case law concerning cross-border surrogacy. Section 5.7 provides a conclusion.

5.2 Access to ART

In its earlier case law focusing on opposite-sex couples in need of IVF using their own gametes or donor insemination, the Court was willing to recognise that Article 8 protected the right to undergo IVF treatment as a method for individuals to make decisions about parenthood.[40] Yet, overall, its early approach towards ART was restrictive. It has only found a violation of Article 8 in two cases of opposite-sex couples.[41] Out of the two judgments, which involve single women, the 2007 judgment in *Evans v UK*[42] is probably the more controversial. The Court reached an absurd outcome in this case where a divorced woman, Ms Natallie Evans, was prevented from using embryos frozen during her marriage after she was diagnosed

36 David HJ Morgan, 'Framing Relationships and Families' in Lynn Jamieson, Roona Simpson and Ruth Lewis, *Researching Families and Relationships: Reflections on Process* (Palgrave MacMillan 2011) 21.

37 ibid 21; Levy (n 4) 124.

38 Levy (n 4) 124–125, 127; Krajewska and Cahill-O'Callaghan (n 20) 90.

39 The parent, who has no genetic or biological connection to the child, is often referred to as the intended or social parent. See *AM* (n 19) para 31.

40 See eg Guillem Cano Palomares, 'Right to Family Life and Access to Medically Assisted Procreation in the Case Law of the European Court of Human Rights' in Maribel Gonzáles Pascual and Aida Torres Pérez (eds), *The Right to Family Life in the European Union* (Routledge 2017) 101.

41 The first case concerned a married Italian couple, who were healthy carriers of cystic fibrosis and which they wanted to rule out, using IVF. See *Costa and Pavan v Italy* App no 54270/10 (ECtHR, 28 August 2012), para 71. The second case concerned a British woman, who could not conceive without the use of IVF because her husband was serving life for murder and would not be released for several years. See *Dickson v UK* App no 44362/04 (ECtHR, 4 December 2007).

42 *Evans v UK* App no 6339/05 (ECtHR, 10 April 2007).

with ovarian cancer. Her access was denied on the grounds that her ex-husband withdrew his consent to the use of his genetic material after their divorce. The Court found that the ex-husband's decision not to become a parent was a fundamental right protected by Article 8 which could not be overridden by Ms Evans's wish to become a mother.[43] In essence, this meant that the former spouse could still exert power over Ms Evans by simply withdrawing his consent even after agreeing for the embryos to be frozen. In the 2012 judgment in *Knecht v Romania*,[44] a dual German-American national, Ms Daniela Knecht, alleged that she was prevented from progressing with her planned IVF treatment in Romania due to a criminal investigation into the Romanian fertility clinic where her embryos were stored. After the Romanian authorities seized the embryos, they refused to transfer the embryos to another licensed clinic. The Court found no violation of Article 8.

The 2011 judgment in *SH and Others v Austria*[45] is the last judgment to adopt a restrictive approach to IVF and to allow States to limit the access to IVF exclusively to married couples. The majority of the Grand Chamber noted that there was uneasiness in Austria about IVF at the time.[46] Therefore, the access to ART was argued to raise sensitive moral and ethical issues as no consensus existed amongst the CoE States.[47] The Court concluded the national legislation, which permitted ART only within a marriage or a relationship similar to marriage, and only if all other methods of conception had been attempted, did not violate Article 8. Although the judgment is restrictive, the Court also addressed the issue in a manner that would allow couples and individuals wishing to have children using IVF to access it outside States that continued to restrict access to ART.[48] It noted that the Austrian legislation did not essentially prohibit individuals from choosing to travel outside Austria to receive similar services.[49] The judgment has been heavily criticised. The dissenting judges noted that the suggestion to travel abroad did not solve the problem that the legal prohibition caused interference with the couples' private life and, therefore, it failed to satisfy the requirements of Article 8.[50] Additionally, the suggestion that couples could access ART abroad does very little to solve the problem for single men and gay men who wish to become fathers but cannot access

43 For commentary on *Evans*, see eg, Craig Lind, '*Evans v United Kingdom*: Judgments of Solomon: Power, Gender and Procreation' [2006] CFLQ 576.

44 *Knecht v Romania* App no 10048/10 (2 October 2012).

45 *SH and Others v Austria* App no 57813/00 (ECtHR, 3 November 2011) (In 2010, the ECtHR held in the same case that the Austrian ban on ART violated art 14 in conjunction with art 8. The Grand Chamber reversed this finding, stating that the ban did not violate art 8).

46 ibid para 99.

47 ibid paras 94 and 97.

48 It has been criticised for such an approach on account that some other State can provide human rights protection outside the jurisdiction of the responding State, while the former can continue to infringe the rights of the applicants. See eg Bracken, 'Accommodations' (n 1).

49 *SH* (n 45) para 114.

50 ibid Joint Dissenting Opinion of Judges Tulkens, Hirvelä, Lazarova Trajkovska and Tsotsoria, para 12.

surrogacy in their country of residence where it is illegal.[51] A single man or a same-sex male couple wishing to become a parent using ART will thus need the help of a surrogate who agrees to carry the child.[52] Even if lesbian couples and single women could easily travel to other European States to receive IVF treatment, the reality is that becoming a parent using ART is linked to an individual's economic privilege and social capital as doing so is financially, logistically, and emotionally demanding.[53] Bracken has criticised the Court for leaving the CoE States a window of opportunity in *SH* to disregard their obligations under the Convention by suggesting that as long as human rights protection is available in another State, the denial of Convention rights is not an issue.[54] It is useful to note that scholars have argued that reproductive rights should be seen primarily as human rights, rather issues involving moral questions, the concept to which the Court often makes a reference to justify granting a wide margin of appreciation to States in this area of law.[55] Although there are only a handful of cases concerning access to IVF, it may be possible to argue that the Court has been unwilling to uphold the rights of single women and unmarried couples to access IVF in the past. As single women and lesbian couples often create families using IVF, they have long struggled to become parents due to their inability to access IVF in many CoE States.[56]

5.3 International Adoption

The right of single persons to adopt a child from abroad was the subject of the 2007 judgment in *Wagner and JMWL v Luxembourg*[57] where the national authorities, including the courts, refused to recognise the child-parent relationship between an unmarried woman, Ms Jeanne Wagner, and a three-year old girl she legally adopted in Peru. The ECtHR found that the refusal to recognise the adoption order, established in a Peruvian court's judgment, was an interference in the exercise of the rights guaranteed by Article 8. This was specifically so as it was impossible for Ms Wagner to adopt the child under the national legislation. Therefore, the authorities' refusal represented an interference with the right to respect for family life of both the mother and the child.[58] The national authorities' approach in *Wagner*

51 Gestational surrogacy is illegal in France and Germany. See eg Isabelle Rein-Lescastereyres, 'Recent Case Law on Cross-Border Surrogacy' in Katharina Boele-Woelki and Angelika Fuchs (eds), *Same-Sex Relationships and Beyond: Gender Matters in the EU* (Intersentia 2017).

52 Krajewska and Cahill-O'Callaghan (n 20) 91.

53 ibid 90.

54 Bracken, 'Accommodations' (n 1).

55 Liiri Oja and Alicia Ely Yamin, '"Woman" in the European Human Rights System: How is the Reproductive Rights Jurisprudence of the European Court of Human Rights Constructing Narratives of Women's Citizenship?' (2016) 32(1) Colum J Gender & L 62, 66.

56 Florence Binard, *Lesbian Motherhood from the Social Recognition of Female Homosexuality to the 'Lesby-Boom': A Comparison between Britain and France* (Routledge 2019).

57 *Wagner and JMWL v Luxembourg* App no 76240/01 (ECtHR, 28 June 2007).

58 ibid para 123.

echoes the sentiment of the 1979 landmark judgment in *Marckx v Belgium*,[59] where the issue was that Belgium required unmarried women to seek the recognition of their parental relationship with their children through adoption.[60] The aim of the legislation was to regulate the conduct of unmarried women by discouraging them from having children outside marriage.[61] The Court confirmed that States cannot discriminate against unmarried women in their national legislation.[62] Although it seems grotesque now that the State would wish to exert its power over an individual's decision whether or not to become a parent this way, unfortunately these types practices have not entirely disappeared. In many judgments concerning adoption by lesbian women, the national authorities and courts, alongside the dissenting judges of the ECtHR, have expressed their views about suitability of single women or lesbian women as parents due to the lack of a male role model in the children's lives.[63] The cases highlight the continued attempt of the States to control who becomes a parent and who does not.

Two complaints against France and Belgium concern the application for adoption of non-national children placed into the legal care of European citizens under *kafala*, a legal guardianship arrangement in place in many Muslim countries.[64] The Court has specifically noted that national authorities have refused adoption applications when the child has been placed into the care of a European citizen under *kafala* for three principal reasons.[65] First, according to it, national laws of the child's country of origin prohibit the child's adoption under another country's legal system.[66] Second, States disagree whether the prohibition of adoption under the legal system of the child's country of origin constitutes an obstacle to adoption.[67] Third, although *kafala* is considered to produce comparable effects to a guardianship, curatorship, or placement with a view to adoption, no State equates it with adoption.[68] The Court, therefore, concluded that in the absence of European consensus, States enjoy a broad margin of appreciation in the matter, and the denial of adoption does not constitute a violation of Article 8 rights of the child or the guardians.[69]

59 *Marckx v Belgium* App no 6833/74 (ECtHR, 13 June 1979) (The Court found that a Belgian practice to require unmarried mothers 'recognise' their children for affiliation to be established, whereas married mothers were exempted violated art 14 in conjunction with art 8).
60 Hart (n 28) 143.
61 ibid 145.
62 Claire Fenton-Glynn, *Family Formation and Parenthood* (OUP 2020).
63 See eg *EB v France* App no 43546/02 (ECtHR, 22 January 2008); *X and Others v Austria* App no 19010/07 (ECtHR, 19 February 2013) Joint Partly Dissenting Opinion of Judges Casadevall, Ziemele, Kovler, Jociene, Sikuta, De Gaetano and Sicilianos, OII-8.
64 *Kafala* is defined as a voluntary undertaking to provide for a child's welfare, education, and protection under Islamic law. See eg *Harroudj v France* App no 43631/09 (ECtHR, 4 October 2012), para 16.
65 ibid.
66 ibid para 11.
67 ibid para 48.
68 ibid.
69 ibid.

The ECtHR's 2012 judgment in *Harroudj v France*[70] concerned an adoption application submitted by 42-year-old French national, Ms Katya Harroudj, who unsuccessfully sought to adopt a two-year-old Algerian girl, Hind, whom an Algerian court placed into her legal care as a baby.[71] The ECtHR took the view that French law created the means to alleviate the effects of the Algerian prohibition to adopt children placed into the care of a French national under the *kafala* arrangement as it was possible for Hind to obtain French citizenship within a reduced period of time, which enabled her adoption afterwards.[72] According to the Court, these measures showed respect for cultural pluralism and aimed to encourage the integration of non-national children to the French society.[73] By doing so, France struck a fair balance between the public interest and that of Ms Harroudj.[74] As Ms Harroudj could adopt Hind after she obtained the French citizenship, there was no violation of Article 8.[75]

The 2014 judgment in *Chbihi Loudoudi and Others v Belgium*[76] concerned the Belgian authorities' refusal to allow a married couple with dual Belgian and Moroccan nationality, Ms Ben Said and Mr Chbihi Loudoudi, to adopt KB, their 16-year-old niece of Moroccan nationality. The ECtHR noted that KB's biological parents, who remained in Morocco, placed her in the couple's care under *kafala* at the age of seven. The couple argued that the Belgian authorities' delay in ruling on their adoption application created a situation of instability and uncertainty for KB as her residence in Belgium was based on several successive fixed-term residence permits. The Court considered that the couple's cohabitation with their niece established family bonds protected by Article 8.[77] Yet, their rights under Article 8 were not violated by the refusal of the adoption because the statutory conditions were not met for an adoption, as KB's genetic parents were still alive. Additionally, her adoption would have created a legal parent-child relationship, which was not constituted by the *kafala* arrangement. According to the ECtHR, the Belgian authorities' refusal to grant the adoption was based on the prevention of improper use of international adoption.[78] It further highlighted that the ECHR did not guarantee a right to a particular type of residence status. Therefore, it was unreasonable to consider that Belgium was required to grant KB unlimited leave

70 ibid.
71 ibid para 7.
72 ibid para 51.
73 ibid.
74 ibid.
75 ibid para 52.
76 *Chbihi Loudoudi and Others v Belgium* App no 52265/10 (ECtHR, 16 December 2014).
77 *Chbiti* (n 76) para 78.
78 It has been suggested that the lack of Belgian efforts to make allowance for the *kafala* under Belgian law are linked to the arguments that the arrangements have been used as a means of circumventing Belgian immigration rules. See Jinske Verhellen and Patrick Wautelet, 'The Treatment of Diversity in Family Law in Belgium: Between Acknowledgment and Indifference' in Nadjma Yassari and Marie-Claire Foblets (eds), *Normativity and Diversity in Family Law: Lessons from Comparative Law* (Springer 2022) 250.

to remain in order to protect her private life under Article 8, despite the fact that she had lived in Belgium for almost ten years. As regards the claim that the couple and their niece were discriminated against on the grounds of their origin as Moroccan citizens, the Court concluded that as the case was considered under Article 8, there was no separate violation of Article 14 in conjunction with Article 8. It is possible that the Court wanted to avoid making a finding on ethnic, racial, and religious discrimination in this case. As both *kafala* and adoption are argued to produce equivalent results from the child's perspective, it seems that the differences between the two institutions may be merely technical and aimed to avoid triggering various rules tailored for adoption, such as, the right of residence and access to child allowance.[79]

5.4 LGBT Parenthood through Adoption

Discussing LGBT cases in aggregate can reveal discriminatory experiences of some LGBT applicants before the ECtHR.[80] While the Court is increasingly more sympathetic to LGBT claims, the Convention organs' response to the complaints brought by lesbian women in particular has rendered the ECtHR's approach to lesbians neither gender-sensitive nor intersectional.[81] The Court's failure to respond to intersectional discrimination faced by LGBT persons, including trans men and trans women, diminishes the potential of the Court's jurisprudence to address gender-based injustices.[82] Therefore, case law can be argued to have a significant impact on family relationship claims of single women, lesbian couples, trans individuals.

Although marriage and civil partnerships offer same-sex couples the most direct means to formalise links between spouses and their non-genetic children,[83] there are three major problems with this logic. First, the lack of legal recognition of same-sex unions impacts the parenting rights of same-sex couples in cases where national legislation fails to provide recognition of filiation between children and their non-biological parent(s). Bracken has argued that the lack of same-sex marriage has had long-standing impact on same-sex parenthood as the Court has afforded States a wide margin of appreciation in cases concerning same-sex relationships.[84]

Second, same-sex couples have been able to access marriage and civil partnerships relatively recently, only around 2010 and principally only in Western European States.[85] Although the Court held in 2015 that Article 8 placed on States an obligation to afford same-sex couples the possibility to obtain legal recognition

79 ibid 249.
80 Hodson (n 5).
81 ibid 384, 388–389.
82 ibid
83 Digoix (n 24) 2; Dunne, 'Who Is a Parent' (n 27).
84 Bracken, 'Strasbourg's Response' (n 7) 361.
85 Digoix (n 24) 2; Dunne, 'Who Is a Parent' (n 27).

and legal protection of their union,[86] States are free to decide the means by which they wish to provide the recognition.[87] The Court's approach has remained largely similar throughout the years. In its 2021 judgment in *Fedotova and Others v Russia*,[88] the Court established that States had a positive obligation under Article 8 to provide an opportunity for two lesbian couples and one gay couple, who sought to enter into marriage, to have their relationships acknowledged. Although States had a wide margin of appreciation in choosing the form of registration of same-sex unions, the Court found a violation of Article 8.[89] The Court confirmed the findings in its 2023 judgment in *Koilova and Babulkova v Bulgaria*[90] where it held that Bulgaria's failure to provide any form of legal recognition and protection of same-sex couples violated Article 8. However, it has taken the Court several decades to accept that States cannot discriminate against same-sex couples when it comes to the recognition of same-sex relationships.

Third, even if States offered a recognition of same-sex civil unions, they often aim to preserve legal differences between opposite-sex marriage and same-sex union and may not guarantee similar parenting rights for lesbian and gay parents.[91] The Court has continually stressed the lack of consensus on claims for same-sex marriage between the 46 CoE States, which has led to a wide margin of appreciation in the area.[92] Scholars have criticised the Court for essentially enabling States to uphold their legislation reserving marriage to opposite-sex couples.[93] When looking at the rights of LGBT applicants in cases concerning second-parent adoption and surrogacy,[94] it is easy to see that the Court's focus on heteronormativity is problematic when parenthood and the right to adopt are linked to marriage. Thus, entering into a marriage or civil union does not guarantee automatic parenting rights for the non-genetic same-sex parent, but in most cases the parent needs to take further steps to formalise the parent-child relationship.[95] Bracken has argued that in practise this has amounted to denial of lesbian and gay adoption, particularly in France.[96]

86 *Oliari and Others v Italy* App no 18766/11 and 36030/11 (ECtHR, 21 July 2015).

87 *Gas* (n 30) para 66: 'Article 12 of the Convention does not impose an obligation on the governments of the Contracting States to grant same-sex couples access to marriage'.

88 *Fedotova and Others v Russia* App no 40792/10 and others (ECtHR, 13 July 2021).

89 ibid para 56.

90 *Koilova and Babulkova v Bulgaria* App no 40209/20 (ECtHR, 5 September 2023).

91 Diego Lasio and Francesco Serri, 'The Italian Public Debate on Same-Sex Civil Unions and Gay and Lesbian Parenting' (2019) 22(4) Sexualities 691.

92 See eg Frances Hamilton, 'The Potential of European Union Law to Further Advance LGBTQ+ Persons and Same-Sex Couples' Rights' in Frances Hamilton and Guido Noto La Diega (eds), *Same-Sex Relationships, Law and Social Change* (Routledge 2020).

93 Margaria argues that essentially the Court's judgments 'validate national bans on same-sex marriage'. See Margaria, 'Trans Men' (n 26) 240.

94 For cases concerning second parent adoption, see s 4.2. For cases concerning surrogacy, see s 6.

95 Dunne, 'Who Is a Parent' (n 27).

96 Bracken, 'Strasbourg's Response' (n 7) 361 and 363.

In earlier case law, the ECtHR adopted a reasoning according to which same-sex couples were treated as any unmarried couple would, thereby denying that its case law was based on the couple's sexual orientation.[97] Yet, treating same-sex couples and unmarried opposite-sex couples equally ignores the lack of legal recognition of legal unions for same-sex couples. Additionally, the Court has distinguished registered partnerships from marriage.[98] For these reasons scholars have argued that the case law on LGBT families is overwhelmingly hindered by the perceived need to protect the institutions of opposite-sex marriage and gender-specific parental roles.[99] Marriage rights of trans individuals serve an apt illustration. Although trans persons have the right to marry,[100] the Court has recognised that States could require that a trans person converts their marriage into a civil partnership with practically identical legal protection.[101] This has meant that the marriages of LGBT individuals are socially acceptable only when they mirror those of opposite-sex couples.[102]

5.4.1 Single Parent Adoption

Major cases concerning the adoption rights of the single persons, particularly gay men and lesbian women, have involved complaints against restrictive national legislation in France. This area has been explored in the scholarship extensively.[103] Although French law allowed single persons to adopt in the early 2000s, French authorities rejected adoption applications on grounds of sexual orientation. The Court's 2002 judgment in *Fretté v France*[104] concerning the inability of a single man to adopt a child is exceptionally restrictive. Although the Court found that the adoption authorities denied the possibility of a gay man, Mr Philippe Fretté, to adopt a child, it found no violation of Article 14 taken in conjunction with Article 8.[105] This was because the refusal did not infringe the principle of proportionality as the French government provided an objective and reasonable justification for the refusal.[106] The government argued, *inter alia*, that more parents wanted to adopt than there were available children to adopt.[107] As no common European consensus existed on the right of LGBT persons to adopt, nor was the scientific consensus conclusive about the likely significance of adoption by same-sex parents in the face

97 Hodson (n 5).
98 The ECtHR long considered that the situation of a lesbian couple, who had entered a registered partnership, could not be likened to situation of an opposite-sex married couple. See *Boeckel* (n 23).
99 Hart (n 28) 98; Hodson (n 5); Margaria, 'Trans Men' (n 26) 240.
100 *Christine Goodwin v UK* App no 28957/95 (ECtHR, 11 July 2002).
101 *Hämäläinen v Finland* App no 37359/09 (ECtHR, 16 July 2014), para 87 (A case concerning a requirement of change of marital status to be recognised as a trans woman). See also Hodson (n 5).
102 Hodson (n 5).
103 See eg Liesker (n 7); Bracken, 'Strasbourg's Response' (n 7) 361.
104 *Fretté v France* App no 36515/97 (ECtHR, 26 May 2002).
105 ibid para 35.
106 ibid paras 42–43.
107 ibid para 42.

of a limited number of scientific studies, the Court concluded the French government enjoyed a wide margin of appreciation in the area.[108] The Court's reasoning is unsatisfactory because the separate opinions annexed to the majority judgment indicated that French law authorised all single persons and same-sex couples to submit an application for adoption.[109] The Court had a real opportunity in this case to address discrimination against gay men and lesbian women but decided not to use this opportunity.

Although it has been suggested that the 2008 judgment in *EB v France*[110] made it clear that an adoption application cannot be rejected on the grounds of a prospective adoptive parent's sexual orientation, discrimination against gay and lesbian applicants, as expressed in the separate opinions annexed to this judgment, is anything but subtle. In *EB*, the Court found that the French authorities violated Article 14 in conjunction with Article 8 by refusing to allow a lesbian applicant, Ms EB, to adopt a child as a single parent. Yet, the judges, disagreeing with the majority, scandalised the fact that she cohabited with a lesbian partner who did not intend to adopt the child, and the child was not going to have a male role model. None of these opinions mention the fact that Ms EB was a 47-year-old nursery teacher with years of experience in educating and caring for small children. Even though *EB* is often cited as one of significant judgments that has advanced the LGBT parenting rights in Europe,[111] problems remain particularly in the context of second parent adoption, which in the case of lesbian couples has meant that the non-genetic parent has no mechanisms for establishing legal ties with the couple's children.

5.4.2 Second Parent Adoption

The ways in which national laws have restricted parental rights of lesbian couples is illustrated by cases concerning recognition of parenting rights of a same-sex partner in the case of donor insemination. The 1992 inadmissible decision in *Kerkhoven and Others v Netherlands*[112] was the first complaint before the Convention organs involving adoption of the child born to one of the partners in a cohabiting unmarried lesbian couple. Ms Catharina Kerkhoven sought to adopt the son of her partner, Ms Anna Maria Hinke. The European Commission of Human Rights considered the case inadmissible on the grounds that the relationship between the two women could not be equated to that of an opposite-sex cohabiting couple, and, therefore, it did not constitute family life under Article 8. The national legislation at the time allowed only men, whether the genetic father or not, to recognise a child, which meant that Ms Kerkhoven, as the non-genetic mother, had no mechanism

108 ibid

109 ibid Partly concurring opinion of Judge Costa joined by Judges Jungwiert and Traja 27. See also *Fretté* (n 104) Joint partly dissenting opinion of Judge Bratza and Judges Fuhrmann and Tulkens.

110 *EB* (n 63).

111 Bracken, 'Strasbourg's Response' (n 7).

112 *Kerkhoven and Others v Netherlands* App no 15666/89 (Commission Decision, 19 May 1992).

for establishing legal ties with her unmarried partner's son.[113] The Commission's response was that the inability to establish legal ties between Ms Kerkhoven and the child did not amount to an interference with Article 8.[114]

Several other cases have continued along similar lines. The restrictive approach is deeply problematic, considering that several northern European States permitted second parent or joint adoption by same-sex couples in the 2000s.[115] The authorities' refusal to allow one of the partners in a lesbian couple to adopt the child by insisting that simple adoption terminates the child's relationship with the birth mother has made it virtually impossible for the non-genetic parent to establish legal ties with the couple's child. The 2012 judgment in *Gas and Dubois v France*[116] illustrates this point. Ms Nathalie Dubois gave birth to a daughter, who was conceived by anonymous donor insemination in Belgium.[117] In 2006, Ms Valérie Gas unsuccessfully applied to adopt the daughter with the consent of her civil partner.[118] The French courts rejected the application on the grounds that under French law simple adoption would have transferred the parental responsibility to Ms Gas while depriving Ms Dubois of parental responsibility altogether. Yet, French law permitted opposite-sex married spouses to adopt one another's genetic children, allowing the adopting spouse and the genetic parent to share the parental responsibility. Although Ms Gas and Ms Dubois were in a civil partnership, French law did not at the time recognise the right of same-sex couples to marry. The authorities failed to see that the law treated civil partners and married couples differently as Ms Gas had no way of establishing legal ties to their daughter.[119] In dismissing the couple's complaint, the Court noted that marriage conferred a special status, and denying the lesbian couple access to that status did not amount to a violation of their rights.[120] These judgments reveal that the focus on the two-parent opposite-sex married couple is deeply embedded in how the Court views families.[121] It also reveals the failure of the Court to see the privilege created by a heterosexual institution of marriage when it was impossible for the lesbian couple to marry.

The 2013 judgment in *X and Others v Austria*[122] similarly concerned second parent adoption by the non-genetic mother. However, the outcome is different.[123] The Court found discrimination on the grounds of sexual orientation,[124] resulting

113 Hodson (n 5) 388.
114 ibid.
115 Liesker (n 7) 183.
116 *Gas* (n 30).
117 See Dondoli (n 33).
118 Hodson (n 5).
119 ibid.
120 Hodson (n 5).
121 See eg Fenton-Glynn (n 62); Michael Wells-Greco, 'Reflections on *Gas and Dubois v France* (2012): Same-Sex Second Parent Adoption–A Missed Opportunity' (2012) Intl Family LJ 224.
122 *X* (n 63) para 92.
123 Hodson (n 5).
124 *X* (n 63) paras 10–11.

in violation of Articles 8 and 14.[125] It accepted that where second-parent adoption was available to unmarried opposite-sex couples, same-sex partners could not be omitted without particularly weighty reasons.[126] The Court held that although the Convention did not oblige States to extend second parent adoption to unmarried couples, as Austria had chosen to do so, it could not discriminate against same-sex couples. The restrictive line continued in the 2013 inadmissible decision in *Boeckel and Gessner-Boeckel v Germany*,[127] which concerned the refusal by German authorities to recognise Ms Sabine Boeckel as the second parent of the child of her civil partner, Ms Anja Gessner-Boeckel. Although Ms Boeckel was not prevented from adopting the child in order to create legal ties with the child, the domestic courts rejected the couple's request and subsequent appeal to amend their son's birth certificate.[128] The ECtHR noted that according to German legislation, the child's genetic father was the birth mother's husband. The lesbian couple, who were a civil partnership, argued that this principle should be applied *mutatis mutandis* to a situation of a birth mother, who was in a civil partnership with a woman. The Court rejected their argument by stating that their situation was not equal to that of a married opposite-sex couple because of the absence of direct genetic link between the child and Ms Boeckel.[129] According to the Court, the discrimination did not result from the couple's sexual orientation but from their unmarried status.[130] Consequently, there was no violation of Article 14 read in conjunction with Article 8.

Even though States have amended their laws to eliminate discrimination against same-sex couples, the effects of the Court's approach have continued to be felt in subsequent case law.[131] Although the French marriage law has, since 2013, allowed same-sex couples to marry and adopt children, secondparent adoption is still not possible for same-sex couples in France on the grounds that simple adoption results in the deprivation of parental responsibility of the birth mother.[132] Additionally, even though France has made access to ART legal for single women and lesbian couples in 2021, the opposition to lesbian parenthood remains strong.[133] The 2018 inadmissible decision in *Bonnaud and Lecoq v France*[134] concerned the inability of Ms Francine Bonnaud to exercise parental responsibility of the child of her partner, Ms Patricia Lecoq, and *vice versa*. This was despite the fact that the couple's two children were born after the couple entered a civil partnership.[135] Adopting its usual

125 ibid 151–152.
126 ibid paras 105–53.
127 *Boeckel* (n 23).
128 Hodson (n 5).
129 *Boeckel* (n 23) para 8.
130 Hodson (n 5).
131 See eg *CE* (n 30). See also Matthias Thibeaud, 'Same-Sex Families Challenging Norms and the Law in France' in Carlson, Gietel-Basten, and Digoix (n 24).
132 See eg *CE* (n 30).
133 See eg Binard (n 56).
134 *Bonnaud and Lecoq v France* App no 6190/11 (ECtHR, 6 February 2018).
135 Hodson (n 5).

reasoning, the Court held that the decision was not based on their sexual orientation as the couple was treated as any unmarried couple would be.[136] The 2022 judgment in *CE and Others v France*[137] is another judgment in the long line of cases demonstrating that one of the partners in a lesbian couple still struggles to create legal ties with the couple's children. What is striking about the judgment is that the Court found that France had adopted new legislation enabling the recognition of filiation while the cases were pending before the ECtHR, and, therefore, the non-genetic parents should have used the new legal mechanisms, even though by its own admission, the legislation did not create a legal relationship between the child and the non-genetic parent. Consequently, it found no violation of Article 8.

The Court's approach in *CE* is perplexing. It essentially accuses the non-genetic parents, Ms CE and Ms AE, for not having taken any steps to obtain legal recognition of the parent-child relationship at the time of their children's birth in the early–late 2000s when it would have been impossible to formalise the child-parental relationship anyway. Both women essentially sought the recognition only after their relationships with the birth mothers had ended. According to the Court, the matter could have been solved easily, had the child's genetic parent obtained a court order for the exercise of joint parental responsibility with their former partner. The Court noted that while such an order would not have entailed the establishment of a legal parent-child relationship, it would have amounted to a degree of legal recognition of the relationship as it allowed the former partner to exercise certain rights and duties associated with parenthood. Furthermore, where the couple had failed to reach an agreement upon separation, the family-affairs judge could determine the arrangements concerning the child's relationship with the non-genetic parent, if the child's interests so required.

In the case of Ms AE, the ECtHR noted that because her non-genetic son, TG, was born in 2008 via an ART procedure carried out abroad when she and her former partner were in a civil partnership, French legislation adopted in 2021 enabled the establishment of a legal parent-child relationship between TG and Ms AE. The couple's subsequent separation had no implications for the application of this legislation.[138] It was sufficient for the couple to have been married, in a civil partnership or cohabiting at the time of the ART treatment, and for them to have had recourse to that treatment with the intention of having a child together. In the case of Ms CE, the ECtHR observed that Ms CE was unable to adopt her non-genetic daughter, MB, born through donor insemination in France, until the latter turned 18. However, the simple adoption procedure became possible after MB's eighteenth birthday.[139] According to the Court, this was apt to satisfy Ms CE's legitimate expectations as it would enable a legal mother-child relationship to be established

136 ibid.

137 *CE* (n 30).

138 French Bioethics Law 2021, art 1 amended French Public Health Code, art 2141-2 to make ART available to 'any couple formed by a man and a woman or two women, or any single woman'. See George (n 7) 343.

139 *CE* (n 30) para 112.

between her and MB. The judgment is disappointing as it does not rectify the longstanding inability of a non-genetic parent in a lesbian couple to legalise their relationship with the couple's children. It has been argued that although the Court did not find discrimination, Ms CE's access to parental rights was differentiated on the basis of her marital status, or absence of it, and Ms AE's parental rights were affected by her sexual orientation, both of which are grounds of discrimination covered by Article 14.[140]

5.5 Trans Parenthood

One area where case law still lags behind social developments is the establishment of legal parenthood for trans persons.[141] Ammaturo has validly argued that the case law reveals that the Court lacks knowledge of the 'experiences, identities, and kinship and life arrangements of trans* persons'.[142] Establishing trans parenthood is vital as, with the rest of the population, trans individuals seek to become parents after legal transition. This is logical, considering that many people are of reproductive age at the time of their transition and engage in post-transition relationships.[143] The Court's first case on trans parenthood is the 1997 judgment in *X, Y and Z v UK*,[144] which concerned parenting rights of a trans man, Mr X. He and his female partner, Ms Y, sought Mr X's registration as the father of their daughter, Z, on the child's birth certificate. The request was rejected as Mr X's reassigned male gender was not yet fully recognised at the time.[145] The couple argued that the refusal violated their right to respect for private and family life under Article 8. The majority of the Court found that Article 8 did not imply an obligation for the UK to formally recognise Mr X, who was not the genetic father, as the father of Z, born through donor insemination.[146] Persuaded by the lack of a common European consensus and the sensitive nature of the ethical and moral issues raised by fatherhood of a trans man, the Court granted a wide margin of appreciation to the UK.[147] Subsequently, it concluded that the authorities had struck a fair balance between the family's rights under Article 8 and the interest of the community 'in maintaining a coherent

140 Charly Derave and Hania Ouhnaoui, '*CE & al v France*: Legal Recognition of Intended Parenthood prem previous same-sex relationships (Between Women)' (*Strasbourg Observers*, 7 October 2022) <https://strasbourgobservers.com/2022/10/07/c-e-al-v-france-legal-recognition-of-intended-parenthood-from-previous-same-sex-relationships-between-women/> accessed 30 June 2024.

141 See eg Alan Brown, 'Trans Parenthood and the Meaning of 'Mother', 'Father' and 'Parent'—*R (McConnell and YY) v Registrar General for England and Wales* [2020] EWCA Civ 559' (2021) 29(1) Med L Rev 157.

142 Francesca R Ammaturo, *European Sexual Citizenship: Human Rights, Bodies and Identities* (Palgrave 2017) 71.

143 Margaria, 'Trans Men' (n 26) 228.

144 *X, Y and Z v UK* App no 21830/93 (ECtHR, 22 April 1997).

145 ibid para 36.

146 ibid para 52.

147 ibid para 44.

system of family law which places the best interests of the child at the forefront'.[148] Hart argues that although the relationship between Mr X and Z was protected by Article 8, it nevertheless fell short of family life as Mr X and Ms Y were legally considered to be a same-sex couple.[149]

5.5.1 Access to Genetic Children Post-Transition

Only a few cases before the ECtHR concern access to genetic children after transition. In its 1997 inadmissible decision in *LF v Ireland*,[150] a dual UK-Irish citizen, Ms LF, residing in Northern Ireland, complained, among others, that the denial of her access to her two teenage children violated Article 8 alone and in conjunction with Article 14. She also complained that because of her gender reassignment, her fixed-term contract as a dental surgeon with the local health board was not renewed and she was subsequently denied access to unemployment benefits. The Commission rejected all claims. In two subsequent cases, the former spouse of a trans woman sought to deprive the latter from parental responsibility and contact rights on the grounds that the children's contact with their parent, who was undergoing gender reassignment, was psychologically harmful for the children. Although in its 2010 judgment in *PV v Spain*,[151] the Court held that gender reassignment was indisputably covered by Article 14, it found no violation of Article 14 in conjunction with Article 8. In *PV*, the initial contact arrangements of Ms PV with her son, born before her transition, were amended on a reviewable basis after her ex-wife sought her deprivation of parental responsibility and contact. The ECtHR found no violation of Article 8, stating that Ms PV's transition was not the decisive factor in the decision to amend the contact arrangements, but these were amended to allow her son to become gradually accustomed to her gender reassignment as her gender transition was ongoing.

When the two first cases are compared with the 2021 judgments in *AM and Others v Russia*,[152] there is a visible difference in the Court's reasoning. The case highlighted elements to be factored in when assessing the restriction of parental rights and deprivation of contact with children following the applicant's gender transitioning.[153] The case concerned the attempt of the former spouse of Ms AM, a trans woman, to restrict her parental rights, including contact with their children. The ECtHR held that the Russian courts violated her rights under Articles 8 and 14 by terminating all contact due to their failure to conduct an extensive examination of the respective interests of the family members and other factors that may have

148 ibid para 47.
149 Hart (n 28) 90.
150 *LF v Ireland* App no 28154/95 (Commission Decision, 2 July 1997).
151 *PV v Spain* App no 35159/09 (ECtHR, 30 November 2010).
152 *AM and Others v Russia* App no 47220/19 (ECtHR, 6 July 2021), paras 53–61.
153 ibid paras 53–61.

been of relevance.[154] It concluded that as terminating contact was not necessary in a democratic society, Russia violated Ms AM's rights under Article 8.[155] The ECtHR also found a violation of Article 14 together with Article 8 when the national courts differentiated Ms AM from parents whose gender identity matched their gender assigned at birth.[156] In so doing, they singled Ms AM out on the grounds of her status as a trans woman.[157] Dunne notes that the case is a welcome addition to the Court's growing jurisprudence on trans families.[158]

5.5.2 Pregnant Man

Whereas legislation in most jurisdictions previously required individuals to undergo gender confirmation surgery, sterilisation, or the combination of the two, the legitimacy and indispensability of such requirements have been challenged before the ECtHR.[159] The Court has established that surgical or medical procedures involving a high probability of sterility are not acceptable requirements for obtaining gender recognition under the Convention.[160] The prohibition for States to require surgery and sterilisation as a precondition of gender recognition has meant that trans men, who have not undertaken surgery to remove their reproductive organs, may be able to become pregnant and give birth to their genetic children after transitioning as hormone therapy does not impact their egg yields.[161] Whereas ART, such as, freezing of oocytes, embryos, or ovarian tissue provide trans men with the opportunity to have children, using their own gametes, national legislation has resulted in trans men being recorded as mothers of their genetic children.[162] Cases concerning women and men, who have become parents after transitioning, particularly those involving a pregnant man,[163] demonstrate that national authorities and courts struggle with questions whether a trans man is their child's mother, father, or simply the parent for the purposes of birth registration.

154 ibid paras 61 and 81. For commentary of the case, see Peter Dunne, '*AM and Others v Russia*: Protecting the Rights of Transgender Parents' *Oxford Human Rights Hub* 21 August 2021 <https://ohrh.law.ox.ac.uk/a-m-and-others-v-russia-protecting-the-rights-of-transgender-parents/> accessed 28 April 2024.

155 *AM and Others* (n 152) paras 61.

156 ibid para 76.

157 ibid para 79.

158 Dunne, '*AM and Others*' (n 154).

159 Margaria, 'Trans Men' (n 26) 228.

160 *YY v Turkey* App no 14793/08 (ECtHR, 10 March 2015); *AP, Garçon and Nicot v France* App nos 79885/12 52471/13 and 52596/13 (ECtHR, 6 April 2017). See also Peter Dunne, 'Legal Gender Recognition in Europe: Sterilisation, Diagnosis and Medical Examination Requirements' (2017) 39 (4) J Soc Wel & Fam L 497.

161 Margaria, 'Trans Men' (n 26) 228–229.

162 Margaria, 'Trans Men' (n 26) 228.

163 Gonzalez-Salzberg (n 12) 193.

Although the ECtHR had the opportunity to review the legal position of parents whose children were born after the parent's legal gender transition in two German cases,[164] the outcome of these cases is disappointing. Essentially, the Court held that the trans individuals' parenthood was not called into question by the authorities' refusal to recognise the parent's new gender on the child's birth certificate. As the risk that the parent's gender identity would be revealed upon presentation of the child's birth certificate was low, there was no violation of their rights under Article 8. In the 2019 judgment in *OH and GH v Germany*,[165] Mr OH, a trans man, complained that he was incorrectly registered as the mother on his son's birth record. After obtaining legal recognition as a male, Mr OH discontinued his hormonal treatment and gave birth to a son, using sperm from a donor. His request was referred to the German courts, which ordered that in accordance with German law, Mr OH was recorded as his son's mother. He unsuccessfully appealed against the decision. In the ECtHR's view, the precautions provided under German law were such as to reduce the need for him to disclose his gender identity.

The 2023 judgment in *AH and Others v Germany*[166] similarly concerned the refusal of German authorities to record a trans woman, Ms AH, as the mother on the birth certificate of her child on the grounds that she was not the birth mother. The German authorities recognised Ms GH, a citizen of Israel, as the child's legal mother, on the grounds that she was the child's birth mother, whereas Ms AH was recorded as father in the birth register as the child was conceived with Ms AH's sperm. The ECtHR found that the German legislature had intended that the former gender and former first name of a parent should be indicated in all cases, regardless of whether the child was born before or after the parent's gender transition become final. The ECtHR found in both cases that the German courts struck a fair balance between the rights of the genetic parent, the interests of the child, considerations as to the child's welfare, and the public interests at stake. Accordingly, there was no violation of Article 8. Both judgments are disappointing, invalidating the gender experiences of trans parents.

5.6 Cross-Border Surrogacy

Most judgments concerning cross-border surrogacy focus on opposite-sex parents even though there are a handful of cases featuring same-sex parents.[167] It is striking that the ECtHR has rarely found a violation of the rights of the intended

164 *OH and GH v Germany* App nos 53568/18 and 54941/18 (ECtHR, 6 February 2019); *AH and Others v Germany* App no 7246/20 (ECtHR, 4 April 2023).

165 *OH* (n 164).

166 *AH* (n 164).

167 Elena Brodeala and Marie-Hélène Peter-Spiess, 'Surrogacy and Same-Sex Parenthood before the European Court of Human Rights: Reflections in Light of Cases against Switzerland' (2022) 32 Swiss Rev Intl & Eur L 397.

parents, even where one of them was genetically related to the child.[168] Instead, the Court has noted that the lack of recognition of filiation may violate the right to private life of the child under Article 8, especially if the child has a genetic link with their intended father.[169] The authorities' refusal to recognise a birth certificate of a child born abroad can be explained by two principal reasons: First, the refusal is aimed at discouraging cross-border surrogacy;[170] second, CoE States adopt different approaches to surrogacy.[171] Whereas some States, such as France and Germany, strictly prohibit surrogacy, others may allow non-commercial surrogacy.[172] Restrictions on surrogacy are frequently maintained based on arguments, such as, the child's best interests; protection of children against trafficking; commercialisation of the female body and pregnancy; and protection of vulnerable women against exploitation.[173] It is, however, recognised that children born through cross-border surrogacy can face difficulties with respect to certain fundamental rights, including issues relating to immigration and nationality, voting rights, residence rights, inheritance rights,[174] and parental care.[175] Additionally, the non-recognition of filiation creates uncertainty for the intended parents as regards their parental rights and obligations, which may result in problems in claiming social benefits associated with the parent-child relationship, such as parental leave[176] and child benefits.[177] Further problems relating to the legal relationship between the child and the non-genetic parent may arise because of the dissolution of a marriage, civil partnership, end of cohabitation, or death of the parents.[178]

5.6.1 Genetic Link

In the ECtHR's case law on cross-border surrogacy, the complaint usually revolves around the State's refusal to recognise the filial link between the intended parents

168 An exception to this is a case concerning the refusal of French courts to establish the paternity of Mr AL who concluded a gestational surrogacy arrangement in France. The ECtHR concluded that France violated art 8 (private life) in respect of Mr AL as it was no longer in the child's best interest to remove his son from the care of a third couple after six years. See *AL v France* App no 13344/20 (ECtHR, 24 March 2022).

169 *Mennesson and Others v France* App no 65192/11 (ECtHR, 26 June 2014); *DB and Others v Switzerland* App nos 58817/15 and 58252/15 (ECtHR, 22 November 2022).

170 Levy (n 4) 172.

171 Rein-Lescastereyres (n 51); Brodeala and Peter-Spiess (n 167) 398; Levy (n 4) 173.

172 Some States do not have any legislation concerning surrogacy. See Levy (n 4) 136; Rein-Lescastereyres (n 51).

173 Levy (n 4) 136.

174 *Mennesson* (n 169) para 98.

175 Brodeala and Peter-Spiess (n 167) 389; Levy (n 4) 124–125; Rein-Lescastereyres (n 51).

176 *Karine Hallier and Others v France* App no 46386/10 (ECtHR, 12 December 2017) (The non-genetic parent in a lesbian couple unsuccessfully applied for parental leave identified as 'paternity' leave, which was denied. The Court held that the purpose of paternity leave was to address inequality between men and women).

177 Brodeala and Peter-Spiess (n 167) 389; Levy (n 4) 124–125.

178 Levy (n 4) 137.

and the child born via gestational surrogacy. The case law highlights the centrality of a genetic link in the recognition of the parent-child relationship when at least one of the intended parents is also the genetic parent of the child. The analysis reveals that in the vast majority of complaints concerning cross-border surrogacy, the intended parents have entered into an agreement outside Europe, usually the US, where a surrogate agrees to carry the child.[179] In gestational or IVF surrogacy, the intended father usually uses his own gametes, which means that he is also the genetic father.[180] In contrast, the intended mother does not usually have either a genetic and gestational link to the child because the couple has used a donated ovum from another woman.[181] The Court has only once dealt with a case where the intended mother used her own ovum while the child was carried to term and delivered by a surrogate.[182]

The ECtHR was first called to decide a complaint involving cross-border surrogacy in its 2014 judgment in *Mennesson and Others v France*.[183] The case concerned the French authorities' refusal to grant a legal recognition of filiation legally established in California between opposite-sex parents and twin girls born via surrogacy.[184] The couple, Mr Dominique Mennesson and Ms Sylvie Mennesson, used an egg from a donor and the gametes of Mr Mennesson.[185] The ECtHR took the view that although France was not required to recognise the parent-child relationship established on the American birth certificates of the twins, it should nevertheless offer another possibility, such as, adoption, of establishing a family relationship between the twins and their intended mother, Ms Mennesson. Although the ECtHR noted that France may wish to deter its nationals from travelling abroad to utilise methods of ART, the effects of non-recognition of the legal parent-child relationship affected both the parents and the children.[186] It further noted that as Mr Mennesson was the twins' genetic father, the refusal to recognise the filial link was incompatible with the children's best interests.[187] Consequently, France overstepped the permissible limits of its margin of appreciation.[188] Although the Court found no violation of Article 8 with regard to the right to respect for family life, France violated the right of the twins as regards their private life.[189] Fenton-Glynn argues that in *Mennesson*, the Court followed the reasoning in *Wagner*[190] where

179 Krajewska and Cahill-O'Callaghan (n 20) 91.
180 ibid.
181 See Krajewska and Cahill-O'Callaghan (n 20) 91.
182 *D v France* App no 11288/18 (ECtHR, 16 July 2020).
183 *Mennesson* (n 169). See also *Labassee v France* App no 65941/11 (ECtHR, 26 June 2014); *D and Others v Belgium* App no 29176/13 (ECtHR, 8 July 2014).
184 O'Halloran (n 18) 150.
185 *Mennesson* (n 169) para 8.
186 ibid para 99.
187 ibid para 100.
188 ibid.
189 ibid paras 101–102.
190 *Wagner* (n 57).

it found that a refusal to recognise an intercountry adoption breached the child's rights under Article 14 in conjunction with Article 8.[191]

Levy argues that after *Mennesson*, the national authorities readily accept to designate the intended genetic father as the legal father on the presentation of a foreign birth certificate.[192] In its 2016 judgment in *Foulon and Bouvet v France*,[193] the Court confirmed that the principles established in *Mennesson* apply equally to cases where the genetic father is a gay or bisexual man who is in a relationship with a male partner.[194] Accordingly, national law must provide for the means to recognise the legal parentage of the genetic father, who is listed on the child's birth certificate following surrogacy abroad, regardless of his sexual orientation.[195] The 2022 judgment in *DB and Others v Switzerland*[196] concerned the Swiss authorities' failure to recognise the filial link between a child born in the US through gestational surrogacy and the intended father, who was married to another man. The couple used the gametes of one of the spouses and a donated ovum. The ECtHR stated in matters relating to establishing or recognising parentage between a child and their parents, the States' margin of appreciation was limited.[197] It concluded that the Swiss authorities' failure to recognise the parent-child relationship violated the child's rights under Article 8.[198] It also noted that the States had no margin of appreciation in the area of birth registrations. The respect for the child's private life required that domestic law offered the possibility of recognising filiation between the child and the intended parent, whether or not the latter was the genetic parent.[199]

The recognition of parenthood in cross-border surrogacy cases has also been argued to raise issues of gender asymmetry.[200] The 2020 judgment in *D v France*[201] concerning the recognition of filial link between an intended mother and a child born through surrogacy demonstrates that authorities often take a restrictive approach towards women in cross-border surrogacy cases. The French authorities recognised the legal relationship between the child's intended genetic father, but not the intended genetic mother.[202] The refusal was based on the fact that under French law, the birth mother is the legal mother.[203] The Court maintained that while the child's right to private life required the recognition of the filial link to the intended

191 Fenton-Glynn (n 62).
192 *D* (n 182) paras 43, 62, 85, and 86.
193 *Foulon and Bouvet v France* App nos 9063/14 and 10410/14 (ECtHR, 21 July 2016).
194 Brodeala and Peter-Spiess (n 167) 408; Lydia Bracken, 'The ECtHR's First Advisory Opinion: Implications for Cross-Border Surrogacy Involving Male Intended Parents' (2021) 21 Med L Intl 3, 13–18.
195 Bracken, 'The ECtHR's First' (n 194) 15.
196 *DB* (n 169).
197 ibid para 85.
198 ibid.
199 *DB* (n 169) paras 84–85.
200 Levy (n 4) 124–125.
201 *D* (n 182).
202 Brodeala and Peter-Spiess (n 167) 412.
203 ibid.

mother, this could take any form, including adoption, even when the parenthood of the genetic father was recognised directly accepting the validity of the child's foreign birth certificate.[204] In addition, the Court refused to accept the claim that such an asymmetric recognition procedure regarding the intended parents discriminated against the child based on birth.[205] Yet, it is unreasonable to require the intended mother, who has donated the ovum, to adopt her own child while no similar requirements exist for intended fathers who have used their own gametes.[206] Therefore, the additional procedural steps imposed on the intended mother can be argued to be discriminatory against women as this represents a significant hurdle to parenthood, considering that adoption can be lengthy and costly.[207]

The 2022 judgment in *KK and Others v Denmark*[208] presents a departure from previous case law in terms of the intended mother's right to adopt. It concerned the Danish authorities' refusal to allow Ms KK to adopt twin girls born in Ukraine.[209] Although Ms KK was named as the twins' mother on their Ukrainian birth certificates, she was not considered their mother under Danish law on the grounds that the birth mother is the legal parent of a child, even in cases where the eggs are donated by another woman.[210] Although the ECtHR did not find a violation of Ms KK's or her children's right to respect for their family life, it found a violation of Article 8 in respect of the twins' right to respect for their private life.[211] It held that it was in the best interests of the twins to have the same legal relationship with their intended mother as they had with their genetic father.[212] Bracken has criticised the Court for failing to explain why the custody arrangement was insufficient, essentially forcing Denmark to allow step-parent adoption when Ms KK did not meet the legislative criteria.[213]

In the 2023 inadmissible decision in *SC and Others v Switzerland*,[214] the intended non-genetic father of a child complained that the Swiss authorities' refusal to register him as the child's father upon presentation of the child's Californian birth certificate was a violation of his right under Article 8.[215] Mr VC and his partner, Mr SC, who was the child's intended genetic father, further argued that adoption was an unsuitable means of remedying the issue due to the length of the adoption procedure.[216] The Court found that the means as to how to allow recognition of filiation of the second parent, who had no genetic link with the child, fell within the State's

204 ibid 402 and 412.
205 ibid 412.
206 Levy (n 4) 124–125.
207 ibid 124–125, 171.
208 *KK* (n 19).
209 ibid paras 6 and 11.
210 ibid para 8.
211 *KK* (n 19) paras 50–51 and 74.
212 ibid para 77.
213 Bracken, 'Accommodations' (n 1).
214 *SC and Others v Switzerland* App no 26848/18 (ECtHR, 28 November 2023).
215 *SC* (n 214) para 18.
216 ibid.

margin of appreciation.[217] Consequently, the recognition could take place by transcription of the foreign birth certificate or other means. In the Court's opinion, adoption constituted an effective and sufficiently rapid mechanism.[218] Although Bracken argues that extending the legal recognition to the non-genetic father is a logical next step in the Court's jurisprudence,[219] the non-recognition has a greater impact on intended mothers as they are consistently being required to adopt the child in cross-border surrogacy cases, regardless of whether they have a genetic link to the child or not.[220] Even if the Court has accepted that States may recognise the foreign birth certificate, it has not required States to do so consistently in all cases concerning cross-border surrogacy. As *SC* and cases concerning lesbian couples challenge the Court's understanding on parenthood, it remains to be seen whether the Court will accept such arguments in the immediate future.

5.6.2 The Absence of a Genetic Link

Issues remain in cases where neither of the intended parents is genetically related to the child or the parents' relationship has ended. The following three cases demonstrate the consequences of the absence of a genetic link between the parent and the child. While the reasons for the outcome in each case were very different, the Court did not find a violation of either of the child's or the parent's rights in any of the cases. Scholars have criticised the Court for privileging families where parents and children are genetically linked despite the fact the children's position in virtually all cases is comparable, regardless of the parents' position.[221] Additionally, Levy notes that the ECtHR fails to recognise the reality that during the lengthy adoption process, the adopting parents are legal strangers to the child.[222] The issue in the 2017 judgment of *Paradiso and Campanelli v Italy*[223] was the absence of a genetic link between the child and both intended parents. Drastically, the Court sided with the Italian authorities, which meant that the dream of an Italian opposite-sex couple, Ms Donatina Paradiso and Mr Giovanni Campanelli, to become parents via cross-border surrogacy was crushed. The couple made surrogacy arrangements with a Russian clinic, which certified that they used Mr Campanelli's gametes for the embryos.[224] When Ms Paradiso sought to have their two-month-old son's birth

217 ibid para 24.

218 ibid citing *D* (n 182) paras 51–54, 70.

219 Bracken, 'The ECtHR's First' (n 194) 15.

220 Levy (n 4).

221 Julian W März, 'What Makes A Parent in Surrogacy Cases? Reflections on the Fjölnisdóttir et al. v Iceland Decision of the European Court of Human Rights' (2021) 21 Med L Intl 272, 280 and 285; Lydia Bracken, 'Cross-Border Surrogacy Before the European Court of Human Rights: Analysis of *Valdís Fjölnisdóttir* and Others v Iceland' (2022) 29 Eur J Health L 194; Bracken, 'Accommodations' (n 1).

222 Levy (n 4) 171 referring to *Fjölnisdóttir and Others v Iceland* App no 71552/17 (ECtHR, 18 May 2021).

223 *Paradiso and Campanelli v Italy* App no 25358/12 (ECtHR, 24 January 2017).

224 ibid paras 11–12.

registered in Italy, the prosecutor's office suspected that the couple violated Italian legislation on surrogacy and the rules on international adoption by presenting a falsified birth certificate attesting their parentage.[225] After the DNA testing ordered by an Italian court showed that their son bore no genetic relationship to the couple, they were placed under a formal criminal investigation for breaching the rules on international adoption.[226] The ECtHR concluded that allowing the couple to adopt the child would have been equal to legalising the situation they created by violating Italian law.[227] As the child was not genetically related to either parent, no family life with the meaning of Article 8 existed between them.[228] Subsequently, there was no violation of Article 8 as the fundamental component in the creation of best interest of child and child's right to private life was missing.[229]

The 2021 judgment in *Fjölnisdóttir and Others v Iceland*[230] and the 2022 judgment in *AM v Norway*[231] demonstrate how the breakdown in the intended parent's relationship influences the outcome of surrogacy cases. *Fjölnisdóttir* concerned the non-recognition of filiation between X, a child born in California via a surrogate mother, and a married lesbian couple, Ms Valdís Fjölnisdóttir and Ms Eydís Agnarsdóttir's. As X was conceived using IVF with donor gametes, he was genetically unrelated to the couple.[232] Before their adoption of X was final, the couple filed for divorce, which meant that they could no longer adopt him jointly. Instead, X was placed into foster care with one ex-spouse with the other enjoying equal custody of him.[233] Although the Court noted that practical problems might arise from the inability of the former spouses to adopt X jointly in line with the national adoption rules, it did not find a violation of Article 8 in respect of either the intended mothers' or the child's right to respect for family life or private life.[234] According to the Court, the interference to the enjoyment of family life created by the non-recognition of a parental link were limited because X was granted Icelandic citizenship, he was fostered by the couple, and a joint adoption was possible for them until their divorce.[235]

AM concerned former partners, Ms AM and Mr EB, who had a son, X, through gestational surrogacy arrangements in the US after their ten-year relationship ended. They used Mr EB's gametes and a fertilised donor egg.[236] While the child's American birth certificate recorded Ms AM as X's mother, her request to be registered as his mother in the Norwegian population register was refused on the

225 ibid paras 20–21. See also O'Halloran (n 18) 150.
226 *Paradiso* (n 223) para 28.
227 ibid para 215.
228 Fenton-Glynn (n 62).
229 ibid.
230 *Fjölnisdóttir* (n 222) para 67.
231 *AM* (n 19) para 131.
232 *Fjölnisdóttir* (n 222) para 5.
233 ibid para 71.
234 ibid para 74.
235 ibid paras 71–72.
236 *AM* (n 19) paras 9 and 11.

grounds that Norwegian law provided that the woman giving birth was the legal mother.[237] In the absence of a valid adoption, Mr EB, as the genetic intended father, was granted sole parental responsibilities.[238] After X's first birthday, Mr EB prevented Ms AM from seeing him due to their disagreement over his upbringing. She unsuccessfully applied for recognition of her maternity, or, in the alternative, adoption.[239] The ECtHR concluded that Norway did not breach Article 8 as the child's adoption required Mr EB's consent and the foreign judgment was not binding on the Norwegian judiciary.[240] Therefore, it found no violation of Ms AM's private life.[241] In her concurring opinion in *AM,* Judge O'Leary raised the issue of a power imbalance between the former partners. She noted that the authorities' failure to award Ms AM with legal recognition of motherhood resulted in Mr EB retaining sole authority to refuse Ms AM any right to visit or stay in contact with X.[242] Although the couple had agreed that Ms AM was intended to be the child's mother, Mr EB not only denied her the motherhood, but also designated his new partner as X's adoptive mother.[243] The case, therefore, raises issues of power imbalance in intimate partner relationships, even after the end of such a relationship.

5.7 Conclusion

This chapter has focused on the ECtHR's jurisprudence on gendered parenthood. The Court has arguably become an increasingly important actor, contributing to the normalising of non-conventional forms of parenting and alternative ways to form a family.[244] In the past, the ECtHR has taken a cautious approach to family formation and responded to change only once, sufficiently wide consensus exists between States.[245] The pressing question is how the Court's case law can improve parental rights of single women and men, lesbian and gay couples, and trans individuals or even women in opposite-sex relationships, who are not the genetic mothers of children born through surrogacy agreements concluded outside Europe. Even if the legislation governing non-conventional parenting has lagged behind societal developments, single parents, same-sex couples, opposite-sex couples, and trans persons have found solutions to start families that are not covered by law, such as, co-parenting, donor insemination, or surrogacy outside the State's jurisdiction.[246] Therefore, diverse families are a social reality in many CoE States. Through its judgments, the Court has reinforced the idea of family as an opposite-sex couple

237 ibid paras 7, 9, 11 and 15.
238 ibid paras 7, 9, 11, 14 and 16.
239 ibid paras 18 and 25.
240 ibid paras 131–132 and 146.
241 ibid para 135.
242 *AM* (n 19) concurring opinion of Judge O'Leary, para 44.
243 ibid.
244 Margaria, 'Trans Men' (n 26) 238.
245 Fenton-Glynn (n 62).
246 Digoix (n 24) 2.

with genetic children. Case law concerning trans individuals, who have children during or after their transition, clearly constitutes an important opportunity for the Court to reframe its understanding of parenthood.[247] In cases where States refuse to amend a child's birth certificate to reflect the reality of modern families means that the children will have to live with a birth certificate that inaccurately records who their parents are. These cases highlight the fact that it is important for the courts to approach cases concerning gender non-conforming individuals in a way that does not diminish or render inauthentic their gender experiences.[248]

The existence of a genetic link emerges as central in the ECtHR's case law on cross-border surrogacy. As a result the Court treats intended fathers and intended mothers differently when recognising the filial link between the intended parents and their children.[249] It has been argued that the Court authorises an additional element of power and control over legal motherhood when it allows States to require that the intended mother adopt the child and, therefore, evaluates her suitability to be a legal mother.[250] This has been considered to violate the intended mother's rights under Articles 8 and 14.[251] The case law analysis demonstrates that as most non-genetic parents in cross-border surrogacy cases are women, the asymmetrical recognition of parenthood has a greater impact on women, regardless whether they are in an opposite-sex couple or same-sex couple . Non-genetic mothers have also been discriminated against in terms of parental rights in cases, particularly originating from France, where their lesbian partners have become pregnant using donor insemination.

The Court has also refused to find a violation of either the rights of the intended parents or the child's rights under Article 8 when there is no direct genetic link between the parents and the child, concluding that the requirements for the intended parent to formalise the parent-child relationship through adoption are proportionate.[252] Yet, the legal means for establishing legal parenthood either by direct recognition, voluntary acknowledgement, or adoption, are not equivalent from the perspective of equal treatment of the parents, even though they eventually produce the same result.[253] Therefore, the Court's approach towards intended mothers and lesbian couples in its case law concerning parenthood perpetuates existing gender inequalities. This ignores the lived diversity of modern families and fails to recognise that States violate not only the rights of non-genetic mothers, regardless of their sexual orientation but also the rights of their children.

247 Margaria, 'Trans Men' (n 26) 227.
248 Alex Sharpe, 'Queering Judgment: The Case of Gender Identity Fraud' (2017) 81(5) J Crim L 417.
249 Brodeala and Peter-Spiess (n 167) 401.
250 Levy (n 4) 131 and 170.
251 ibid.
252 Levy (n 4) 131 and 170.
253 ibid 171.

References

Ammaturo FR, *European Sexual Citizenship: Human Rights, Bodies and Identities* (Palgrave Macmillan 2017).

Binard F, *Lesbian Motherhood from the Social Recognition of Female Homosexuality to the 'Lesby-Boom': A Comparison between Britain and France* (Routledge 2019).

Bracken L, 'Accommodations of Private and Family Life and Non-Traditional Families: The Limits of Deference in Cases of Cross-Border Surrogacy Before the European Court of Human Rights' (2024) 32(2) Med L Rev 141.

Bracken L, 'The ECtHR's First Advisory Opinion: Implications for Cross-Border Surrogacy Involving Male Intended Parents' (2021) 21 Med L Intl 3.

Bracken L, 'Strasbourg's Response to Gay and Lesbian Parenting: Progress, then Plateau' (2016) 24 Intl J Child Rts 358.

Brodeala E and Peter-Spiess MH, 'Surrogacy and Same-Sex Parenthood before the European Court of Human Rights: Reflections in Light of Cases against Switzerland' (2022) 32 Swiss Rev Intl & Eur L 397.

Brown A, 'Trans (Legal) Parenthood and The Gender of Legal Parenthood' (2024) 44(1) LS 168.

Brown A, 'Trans Parenthood and the Meaning of 'Mother', 'Father' and 'Parent'—*R (McConnell and YY) v Registrar General for England and Wales* [2020] EWCA Civ 559' (2021) 29(1) Med L Rev 157.

Cano Palomares G, 'Right to Family Life and Access to Medically Assisted Procreation in the Case Law of the European Court of Human Rights' in Maribel Gonzáles Pascual and Aida Torres Pérez (eds), *The Right to Family Life in the European Union* (Routledge 2017).

Derave C and Ouhnaoui H, '*CE & al v France*: Legal Recognition of Intended Parenthood prem previous same-sex relationships (Between Women)' (*Strasbourg Observers*, 7 October 2022) <https://strasbourgobservers.com/2022/10/07/c-e-al-v-france-legal-recognition-of-intended-parenthood-from-previous-same-sex-relationships-between-women/> accessed 30 June 2024.

Digoix M, 'Introduction: LGBT Questions and the Family' in Carlson ED, Gietel-Basten S, and Digoix M (eds), *Same-Sex Families and Legal Recognition in Europe* (Springer 2020).

Dondoli G, 'An Overnight Success A Decade in The Making: Indirect Discrimination on The Grounds of Sexual Orientation' (2018) 18(1) IJDL 5.

Dunne P, '*AM and Others v Russia*: Protecting the Rights of Transgender Parents' (*Oxford Human Rights Hub*, 21 August 2021) <https://ohrh.law.ox.ac.uk/a-m-and-others-v-russia-protecting-the-rights-of-transgender-parents/> accessed 28 April 2024.

Dunne P, 'Legal Gender Recognition in Europe: Sterilisation, Diagnosis and Medical Examination Requirements' (2017) 39(4) J Soc Wel & Fam L 497.

Dunne P, 'Who Is a Parent and Who Is a Child in a Same-Sex Family? Legislative and Judicial Issues for LGBT Families Post-Separation, Part I: The European Perspective' (2017) 30 J Am Acad Matrimonial Lawyers 27.

Dzehtsiarou K, *European Consensus and The Legitimacy of the European Court of Human Rights* (CUP 2015).

George M, 'Using the European Court of Human Rights to Expand Access to *In Vitro* Fertilization for Straight Women and Lesbian Couples in Europe' (2021) 53(2) Geo Wash Intl L Rev 321.

Gonzalez-Salzberg D, *Sexuality and Transsexuality under the European Convention on Human Rights: A Queer Reading of Human Rights Law* (Hart 2019).

Hamilton F, 'The potential of European Union law to further advance LGBTQ+ persons and same-sex couples' rights' in Hamilton F and Noto La Diega G (eds), *Same-Sex Relationships, Law and Social Change* (Routledge 2020).

Hart L, Relational Subjects: Family Relations, Law and Gender in the European Court of Human Rights (PhD Thesis, University of Helsinki 2016).

Hodson L, 'Sexual Orientation and the European Convention on Human Rights: What of the "L" in LGBT?' (2019) 23(3) J Lesbian Studies 383.
Johnson P, 'UK Withdrawal from the European Convention on Human Rights: A Disaster for LGBT People' (2024) 5 ECHR L Rev 83.
Krajewska A and Cahill-O'Callaghan R, 'When a Single Man Wants to be A Father: Revealing the Invisible Subjects in the Law Regulating Fertility Treatment' (2020) 29(1) Social and Legal Studies 85.
Lasio D and Serri F, 'The Italian Public Debate on Same-Sex Civil Unions and Gay and Lesbian Parenting' (2019) 22(4) Sexualities 691.
Levy M, 'Surrogacy and Parenthood: A European Saga of Genetic Essentialism and Gender Discrimination' (2022) 29 Mich J Gender & L 121.
Liesker HJ, 'Caught in a Balancing Act: The European Court of Human Rights and the Road to Recognition for Sexual Minorities' (2017) 4(3) Oslo L Rev 172.
Lind C, '*Evans v United Kingdom*: Judgments of Solomon: Power, Gender and Procreation' (2006) 18 CFLQ 576.
Lorenzetti A, 'The European Courts and Transsexuals: The Binary Distinction and the Pattern of Family' in Maribel Pascual and Aida Torres Pérez (eds), *The Right to Family Life in the European Union* (Routledge 2017).
Macdougall B, *Queer Judgments: Homosexuality, Expression, and the Courts in Canada* (University of Toronto Press 2000).
Margaria A, *The Construction of Fatherhood: The Jurisprudence of the European Court of Human Rights* (CUP 2019).
Margaria A, 'Trans Men Giving Birth and Reflections on Fatherhood: What to Expect?' (2020) 34(3) IJLPF 225.
Minnerop P, 'European Consensus As Integrative Doctrine of Treaty Interpretation: Joining Climate Science and International Law under the European Convention on Human Rights' (2023) 40(2) Berk J Intl L 206.
Morgan DHJ, 'Framing Relationships and Families' in Jamieson L, Simpson R, and Lewis R (eds), *Researching Families and Relationships: Reflections on Process* (Palgrave Macmillan 2011).
O'Halloran K, *The Politics of Adoption* (Springer 2021).
Oja L and Yamin AE, '"Woman" in the European Human Rights System: How is the Reproductive Rights Jurisprudence of the European Court of Human Rights Constructing Narratives of Women's Citizenship?' (2016) 32(1) Colum J Gender & Law 62.
Otto D, 'Between Pleasure and Danger: Lesbian Human Rights' (2014) 6 EHRLR 618.
Otto D, 'Lesbians? Not in My Country' (1995) 20 Alt LJ 288.
Radacic I, 'The Margin of Appreciations, Consensus, Morality and the Rights of Vulnerable Groups' (2010) 31 Zb Prav Fak Sveuc Rij 599.
Rein-Lescastereyres I, 'Recent Case Law on Cross-Border Surrogacy' in Boele-Woelki K and Fuchs A (eds), *Same-Sex Relationships and Beyond: Gender Matters in the EU* (Intersentia 2017).
Sharpe A, 'Queering Judgment: The Case of Gender Identity Fraud' (2017) 81(5) J Crim L 417.
Thibeaud M, 'Same-Sex Families Challenging Norms and the Law in France' in Carlson ED, Gietel-Basten S, and Digoix M (eds), *Same-Sex Families and Legal Recognition in Europe* (Springer 2020).
Tobin B, 'The (D)evolving Nature of Guardianship Rights for Unmarried Fathers under Irish Law' (2020) 32(3) CFLQ 285.
Verhellen J and Wautelet P, 'The Treatment of Diversity in Family Law in Belgium: Between Acknowledgment and Indifference' in Yassari N and Foblets MC (eds), *Normativity and Diversity in Family Law: Lessons from Comparative Law* (Springer 2022).
Viljanen J, *The Role of the ECtHR as a Developer of International Human Rights Law* (Tampereen Yliopisto 2003).
Wells-Greco M, 'Reflections on *Gas and Dubois v France* (2012): Same-Sex Second Parent Adoption–A Missed Opportunity' (2012) Intl Family LJ 224.

6 Gendered Asylum

6.1 Introduction

Although no right to asylum exists in the European Convention on Human Rights (ECHR)[1] or its protocols, the European Court of Human Rights (ECtHR) often considers complaints by individuals who seek asylum in Europe. In general, the Court deals with two types of asylum-related complaints where the individuals are at different stages of the asylum process. First, there are cases concerning individuals whom the member State of the Council of Europe (CoE) seeks to return to the country of origin after they have been deemed unsuccessful in their asylum claim and subsequent appeal(s) on the grounds that they do not meet the term refugee in the 1951 United Nations (UN) Refugee Convention.[2] Second, the Court examines complaints where the individual's asylum application is yet to be processed. These cases may concern the detention of asylum-seeking women and their families in border transit zones, or their stay in asylum detention or at a reception centre. Alternatively, the women may be summarily expelled to another country without the ability to submit an asylum application in the first place.[3] Some asylum-related complaints brought to the attention of the ECtHR have also involved a legal challenge against the removal of an asylum-seeking woman to another CoE State that is considered responsible for her asylum application. These cases usually concern the so-called Dublin transfer decisions and are often raised as part of a complaint concerning another issue, such as, asylum detention[4] or the removal to the country of origin.[5] Although the chapter does not intend to examine the complaints concerning Dublin transfer decisions in detail, it is worth noting that different judicial bodies have

1 Convention for the Protection of Human Rights and Fundamental Freedoms (European Convention on Human Rights, as amended).

2 Convention on the Status of Refugees (adopted 28 July 1951, entry into force 22 April 1954) 189 UNTS 150 as amended by the Protocol relating to the Status of Refugees (adopted 31 January 1967, entry into force on 4 October 1967) 606 UNTS 267.

3 See eg *OM and DS v Ukraine* App no 18603/12 (ECtHR, 15 September 2022); *MH and Others v Croatia* App nos 15670/18 and 43115/18 (ECtHR, 18 November 2021); *SS and Others v Hungary* App nos 56417/19 and 44245/20 (ECtHR, 12 October 2023).

4 *Aden Ahmed v Malta* App no 55352/12 (ECtHR, 23 July 2013) (A violation of art 3 in relation to Ms Aslya Aden Ahmed's detention in Malta).

5 *RH v Sweden* App no 4601/14 (ECtHR, 10 September 2015).

DOI: 10.4324/9781003435099-6

reached different outcomes in cases concerning these transfers. In September 2015 the Human Rights Committee found that the return of a Somali woman Ms Warda Osman Jasin and her three children from Denmark to Italy would violate Article 7 of the International Covenant on Civil and Political Rights,[6] which codifies the principle of *non-refoulement*.[7] Ms Jasin and her minor daughter were granted subsidiary protection and a residence permit in Italy in 2008 after which they were no longer entitled to remain at the reception centre, making the mother and her daughter homeless, with no means of subsistence. The Human Rights Committee stated that Denmark should reconsider their asylum application and the need to obtain individual assurances from Italy that their removal there would not result in a violation of Article 7. In a factually similar decision delivered only a few months later in *ATH v Netherlands*,[8] the ECtHR found that a HIV-positive single mother, of an Eritrean nationality, Ms ATH, who claimed asylum in the Netherlands on the grounds that she was left destitute in Italy, should return there, despite her vulnerability in light of her health, status as an asylum seeker, a single parent with a minor child, and the inability to access medical, social, housing or other forms of assistance in Italy.

The long-standing asylum related jurisprudence of the ECtHR has largely focused on the question of whether the return of an individual by the CoE State may give rise to an issue under Articles 2[9] and 3[10] ECHR. As *non-refoulement* claims often coincide with or follow an unsuccessful asylum application,[11] these cases are of central relevance to this chapter. While scholars have highlighted the need to address the issue that women's experiences are often ignored in the national asylum determination process,[12] the ECtHR has only recently started to address issues relating to gender in its jurisprudence, with the consequence that there is a visible change in 2023. While this is a welcome development, it is useful to examine how the Court takes gender and other intersecting externally perceived identities, such as, religious beliefs, race, and sexual orientation into account in its jurisprudence. The case law analysis reveals that although the Court rarely investigates asylum-seeking women's complaints from a gendered perspective, it may sometimes consider an asylum-seeking woman to be more vulnerable than others in a comparable situation.

6 (adopted 16 December 1966; entry into force 23 March 1976) 999 UNTS 171.

7 *Warda Osman Jasin and Others v Denmark* Communication No 2360/2014 (4 September 2015).

8 *ATH v The Netherlands* App no 54000/11 (ECtHR, 10 December 2015).

9 ECHR, art 2(1): 'Everyone's right to life shall be protected by law. No one shall be deprived of his life intentionally save in the execution of a sentence of a court following his conviction of a crime for which this penalty is provided by law'.

10 ibid, art 3: 'No one shall be subjected to torture or to inhuman or degrading treatment or punishment'.

11 Lore Roels, 'Rape Myths in the European Court of Human Rights' Non-Refoulement Case Law on Sexual and Gender-Based Violence' (2024) 36(1-2) IJRL 77, 79.

12 Nora Honkala, 'She, Of Course, Holds No Political Opinions: Gendered Political Opinion Ground in Women's Forced Marriage Asylum Claims' (2017) 26 Social & L Stud 166; Janna Wessels, 'The Boundaries of Universality: Migrant Women and Domestic Violence Before the Strasbourg Court' (2019) 37(4) NQHR 336.

The structure of the chapter is as follows: Section 6.2 briefly outlines the main scholarly arguments relating to gendered asylum in Europe. Section 6.3 analyses the Court's case law on return of asylum-seeking women (Section 6.3.1) and lesbian, gay, bisexual and transgender (LGBT) asylum applicants (Section 6.3.2) to the country of origin. It also considers the significance of strike out decisions in the Court's asylum jurisprudence relating to returns (Section 6.3.3). Section 6.4 analyses the judgments where women are at the start of their asylum-seeking process and allege human rights violations due to detention, inadequate reception conditions, or summary expulsion. Section 6.5 provides a conclusion.

6.2 Existing Literature on Gender and Asylum

Existing scholarly literature concerning gendered asylum has focused largely on the national asylum determination processes, which have been identified to act as one of the key barriers to women's access to asylum.[13] As national authorities have a significant role in determining the way in which international and European asylum legislation is implemented at the national level, this ultimately affects women's chances of being successful in their claims.[14] One of the key reasons why women are unable to benefit from asylum is arguably that the authorities assessing their applications often consider women's claims to lack credibility, if their behaviour does not follow expected patterns.[15] In order to process applications quickly, officials conducting asylum interviews may be willing to have recourse to stereotypical gender roles.[16] Yet, in its gender equality case law under Article 14 ECHR, the Court has condemned the reliance on gender stereotypes.[17] States also increasingly use the accelerated asylum procedures, which have been argued to make the asylum procedures inconsistent with the ECHR.[18] Scholars have also observed that the perception of gender shapes the way the asylum appeal courts or tribunals

13 Catherine Dauvergne and Hannah Lindy, 'Excluding Women' (2019) 31(1) IJRL 1.

14 Hana Cheikh Ali, Christel Querton and Elodie Soulard, *Gender Related Asylum Claims in Europe: Comparative Analysis of Law, Policies and Practice Focusing on Women in Nine EU Member States* (European Parliament 2012). <www.europarl.europa.eu/RegData/etudes/etudes/join/2012/462481/IPOL-FEMM_ET(2012)462481_EN.pdf> accessed 2 May 2024.

15 Malak Benslama-Dabdoub, 'Epistemic Violence and Colonial Legacies in the Representation of Refugee Women: Contesting Narratives of Vulnerability and Victimhood' (2024) 20(1) Int JLC 54; Nazanin Gifani, 'The Code of Gender in Judgments of the European Court of Human Rights: The Case of Traditional Harmful Practice' (2016) 10(2) Helsinki Law Review 12, 21–22 <https://journal.fi/helsinkilawreview/article/view/74533> accessed 31 March 2024; Debora Singer, 'Falling at Each Hurdle: Assessing the Credibility of Women's Asylum Claims in Europe' in Efrat Arbel, Catherine Dauvergne, and Jenni Millbank (eds), *Gender in Refugee Law: From Margins to the Centre* (Routledge 2014) 98; Thomas Spijkerboer, 'Stereotyping and Acceleration: Gender, Procedural Acceleration and Marginalised Judicial Review in the Dutch Asylum System' in Noll G (ed), *Proof, Evidentiary Assessment and Credibility in Asylum Procedures* (Martinus Nijhoff 2005) 88.

16 Spijkerboer, 'Stereotyping' (n 15) 67. See also Benslama-Dabdoub (n 15) 58.

17 Gifani (n 15) 21. See also ch 4.

18 Spijkerboer, 'Stereotyping' (n 15) 67.

view the asylum claims, particularly when the individual is fleeing gender-related violence.[19] Additionally, time pressures may mean that judicial control in the area of asylum is less effective.[20]

As a result of these flaws, women seeking asylum in Europe are argued to routinely face national legislation and policy that falls below the standards required by the 1951 Refugee Convention and the ECHR as asylum-seeking women are argued to be afforded reduced rights, protections, and privileges in national asylum policies.[21] It has also been suggested that due to inadequate implementation of the UN Gender Guidelines,[22] there is considerable variation in the processing of gender-related asylum claims at the national level.[23] Consequently, the UN High Commissioner for Refugees (UNHCR) has raised concerns about the gender bias in the national credibility assessments.[24] Yet, the UNHCR's own operations are not free from practices that negatively affect asylum-seeking women. It has been noted that women did not initially receive the prepaid cash cards distributed at the beginning of the UNHCR programme during the so-called Mediterranean refugee crisis of 2015 because these cards were distributed to men due to their assumed role as heads of their families.[25] The danger in these types of practices is that the stereotypic gender roles result in women's economic vulnerability, which may expose women to various types of gendered violence if they feel that they have no other alternative than to remain in potentially coercive relationships.[26] Consequently, the lack of a systematic approach towards gender in national asylum and appeal procedures has the potential to discriminate against women and further reduce their rights as asylum seekers due to the lack of sensitivity to gender-related claims.[27] The case law analysis in Section 6.3 demonstrates that asylum applications submitted by women and LGBT persons are often not considered credible. Additionally, Section 6.4 demonstrates that women still experience reception conditions that fall

19 Gifani (n 15).
20 Spijkerboer, 'Stereotyping' (n 15) 67.
21 Cheikh Ali, Querton and Soulard (n 14) 16 and 35; Chara Karagiannopoulou, Evangelia Tastsoglou and Sandy Petrinioti, 'Gender and Asylum Seeking in a European Borderland: Intersectional Discriminations and "Lessened" Citizenship' (2024) 40(1) Refuge 1, 5 doi:10.25071/1920-7336.41162.
22 UNHCR, Guidelines on International Protection: Gender-Related Persecution within the context of Article 1A(2) of the 1951 Convention and/or its 1967 Protocol relating to the Status of Refugees HCR/GIP/02/01 (7 May 2002) (UN Gender Guidelines) <www.unhcr.org/3d58ddef4.pdf> accessed 31 March 2024.
23 Cheikh Ali, Querton and Soulard (n 14) 16 and 35.
24 Roels (n 11) 78. See also UNHCR, Beyond Proof: Credibility Assessment in EU Asylum Systems (May 2013) 70.
25 Karagiannopoulou, Tastsoglou and Petrinioti (n 21) 8.
26 ibid 7.
27 Patrick Emmenegger and Katarina Stigwall, 'Women-Friendliness in European Asylum Policies: The Role of Women's Political Representation and Opposition to Non-EU Immigration' (2019) 52(9) Comp Pol Stud 1293, 1295; Annemarie Middelburg and Alina Balta, 'Female Genital Mutilation/Cutting as a Ground for Asylum in Europe' (2016) 28(3) IJRL 416; Jane Freedman, *Gendering the International Asylum and Refugee Debate* (2nd edn, Palgrave McMillan 2015).

short of standards, they may be subject to detention while being pregnant, or they may be subject to summary expulsion.

An intersectional feminist approach can be useful in the context of asylum jurisprudence.[28] This is because the 1951 Refugee Convention has been widely argued to be framed around the experiences of men, with the consequence that women's experiences of persecution are often rendered invisible in the national assessment procedures.[29] The intersectional approach describes the idea that different social markers, such as, gender, nationhood, race, age, and social class do not operate in isolation but interact and create positions of privilege and marginalisation.[30] Scholars have challenged overgeneralisation of the experiences of asylum-seeking women by arguing that ignoring class, cultural, religious, and racial differences between women fails to recognise that women experience multiple forms of discrimination concurrently.[31] Kapur points out that racialised women's experiences of gender discrimination cannot be separated from their experiences of racial discrimination because they occur simultaneously.[32] As asylum-seeking women often experience discrimination arising from both their ethnicity and refugee status, refugee law is not only gendered but also racialised.[33] Additionally, adopting a queer lens may make visible some of the challenges surrounding the conceptualisation of the reasons for persecution.[34]

The definition of 'refugee' is formulated in the 1951 Refugee Convention, which states that:

> [T]he term 'refugee' shall apply to any person who … owing to wellfounded fear of being persecuted for reasons of race, religion, nationality, membership of a particular social group or political opinion, is outside the country of his nationality and is unable or, owing to such fear, is unwilling to avail himself of the protection of that country.[35]

There are frequent arguments that the definition of the term refugee has made it challenging for women and LGBT persons to obtain refugee status.[36] Despite scholarly

28 For arguments concerning gender intersecting with race in the US context, see eg Kimberlé Crenshaw, 'Mapping the Margins: Intersectionality, Identity Politics and Violence Against Women of Colour' (1991) 43(6) Stan L Rev 1241.

29 Catherine Dauvergne, 'Women in Refugee Jurisprudence' in Cathryn Costello, Michelle Foster, and Jane McAdam (eds), *The Oxford Handbook of International Refugee Law* (OUP 2021).

30 Natalie Welfens, 'Promising Victimhood: Contrasting Deservingness Requirements in Refugee Resettlement' (2023) 49(5) J Ethnic and Migration Stud 1103.

31 Ratna Kapur, 'The Tragedy of Victimisation Rhetoric: Resurrecting the "Native" Subject in International/Postcolonial Feminist Legal Politics' (2002) 15 Harv Hum Rts J 1, 9.

32 ibid 8.

33 Benslama-Dabdoub (n 15); Karagiannopoulou, Tastsoglou and Petrinioti (n 21) 12.

34 Janna Wessels, *The Concealment Controversy: Sexual Orientation, Discretion Reasoning and the Scope of Refugee Protection* (CUP 2021).

35 1951 Refugee Convention, art 1(A)2.

36 Samuel Ballin, 'Four Challenges, Three Identities and a Double Movement in Asylum Law: Queering the "Particular Social Group" after *Mx M'* (2023) 49(1) Australian Fem L J 141.

criticism focusing on the practicality of the concept of a particular social group (PSG), it is widely used in many national legal systems in the context of women's asylum claims and those relating to persecution arising from sexual orientation or gender identity. It has been argued that national authorities tend to consider women's asylum claims as automatically falling under the PSG category, despite the fact that women explicitly claim asylum under the other four grounds, including political opinion, religion, and ethnicity.[37] Consequently, asylum-seeking women are often forced to claim asylum on the basis of their PSG membership, or due to gender-based persecution, rather than their political autonomy, despite evidence to suggest that many women are fleeing political persecution.[38] Although there are recent developments which recognise resistance to gender-based violence, such as female genital mutilation (FGM), as political,[39] there is no consistent approach among the CoE States in this. Therefore, the outcome of the national asylum determination process is highly dependent on the ways in which the national authorities construct asylum-seeking women's PSG membership.[40] States and courts have long failed to recognise that intimate partner violence, such as marital violence, is discrimination against asylum-seeking women.[41] This raises concerns about the consistency of approach, considering that the ECtHR's extensive jurisprudence in the context of Article 14 ECHR recognises that violence in the context of intimate partner relationships is a form of gender discrimination.[42]

Another helpful theoretical lens through which the Court's asylum jurisprudence can be analysed is Fineman's vulnerability theory.[43] Although asylum-seeking women are not considered vulnerable in general, the Court has recognised that some asylum seekers are more vulnerable than others.[44] Recognising the vulnerability of asylum-seeking women requires the understanding of situational disadvantages that confront women in different ways due to intersectional discrimination operating through law as well as exclusionary policies, practices, and discourses that are linked to their migratory status.[45] While scholars have analysed the Court's asylum jurisprudence

37 Wessels, *Concealment* (n 34).
38 Benslama-Dabdoub (n 15) 69; Honkala (n 12).
39 Adrienne Anderson, 'There Should Be Equality in Opinions: Political Opinion in Intimate Partner Violence Claims' (2024) 36(1-2) IJRL 123, 127. The UK Home Office guidelines on gender state that '[n]on-conformist behaviour in certain cultures such as refusing to wear a veil, refusing FGM, pursuing an education … could also lead to a woman having a political opinion attributed to her'. See United Kingdom Home Office, 'Gender Issues in the Asylum Claim' (2018) 23.
40 See eg Honkala (n 12); Ballin (n 36).
41 Anderson (n 39) 127.
42 See ch 4.
43 See Martha Fineman, 'The Vulnerable Subject: Anchoring Equality in the Human Condition' (2008) 20(1) Yale J L & Fem 1, 9.
44 Ben Hudson, 'Asylum Marginalisation Renewed: "Vulnerability Backsliding" at the European Court of Human Rights' (2024) 20 Int JLC 16.
45 See eg Karagiannopoulou, Tastsoglou and Petrinioti (n 21); Moritz Baumgärtel and Sarah Ganty, 'On the Basis of Migratory Vulnerability: Augmenting Article 14 of the European Convention on Human Rights in the Context of Migration' (2024) 20(1) Int JLC 92, 94.

using the theory,[46] there are no existing systematic analyses of the ECtHR case law using this theory that focus specifically on asylum-seeking women. As the requirements for vulnerability are argued to be racialised, gendered, classed, and age-differentiated,[47] the ECtHR's asylum jurisprudence influences the ways in which the vulnerabilities of asylum seekers are framed.[48] However, as the ECtHR has not explained the precise meaning of the concept of vulnerability in its case law, the scholars disagree as to how the Court understands and employs this concept in the area of asylum.[49] Hudson argues that the Court has chosen to preface the discussion of an asylum seeker's vulnerability by comparing their circumstances to other asylum seekers in a similar situation.[50] Thus, unless an asylum seeker is identified to have additional or compound vulnerability, they are not considered any more vulnerable than others in the comparable situation.[51] The next section focuses on the case law on returns.

6.3 Return to the Country of Origin

The ECtHR has accumulated substantial jurisprudence concerning the alleged risk of violation of Articles 2 and 3 in the context of the return of an unsuccessful asylum seeker to the country of origin either because of their individual circumstances or the general situation in that country.[52] It has consequently held that where substantial grounds exist to believe that, if expelled, a person faces a real risk of capital punishment, torture, or inhuman or degrading treatment or punishment in the destination country, Articles 2 and 3 imply that the States must not expel that person.[53] Although the Court usually examines these two Articles together, most cases chosen for the analysis in this chapter focus on the alleged violation of Article 3. The Court has established that the existence of the risk of ill treatment must be assessed with reference to the facts the State knew, or should have known, at the time of the expulsion.[54] Accordingly, ill-treatment must attain a minimum level of

46 See eg Hudson (n 44).

47 Welfens (n 30).

48 See eg Raoul Wieland and Edward J Alessi, 'Do the Challenges of LGBTQ Asylum Applicants Under Dublin Register with the European Court of Human Rights?' (2021) 30(3) Social & L Stud 405; Violeta Moreno-Lax and Niovi Vavoula, 'Vulnerability's Legal Life: An Ambivalent Force of Migration Governance' (2024) 20(1) Int JLC 1.

49 Hudson (n 44). See also So Yeon Kim, '*Les Vulnérables*: Evaluating the Vulnerability Criterion in Article 14 Cases by the European Court of Human Rights' (2021) 41(4) LS 617.

50 Hudson (n 44) 27.

51 ibid 30.

52 *EP and AR v Netherlands* App nos 43538/11 and 63104/11 (ECtHR, 11 July 2017) (The Court found that denying an asylum for two Afghan men pursuant to art 1F of the 1951 Refugee Convention on the grounds that the men had worked for the Security Services in Communist Afghanistan did not violate art 8 as the cruel nature of the organisation was widely known in Afghanistan).

53 See ECtHR, 'Guide on the Case-Law of the European Convention on Human Rights: Immigration' (Updated on 31 December 2021) 21 (ECtHR Guide on Immigration Case-Law).

54 *FG v Sweden* App no 43611/11 (ECtHR, 23 March 2016), para 115.

severity in order to fall within the scope of Article 3.[55] The assessment must focus on the foreseeable consequences of the removal to the country of destination, in light of both the general situation there and the returnee's personal circumstances.[56] Additionally, Articles 60 and 61 of the CoE Istanbul Convention[57] specify that an assessment of an alleged violation of the *non-refoulement* principle must occur in a gender-sensitive manner.[58]

When the general situation in the country of destination is seemingly improving, the Court places more weight on the assessment of the returnee's personal situation.[59] Whereas the expulsion to a country of origin experiencing a general situation of violence does not normally in itself violate Article 3 ECHR,[60] in the cases of extreme general violence, a real risk of ill-treatment may exist simply because an individual may be exposed to such violence on return.[61] In its jurisprudence, the Court does not, however, examine the actual asylum application submitted by the individual or verify how the States honour their obligations under other legal instruments, such as, the 1951 Refugee Convention or the European Union (EU) legislation.[62]

The Court's registry has published a document,[63] listing examples of situations, which may expose an individual to treatment contrary to Article 3 and prevent their return. Accordingly, a real risk of ill-treatment may arise in the absence of safe access to or the dire conditions in the camps for internally displaced persons;[64] due to a membership to a minoritised or diasporic population systematically at risk within a country of origin;[65] various forms of gender-related persecution, such as, forced marriage and honour crimes,[66] FGM,[67] social

55 *MB v Greece* App no 8389/20 (ECtHR, 23 November 2023), para 31.
56 *FG* (n 54) para 115.
57 Council of Europe Convention on Preventing and Combating Violence against Women and Domestic Violence (adopted 11 May 2011, entered into force 1 August 2014) CETS No 210.
58 See eg Roels (n 11) 78.
59 Gifani (n 15) 21.
60 *RH* (n 5) (While the Court acknowledged that Ms RH faced discrimination in Somalia as a woman, this was not sufficient to find a violation of art 3).
61 See eg *JK and Others v Sweden* App no 59166/12 (ECtHR, 23 August 2016), para 121 (The cumulative effect of the personal circumstances of a married Iraqi couple and their minor son and the Iraqi authorities' diminished ability to offer effective protection for the family against threats by al-Qaeda created a real risk of ill-treatment on return. Therefore, Sweden violated art 3).
62 This is in cases where the respondent State is a member of both the CoE and the EU. See, eg, *FG* (n 54) para 117.
63 ECtHR Guide on Immigration Case-Law (n 52).
64 See *Sufi and Elmi v UK* App nos 8319/07 and 11449/07 (ECtHR, 28 November 2011) (Returning two Somali men to Mogadishu despite their criminal records in the UK was a violation of art 3 due to the general situation of violence in the city).
65 See *Salah Sheek v Netherlands* (ECtHR, 13 January 2007). (The proposed deportation of asylum seeker to 'relatively safe area' of Somalia would violate art 3 due to his membership to a minoritised group).
66 See *AA and Others v Sweden* App no 14499/09 (ECtHR, 28 June 2012) (No violation of art 3). Compare with *RD v France* App no 34648/14 (ECtHR, 16 June 2016) (The Court found that Ms RD's return to Guinea would amount to a breach of art 3).
67 The Court found no violation of art 3 in any of the following cases: *Collins and Akaziebie v Sweden* App no 23944/05 (ECtHR, 8 March 2007); *Izevbekhai v Ireland* App no 43408/08 (ECtHR, 17 May

exclusion due to alleged lack of a male support network,[68] widespread sexual violence against women and girls,[69] ill-treatment inflicted by family members,[70] and the risk of trafficking or re-trafficking.[71] The Court has also recognised that the returnee may be at risk of ill-treatment in the country of origin due to reasons of mental or physical illness.[72] Yet, many complaints raising one of the issues listed above have been declared inadmissible, they have been struck from the Court's register, or the Court has not found a violation of Article 3. The case law analysis highlights that asylum-seeking women and LGBT persons have rarely been successful before the ECtHR in proving that their return may constitute a violation of Article 3.[73] It is, therefore, misleading to compile such a list of the grounds for meeting the threshold of severity required to engage Article 3, when so few complaints have been successful in practice.[74] As the jurisprudence of the Court has been argued to set the common European minimum standard,[75] its chosen line of interpretation has had a profound impact on refugee protection in Europe.

6.3.1 Violence against Women in Asylum Cases

The ECtHR has considered several complaints concerning various forms of violence against women committed by civilians or State forces in the country of origin, which have often experienced protracted armed conflicts, such as Afghanistan,

2011); *Ameh and Others v UK* App no 4539/11 (ECtHR, 30 August 2011); *Omoredo v Austria* App no 8969/10 (ECtHR, 20 September 2011); *RW and Others v Sweden* App no 35745/11 (ECtHR, 10 April 2012); *Sow v Belgium* App no 27081/13 (ECtHR, 19 January 2016); *RBAB and Others v Netherlands* App no 7211/06 (ECtHR, 7 June 2016).

68 See *N v Sweden* App no 23505/09 (ECtHR, 20 July 2010); *WH v Sweden* App no 49341/10 (ECtHR, 8 April 2015) (The Court struck the case out of its register because Sweden granted Ms WH, a divorced single mother from Iraq, a permanent residence permit); *RH* (n 5).

69 See *MMR v Netherlands* App no 64047/10 (ECtHR, 24 May 2016) (The risk of sexual violence in Democratic Republic of Congo as minoritised or diasporic Tutsi did not violate art 3).

70 See *RD* (n 66) paras 36–45.

71 For asylum cases concerning complaint that the applicant has been trafficked to Europe and forced into prostitution or forced labour as a domestic servant, see *LR* v *UK* App no 49113/09 (ECtHR, 14 June 2011); *VF v France* App no 7196/10 (29 November 2011); *FA v UK* App no 20658/11 (ECtHR, 10 September 2013); *OGO* v *UK* App no 13950/12 (ECtHR, 18 February 2014).

72 *N v UK* App no 26565/05 (ECtHR, 27 May 2008) (The UK denied subsidiary protection to a Ugandan woman suffering from an advanced state of AIDS. The Court reiterated that art 3 only precluded removal in cases of illness under very exceptional circumstances. Although the Court acknowledged that Ms N's return would decrease her life expectancy as her access to appropriate medical treatment was uncertain in Uganda, it concluded that she was 'stable' and 'fit to travel' and authorised her expulsion to Uganda). See also Diego Ginés Martín, 'In Limbo: Divergent Conceptualisations of Ill-treatment by European Courts and the Creation of Non-Removable Migrants' (2021) 9(2) European Papers 1173, 1177.

73 See s 3.2.

74 For inadmissible decisions, see *SB v Finland* App no 17200/11 (ECtHR, 24 June 2014) (The risk of domestic violence in Morocco did not violate art 3); *RH* (n 5); *MMR* (n 67).

75 Jukka Viljanen and Heta-Elena Heiskanen, 'The European Court of Human Rights: A Guardian of Minimum Standards in the Context of Immigration' (2016) 34(2) NQHR 174, 193.

Iran, Iraq, Nigeria, Somalia, and Yemen. Yet virtually all complaints decided before 2016, apart from one, have been unsuccessful. The slow progress in recognising women's ability to benefit from refugee protection is particularly problematic from the point of view that the Istanbul Convention was opened for signature in May 2011. Article 60(3) of the Istanbul Convention requires the signatory States to develop gender-sensitive asylum procedures and gender guidelines. Further, Article 61 of the same Convention specifically prohibits States from returning victims of gender-based violence to a country where their life would be at risk.[76] The only successful case before the ECtHR for a long time was the 2010 judgment in *N v Sweden*[77] where the ECtHR accepted the argument that an Afgan woman, who had been living in Sweden for six years, lacked a male network in Afghanistan and could not be returned there.[78] The Court's analysis of *N* is problematic as it essentially indicated that the evidence pertaining to Ms N's individual circumstances was insufficient. Ms N claimed persecution due to her political beliefs and because she had taught women in Afghanistan, which was not accepted by parts of the leading elite in Kabul.[79] The ECtHR, however, proceeded to examine her personal circumstances as a woman who wanted to divorce her estranged husband. It concluded that substantial grounds existed for believing that she would face various cumulative risks of reprisals from her husband, his family, her own family, and from the Afghan society upon her return there in light of statistical and international reports, which indicated prevalent violence against women in Afghanistan as well as the absence of prosecution of marital violence.[80] The Court specifically referred to the UNHCR guidelines highlighting that women whose behaviour was perceived as transgressing social and religious norms were systematically exposed to domestic violence and other forms of punishment, including honour crimes.[81]

Scholars have widely criticised the Court for the jurisprudence that followed *N*. Jakulevičienė and Biekša criticise the Court for taking the view that women should invoke the protection of their male relatives, shelters for women, or corrupt police, as they fall short of the standards of protection required by refugee law.[82] Benslama-Dabdoub highlights the flaws in the approach according to which women are considered vulnerable, if they lack protection by male relatives, considering that both women and men are equally powerless to protect themselves and their families in the context of indiscriminate forms of violence due to an armed

76 The Istanbul Convention entered into force in August 2014. See Catherine Warin, 'Gender in EU Asylum Law: The Istanbul Convention as a Game Changer?' (2024) 36(1–2) IJRL 93, 104.

77 *N v Sweden* (n 68).

78 Christel Querton, 'Non-State Actors of Protection and the Sliding Scale of Protection for Refugee Women' (2022) 41(3) Refugee Survey Q 444.

79 *N v Sweden* (n 68) para 8.

80 *N v Sweden* (n 68) paras 57–58. See also Lyra Jakulevičienė and Laurynas Biekša, 'Trends in The Qualification of Asylum Claims Related to Gender-Based Violence Under International and European Law' (2021) 26(5) IJHR 833.

81 *N v Sweden* (n 68) para 34 referring to UNHCR, 'Eligibility Guidelines for Assessing the International Protection Needs of Afghan Asylum-Seekers' (July 2009) 32.

82 Jakulevičienė and Biekša (n 79).

conflict or collective punishment.[83] Spijkerboer argues that the Court's case law challenges the notion that European human rights protection is the most developed globally.[84] He particularly criticises the Court for suggesting in its 2012 judgment in *AA and Others v Sweden,* that forced marriage, with associated physical and sexual violence, does not constitute sufficient evidence preventing a return to Yemen.[85] According to the Court, the family's three daughters could seek protection of their uncle and their two brothers, who had attained majority, while the family sought asylum in Sweden.[86] In her dissenting opinion in *AA*, Judge Power-Forde argued that the violence against the family's women constituted inhuman treatment with the meaning of Article 3.[87]

A similar approach continued in the 2015 judgment in *RH v Sweden*,[88] which concerned the return of a 27-year-old Ms RH to Somalia. The Court noted that as the terrorist group al-Shabaab was no longer in power in Mogadishu, returns were possible.[89] Although it reviewed various reports highlighting widespread sexual and gender-based violence committed against women by civilians and armed forces; the lack of investigation and prosecution of violence against women, and women's subordinate position to men and their general discrimination in the Somali society,[90] it concluded that her return did not violate Article 3.[91] This was because she had access to family support as her brother and uncles still lived there.[92]

Gender-sensitive outcomes in the case law have started to emerge with the 2016 judgment in *RD v France*[93] where the Court found that Ms RD's return to Guinea would violate Article 3.[94] It found three reasons for the breach. First, the Court did not consider Guinea capable of ensuring protection for Ms RD from her father, an influential imam, and her brothers, who threatened to kill her, after she married a non-Muslim man, Mr X.[95] Second, her marriage certificate and the French medical certificates documenting violent retaliation by her brothers and father contributed to the credibility of her claims.[96] Third, the Court did not consider it likely that her family would treat her any differently after her return to Guinea. Another

83 Benslama-Dabdoub (n 15) 59.
84 Thomas Spijkerboer, 'Gender, Sexuality, Asylum and European Human Rights' (2018) 29 Law Critique 2 21, 224; Jakulevičienė and Biekša (n 80); Wessels 'Boundaries' (n 12).
85 Spijkerboer, 'Gender' (n 84) 226-227. See also *AA* (n 66) paras 11 and 13 (Ms AA, and her five children sought asylum in Sweden on grounds that she and her two daughters were forced to marry much older men in their teens and were at risk of honour crimes if they tried to leave their husbands).
86 See Spijkerboer, 'Gender' (n 84) 225; Wessels, 'Boundaries' (n 12); Jakulevičienė and Biekša (n 80).
87 Spijkerboer, 'Gender' (n 84) 229.
88 *RH* (n 5).
89 ibid paras 64 and 68.
90 ibid para 70.
91 *RH* (n 5) para 70.
92 ibid para 74.
93 *RD* (n 66).
94 ibid para 45.
95 ibid para 40.
96 ibid para 42.

gender-sensitive conclusion was reached in the 2024 judgment in *BS v Türkiye*,[97] where an Iranian single mother, Ms BS, initially claimed asylum in Türkiye with her minor son due to marital violence.[98] The Turkish authorities rejected her application and sought to deport her.[99] Ms BS challenged her deportation on the grounds that she would be exposed to a real risk of death or ill-treatment in Iran after her conversion to Christianity.[100] The ECtHR considered that the Turkish authorities failed to conduct a proper examination of her asylum application.[101] Accordingly, Ms BS's conversion to Christianity after her arrival to Türkiye meant that her removal to Iran merited a new assessment whether there would be a violation of Article 3.[102] The Court found that the return would violate Articles 2 and 3 in their procedural aspect, if she was returned to Iran without taking into account the consequences arising from her conversion to Christianity after the Turkish authorities made the final decision on her removal.[103]

Several inadmissible decisions concern complaints by women, who allege that they have been subjected to partial FGM and fear further circumcision, if they are returned to the country of origin.[104] In cases where the women have daughters, they often fear that their daughters are also at risk upon return.[105] Despite the fact that FGM inflicts physical and psychological damage on women specifically due to their gender, the Court is yet to deliver a single successful judgment where the return would have been prevented due to the breach of Article 3, even if it noted in 2016 that exposing a child or an adult to FGM amounted to treatment prohibited by Article 3.[106] In reality, all complaints concerning FGM have been declared inadmissible before 2016, with the Court concluding that the return of women alleging risk of FGM does not violate Article 3 because they can rely on either the authorities or their male family members for protection.[107] The logic of relying on authorities or parents to prevent FGM is faulty because often the authorities are not able to prevent these occurrences, and frequently the family members may wish that the girl or woman undergo FGM.[108] This is because harmful traditional practices such as FGM are deeply rooted in societies where they are practised.[109]

97 *BS v Türkiye* App no 14820/19 (ECtHR, 21 March 2024).
98 ibid para 3.
99 ibid para 4.
100 ibid para 5.
101 See also *JA and AA v Türkiye* App no 80206/17 (ECtHR, 6 February 2024) (The return of a married couple and their four minor children to Iraq without a fresh assessment of their claims breached arts 2 and 3).
102 *BS* (n 97) para 17.
103 ibid para 18. See also *FG* (n 54) paras 115 and 158.
104 See eg *Sow* (n 67).
105 Jakulevičienė and Biekša (n 79).
106 *RBAB* (n 67) para 54.
107 See n 67.
108 Jakulevičienė and Biekša (n 80).
109 Gifani (n 15) 17.

6.3.2 LGBT Asylum Seekers

The existing commentary on the case law pertaining to the return of LGBT asylum applicants to the country of origin is extensive,[110] even though the ECtHR has only decided a handful of cases. All these cases focus on the likelihood of persecution on the grounds of sexual orientation in the country of origin. So far, the Court has only twice concluded that Article 3 prevents return . In its 2020 judgment in *B and C v Switzerland*,[111] the return of a gay man, Mr B, to the Gambia was not possible due to the widespread homophobia and discrimination against LGBT persons in the country. As ill-treatment may also emanate from the conduct of private individuals, other than family members,[112] the Swiss courts had insufficiently assessed the availability of State protection against the risk of ill-treatment emanating from private parties.[113]

In all previous cases concerning LGBT asylum applicants, the reasoning is strikingly similar, with the Court concluding that the return does not violate Article 3. Ferreira noted in 2021 that before 2020, the Court had rejected all LGBT asylum claims, either by declaring them inadmissible, striking them from the list of pending cases,[114] or finding no violation of Article 3.[115] The reasons why the national authorities reject the asylum application focus on the absence of active prosecution of same-sex acts in the country of origin as the legislation criminalising same-sex conduct is rarely enforced.[116] Alternatively, the Court may note that the individuals are unlikely to face arrest, prosecution, or a credible risk of torture or ill-treatment, even where the country of origin imposes a death penalty on same-sex consensual acts.[117] Additionally, in the 2017 decision in *MB v Netherlands*, the national authorities noted that a Guinean

110 See eg Carmelo Danisi and others, *Queering Asylum in Europe: Legal and Social Experiences of Seeking International Protection on Grounds of Sexual Orientation and Gender Identity* (Springer 2021); Nuno Ferreira, 'An Exercise in Detachment: The Council of Europe and Sexual Minority Asylum Claims' in Richard CM Mole (ed), *Queer Migration and Asylum in Europe* (UCL Press 2021).

111 *B and C v Switzerland* App nos 889/19 and 43987/16 (ECtHR, 17 November 2020) (The Court found that Mr B's deportation to the Gambia would violate art 3). For comment, see Liam Davis, 'Gay Asylum Seekers European Court of Human Rights (Third Section): Judgment of 17 November 2020' (2021) 2 EHRLR 218.

112 *B* (n 111) para 61. See also Wieland and Alessi (n 48).

113 *B* (n 111) para 63.

114 In two cases, the applicant was granted a residence permit which resulted in the case being struck out of the Court's register. See *ME v Sweden* App no 71398/12 (ECtHR, 8 April 2015); *AE v Finland* App no 30953/11 (ECtHR, 22 September 2015).

115 Ferreira (n 110) 87. See also Laurence R Helfer and Clare Ryan, 'LGBT Rights as Mega-Politics: Litigating before the ECtHR' (2021) 84 LCP 59.

116 Ferreira (n 110) 87.

117 *IIN v Netherlands* App no 2035/04 (ECtHR, 09 December 2004) (Mr IIN claimed asylum on grounds of repeated rape by police. The Court found that there were no substantial grounds for believing that Mr IIN would be exposed to a real risk of being subjected to treatment contrary to art 3 in Iran on grounds of his sexuality); *IK v Switzerland* App no 21417/17 (ECtHR, 18 January 2018) (The Court considered that Mr IK failed to provide additional evidence that his return would breach art 3. The criminalisation of same-sex conduct in Sierra Leone was insufficient).

man did not plausibly establish that he was in a same-sex relationship in the country of origin,[118] invalidating his experiences as a gay man.

Two specific features stand out in the Court's jurisprudence in this area. First, the ECtHR has considered almost exclusively complaints concerning asylum-seeking gay men.[119] Second, even the LGBT-friendly countries, such as the Netherlands, have rejected most asylum applications by LGBT individuals.[120] A search in the Court's database, HUDOC, brought up only one case concerning a lesbian woman who applied for asylum in Sweden on the basis of persecution arising from her sexual orientation.[121] However, the complaint was brought against Armenia for its failure to offer adequate protection for an Armenian national, Ms Armine Oganezova, from homophobic attacks and hate speech as well as to conduct a proper investigation into the hate-motivated ill-treatment against her.[122] In conclusion, the Court has found a violation of Article 3 only in two cases concerning the return of an LGBT asylum applicant to the country of origin.[123] So far, it does not appear that the Court has considered any complaints concerning applicants who seek asylum due to their gender identity, raising a question as to why this may be.

6.3.3 Strike Out Decisions

What further emerges from the case law analysis concerning returns to the country of origin is that the Court often strikes pending cases out of its register under Article 37 ECHR, which gives it the power to do so. These decisions do not result in a finding of a violation of Article 3 and, therefore, they are not generally considered successful as such. Some cases are struck out because an asylum-seeker has formed a family relationship in the country of asylum, which has resulted in a residence permit for family purposes being granted to them.[124] In other cases the respondent State grants a temporary residence permit for other reasons. Additionally, in many cases, the State grants a temporary residence with the possibility of renewal, but this does not necessarily regularise their stay in the State, unless an indefinite leave to remain is issued. The Court will strike a decision out of the register if it is satisfied with the State's promise not to expel the individual imminently or in the near future.[125] Therefore, the Court has accepted residency of any length and in some

118 *MB v Netherlands* App no 63890/16 (ECtHR, 28 November 2017).

119 Loveday Hodson, 'Sexual Orientation and the European Convention on Human Rights: What of the "L" in LGBT?' (2019) 23(3) J Lesbian Stud 383.

120 Helfer and Ryan (n 114).

121 *Oganezova v Armenia* App nos 71367/12 and 72961/12 (ECtHR, 17 May 2022) (The Court found that Armenia violated art 3 taken in conjunction with art 14).

122 ibid para 123.

123 *B* (n 110). See also *MI v Switzerland* App no 56390/21 (ECtHR, 12 November 2024) (The return of a gay man to Iran without sufficient assessment of the risk of ill-treatment would violate art 3).

124 See eg *ME* (n 114); *RBAB* (n 67) (The Court struck the case out of the list to the extent that it related to one of the family's daughters, who was granted a residence permit for the purpose of residence with her Dutch partner with whom she had a minor child).

125 Elisabeth Lambert Abdelgawad, 'The Practice of the European Court of Human Rights When Striking Out Applications' (2018) 36(1) NQHR 7, 20.

cases, even a so-called tolerated stay, as an indication that the individual is no longer at risk of expulsion.[126] However, the tolerated stay may preclude access from public services, such as welfare programmes, public benefits, and health care.[127]

A series of complaints against the Netherlands concerning FGM are probably the most significant in this area. The Guinean women who unsuccessfully claimed asylum in the Netherlands due to the fear that their minor daughters born in the Netherlands would be subjected to FGM in Guinea resulted in several strike out decisions between 2018 and 2020.[128] The mothers claimed that they were unable to provide protection, given the high FGM rate in Guinea, in general and within their respective ethnic groups, as well as the social and cultural pressure. The Dutch government granted the women and their daughters temporary residence permits after the applications were lodged with the Court's registry. This, however, means that the once the temporary residence permits expire, the women need to reapply. Only one of the women was invited to submit a fresh application for asylum, which would be accepted.[129]

The strike out decisions appear significant for the rights of asylum-seeking women because even if the Court does not find a violation of Article 3 and the State does not have to pay compensation awarded by the Court, the outcome is still positive for the individuals because they are granted a residency permit, even if it may be of temporary nature. Alternatively, the individual may be eligible to submit a fresh asylum application. In cases concerning migration, the Court is acutely aware of the CoE States' reluctance to implement its judgments where it finds a violation of the Convention, which may consequently endanger the legitimacy of the Court.[130] A strike out decision allows the ECtHR to avoid, or at least to postpone, a decision on substance, which may allow CoE governments to resolve the question outside of court.[131] Additionally, the delay may allow for the evolution of European consensus on the issue.[132]

126 ibid referring to *Khan v Germany* App no 38030/12 (ECtHR, 21 September 2016).

127 See also Gianna Eckert, 'Caught in Limbo: The Precarious (Legal) Situation of Non-Removable Migrants Stranded in Europe' (2021) 35(3) JIANL 252.

128 *Zenab Soumah v Netherlands* App no 61452/15 (ECtHR, 5 June 2018); *Kadiatou and Binta Barry v Netherlands* App no 66238/16 (ECtHR, 4 September 2018); *Aminata Kake and Kani Camara v Netherlands* App no 63913/17 (ECtHR, 4 September 2018); *Aichtou Magassouba v Netherlands* App no 37153/17 (ECtHR, 24 October 2019); *Benty Yasmine Chaloub and Latifa Moussoukoura Camara v Netherlands* App no 7338/16 (ECtHR, 15 October 2020). See also *Aida Touré v Netherlands* App no 14778/18 (ECtHR, 3 July 2018); *OTD v Netherlands* App no 49837/20 (ECtHR, 19 May 2022) (The case was struck out of the Court's register because Ms OTD submitted a new asylum application in the Netherlands).

129 *Kadiatou and Binta Barry* (n 128).

130 Lambert Abdelgawad (n 125) 20.

131 Erin F Delaney, 'Analysing Avoidance: Judicial Strategy in Comparative Perspective' (2016) 1 Duke L J 66. See also Lize R Glas, 'Changes in the Procedural Practice of the European Court of Human Rights: Consequences for the Convention System and Lessons to be Drawn' (2014) 14 HRL Rev 671. See also *AA and Others v Sweden* App no 1270/21 (ECtHR, 4 July 2024) where Sweden granted temporaty residency permits to an Afghan mother and her four adult daughters due to changed situation of women following the Taliban takeover. The family had unsuccesfully applied asylum in Sweden twice before).

132 Delaney (n 131).

6.4 New Asylum Applicants

The ECtHR has summarised the general principles concerning the detention and living conditions of asylum-seekers in its case law.[133] As similar issues are often raised in cases concerning asylum detention[134] and reception conditions, this section discusses these types of cases together. In its asylum detention case law, the Court usually establishes whether the conditions of detention exceed the threshold of Article 3 and whether the detention violates the asylum applicant's rights under Article 5 (Right to liberty and security). The Court has also addressed the general principles concerning the living conditions of pregnant women and the duration of ill-treatment suffered.[135] In these cases the Court usually highlights the compound vulnerability of the asylum-seeking women due to ill-health, pregnancy, and history of various forms of violence in order to establish whether their treatment exceeds the threshold of severity required to engage Article 3.

6.4.1 Asylum Detention

In several complaints against Malta before 2015, the Court found that Maltese legislation violated Article 5(4) ECHR in the absence of any remedy by which asylum applicants could challenge the lawfulness of their detention.[136] It made the same finding in four separate judgments issued between 2013 and 2016, where five Somalian asylum-seeking women in their 20s, who travelled alone, complained about the prison-like conditions in the Maltese detention centres.[137] Two of these judgments are significant as they establish the women's vulnerability. In its 2013 judgment in *Aden Ahmed v Malta*,[138] the Court considered that the 22-year-old Somali woman, Ms Aslya Aden Ahmed, was vulnerable on account of her irregular migration status and her fragile health.[139] After being detained for four months, she escaped from detention and travelled to the Netherlands to seek asylum.[140] Her plan was to travel to Sweden where she hoped to be reunited with her three-year-old son, Ahmed; her father; and her siblings, who were in Ethiopia awaiting resettlement in Sweden.[141] Despite the repeated unsuccessful attempts by Ms Aden Ahmed's lawyer to prevent her return to Malta, she was returned to detention there

133 *SAB and SAR v Hungary* App no 17089/19 (ECtHR, 30 November 2023), para 15.

134 The Court increasingly uses the term 'confinement' to characterise the detention of asylum seekers at the Hungarian border transit zones.

135 *Mahmundi and Others v Greece* App no 14902/10 (ECtHR, 31 July 2012), para 70; *RR and Others v Hungary* App no 36037/17 (ECtHR, 2 March 2021) paras 64–65; *AD v Greece* App no 55363/19 (ECtHR, 4 April 2023), paras 32-33; *MB* (n 55) para 34.

136 See eg *Louled Massoud v Malta* App no 24340/08 (ECtHR, 27 July 2010).

137 See eg *Moxamed Ismaaciil and Abdirahman Warsame v Malta* App nos 52160/13 and 52165/13 (ECtHR, 12 January 2016), para 18.

138 *Ahmed* (n 4).

139 ibid para 144. See also Hudson (n 44) 21.

140 *Ahmed* (n 4) para 13.

141 ibid. Her family were eventually resettled in Sweden on 17 March 2011.

while being two months pregnant.[142] The cumulative effect of her two periods of detention over 12 months, irregular migratory status, and fragile health status constituted degrading treatment contrary to Article 3.[143]

Similarly, in its 2016 judgment in *Abdi Mahamud v Malta*[144] the Court found a violation of Article 3 in respect of the detention of a 20-year-old Somalian woman, Ms Sagal Abdi Mahamud, who was detained in Malta for more than 18 months. She was considered vulnerable due to her fragile physical and mental health, and the fact that it took the authorities eight months to release her after they had determined that she should be released.[145] The Court noted that her detention in prison-like conditions diminished her human dignity and aroused feelings of anguish and inferiority capable of humiliating and debasing her.[146] Although the two other complaints against Malta in 2015 and 2016[147] were factually similar, the Court contrasted the personal circumstances of the women with those of Ms Aden Ahmed.[148] In its analysis the Court accepted that the women, who were detained in Malta between eight and 12 months, were vulnerable, by virtue of being asylum seekers. However, according to the Court, they were 'not more vulnerable than any other adult asylum seekers detained at the time'.[149] Consequently, the conditions of their detention did not reach the minimum level of severity needed to constitute a violation of Article 3.[150] In *Mahamed Jama*,[151] the Court additionally found a violation of Article 5(1) ECHR (Right to liberty) concerning 26-year-old Ms Farhiyo Mahamed Jama's continued detention even after the authorities had reached a decision on her asylum claim.

The women in the four cases were detained on average between eight and 18 months when their detention in some cases was no longer necessary. For the Court to find that some of them were more vulnerable than others demonstrates that the Court looks for compound vulnerability, such as, poor physical or mental health and/or pregnancy in order to find a violation of Article 3 in these cases. It is undisputed that the women in these cases were not fluent in English and did not understand their rights when the Maltese authorities gave them the information concerning asylum in writing. They complained about feeling vulnerable in an environment where the detention centre staff was all male, and they received consistent verbal abuse from the male detainees who were housed on the floor above.[152]

142 ibid para 14.
143 ibid paras 98–99.
144 *Abdi Mahamud v Malta* App no 56796/13 (ECtHR, 3 May 2016) (The Court found a violation of arts 3, 5(4) and 5(1) in respect of her two periods of detention).
145 ibid paras 11, 24 and 88.
146 ibid para 89.
147 *Ismaaciil* (n 137) paras 118–119.
148 Hudson (n 44).
149 *Mahamed Jama v Malta* App no 10290/13 (ECtHR, 26 November 2015), para 100; *Ismaaciil* (n 137) para 94. See also Hudson (n 44).
150 See eg *Jama* (n 148) para 102; *Ismaaciil* (n 137) para 99.
151 *Jama* (n 149) paras 18 and 46 (No violation of art 3).
152 See eg *Ismaaciil* (n 136) para 18.

They also raised issues concerning the lack of privacy, non-existence of heating during the winter months, and lack of air-conditioning during summer, as well as inadequate access to outdoors, medical care, and Somali language interpreters during their detention.[153] It could, therefore, be argued that the conditions of their lengthy detention were sufficient in themselves to violate their rights under Article 3, considering that the Court has in its subsequent case law noted that detention should be used only as a last resort.[154]

In the 2016 judgment in *OM v Hungary*,[155] a gay Iranian man claimed that his detention violated his rights. Wieland and Alessi note that *OM* is the first case in which the ECtHR recognised the specific protection needs of LGBT asylum seekers when compared with asylum seekers in general as vulnerable persons.[156] They argue that LGBT individuals are at high risk of encountering harassment, physical, and sexual abuse by other detainees and staff members, leading to feelings of fear, loss of freedom, and aggravation of pre-existing trauma.[157] Ultimately, the ECtHR found that Mr OM's detention violated Article 5(1)(b) ECHR.[158] Accordingly, Hungary failed to consider his situation 'in a sufficiently individualised manner as required by the national law' after his arrest at the border.[159] Mr OM was considered vulnerable as the Court noted that LGBT rights in Iran were virtually non -existent.[160] An individualised analysis was necessary to ensure that Mr OM, as a vulnerable detainee, was safe when placed in detention with other asylum seekers from 'countries with widespread cultural or religious prejudice against' LGBT persons.[161] It is striking how different the Court's approach in *OM* is from its previous decisions concerning the return of LGBT asylum seekers to Iran discussed in Section 3.2.

Several judgments between 2021 and 2023 concern the conditions and alleged ill treatment of Iraqi and Afghan families with minor children in the transit zones at the Hungarian border with Serbia.[162] The analysis focuses on the families' mothers as asylum-seeking women. All families in the following three cases were confined to a border transit zone for four months. In all these cases the Court found that Hungary violated all family members' rights under Article 3. It also found a violation of Articles 5(1) and 5(4) ECHR as no legal basis for detention existed in Hungarian law at the time, no formal documents explaining the reasons for the detention were issued to the families, nor did they have an effective remedy to

153 ibid.
154 *OM v Hungary* App no 9912/15 (ECtHR, 5 July 2016), para 52.
155 ibid.
156 Wieland and Alessi (n 48) 406 and 418.
157 ibid 418.
158 *OM* (n 154) para 52.
159 ibid.
160 ibid para 53.
161 ibid.
162 See *RR* (n 135) para 49; *SF and Others v Bulgaria* App no 8138/16 (ECtHR, 7 December 2017), paras 78–83; *MH* (n 3) paras 183–186.

challenge the lawfulness of their detention.[163] According to Hudson, the children's young age is often determinative in reaching the conclusion that the conditions experienced at the transit zone exceed the minimum severity threshold needed to constitute a violation of Article 3, rather than their asylum seeker status.[164] This is understandable, considering that the Court has previously emphasised that children who do not have the appropriate travel documents are extremely vulnerable, which in a case of an irregular migrant child overrides their irregular migration status.[165] In contrast, a violation of an asylum-seeking woman's rights is usually only found if she is pregnant or suffers from ill health. Even fewer cases recognise the vulnerability of asylum-seeking men, even though the fathers in these cases were subjected to treatment that violates Article 3.

Although the 2021 judgment in *RR and Others v Hungary*[166] is often seen as a landmark judgment in the context of the unlawful detention of asylum seekers in the Hungarian border transit zones, the judgment itself is not gender-aware nor does it focus on the vulnerability of the parents. *RR* concerned an Afghan Iranian family consisting of three minor children and their parents. For a part of their detention in the Röszke transit zone, they were accommodated in particularly restrictive conditions.[167] When assessing whether the detention violated Article 3, the Court specifically noted the children's ages, the length of detention, the serious health condition and pregnancy of the mother, Ms SH, and the fact that the father, Mr RR, was deprived of food during his stay in the transit zone.[168] Hudson notes that the Court did not explicitly mention the parents' particular vulnerability as asylum seekers, even if it noted the 'vulnerabilities associated with Ms SH's health and pregnancy'.[169] It is noteworthy that *RR* was decided several months before the Taliban came to power in Afghanistan in August 2021, after which the Taliban has adopted several restrictive measures systematically targeting women, which

163 See *HM and Others v Hungary* App no 38967/17 (ECtHR, 2 June 2022), para 32; *RR* (n 135) paras 87–92; 97–99; *PS and AM v Hungary* App no 53272/17 (ECtHR, 5 October 2023), para 16. See also Lorenzo Bernardini, '*HM and Others v Hungary*: Immigration Detention, Burden of Proof and Principle of Necessity: Weakening Safeguards at the Borders?' (*Strasbourg Observers*, 19 August 2022) <https://strasbourgobservers.com/2022/08/19/h-m-and-others-v-hungary-immigration-detention-burden-of-proof-and-principle-of-necessity-weakeaning-safeguards-at-the-borders/> accessed 15 August 2024.

164 Hudson (n 44) 25. *RR* (n 135) para 65.

165 Viljanen and Heiskanen (n 75) 179. The ECtHR has previously held that detaining a five-year-old girl in a closed centre for adults for two months violated art 3. See *Mubilanzila Mayeka and Kanini Mitunga v Belgium* App no 13178/03 (ECHR, 12 January 2007).

166 *RR* (n 135).

167 ibid paras 1 and 59.

168 Hungarian authorities denied Mr RR access to food on the grounds that he had already applied for asylum in Hungary before entering the border transit zone with his family. See *RR* (n 135) paras 21 and 52. See also Hudson (n 44) 24.

169 *RR* (n 135) paras 58–65.

have resulted in significant deterioration of the human rights situation for women in Afghanistan.[170]

The 2022 judgment in *HM and Others v Hungary*[171] concerned the detention of an Iraqi family consisting of parents and four minor children in the Tompa transit zone in 2017. The Court considered the mother, Ms JK, as vulnerable due to her advanced stage of high-risk pregnancy.[172] It, therefore, recognised that the detention must have caused her anxiety and psychological suffering, albeit she received the necessary medical attention.[173] It further found a violation of Article 3 in respect of the father, Mr MH, who was handcuffed while accompanying his pregnant wife to the hospital.[174] As there was no evidence that he posed any danger to himself or those around him, or that there was any other security risk related to his previous conduct, handcuffing him diminished his human dignity and was degrading contrary to Article 3, considering that he had endured torture by the Iraqi security services.[175] Here the Court clearly recognised the vulnerability of both parents due to different reasons, but its analysis is more aware of the issues facing asylum seekers upon their arrival to countries like Hungary.

The 2023 judgment in *PS and AM v Hungary*[176] concerned a complaint of detention in the Tompa transit zone and the degrading and inhuman conditions experienced by an Iraqi mother, Ms PS, and her minor son, AM, who had fled Iraq due to marital violence.[177] Ms PS maintained that although the Hungarian authorities were aware of her history of violent abuse, vulnerable situation, and deteriorating mental health, Hungary failed to provide her access to a psychologist or psychiatrist.[178] The Court was not convinced that she was provided with adequate mental health care because professional psychological assistance was not available in the transit zones in 2017.[179] It, therefore, considered that the authorities were aware that the conditions of detention must have caused Ms PS significant psychological suffering.[180] Consequently, Hungary failed to comply with their obligations under Article 3 with regard to providing her with appropriate health care.[181]

Although there are other cases concerning detention of Iraqi and Afghan asylum seekers in the Hungarian border transit zones, the cases chosen for the analysis include those where the Court found a violation of the parents' rights due to their

170 Hülya Kaya, 'Afghan Women Are Under Threat from the Taliban: A Great Test of the Turkish Government and the Courts' (2024) 36(1-2) IJRL 6.
171 *HM* (n 163).
172 ibid para 18.
173 ibid.
174 ibid para 25.
175 *HM* (n 163) paras 25, 27–28.
176 *PS* (n 163).
177 Although Ms PS and AM were placed in an open reception centre due to Ms PS's poor mental well-being, they returned to Iraq voluntarily shortly after. See *PS* (n 162) paras 1–2, 4 and 10.
178 ibid para 10.
179 ibid paras 10–11 citing *RR* (n 135) paras 30, 46 and 63.
180 ibid para 10.
181 ibid para 12.

specific circumstances, such as pregnancy, poor mental health, or history of violence or torture.[182] This is sobering reading, demonstrating the particular vulnerability of asylum-seeking women and men, who not only have fled conflict zones and persecution in the country of origin but who may also have experienced serious violence there or suffer from mental and physical health problems in the border transit zones due to severe restrictions on their rights and freedoms.

6.4.2 Reception Conditions

In its case law concerning reception conditions, the Court usually establishes whether the conditions at the reception centres exceed the threshold of Article 3. All four judgments analysed in this section were issued in 2023 and concern the inadequacy of the reception conditions for vulnerable women and adolescent girls. The relevance of the Istanbul Convention becomes obvious in this context as it requires that States develop 'gender-sensitive reception procedures and support services for asylum-seekers'.[183] One of the judgments concerns the stay of a 17-year-old girl in the adult reception centre in Italy for almost eight months,[184] and three judgments concern the inadequacy of reception centres on the island of Samos. The judgment in *MA v Italy*[185] concerned a violation of Article 3 in respect of a Ghanaian national, Ms MA, due to her accommodation in an adult reception centre when the Italian authorities knew that she was a particularly vulnerable minor as she had disclosed being a victim of sexual abuse in Ghana and Libya as part of her asylum request.[186] The Court noted that as the centre was not equipped to provide Ms MA with appropriate psychological assistance that her situation required, she was at significant risk of developing post-traumatic stress disorder.[187] She was granted international protection in December 2017 because of her forced marriage in Ghana, the practice of which was confirmed by several international sources.[188] Consequently, her continued stay in the adult reception centre, taken together with the national authorities' prolonged inaction regarding her situation and her needs as a particularly vulnerable minor amounted to a breach of Article 3.[189]

182 For cases concerning a lengthy stay between seven months and over a year in the Röszke transit zone, see eg *WO and Others v Hungary* App no 36896/18 (ECtHR, 25 August 2022) paras 9–10 (The Court found a violation of art 3 in respect of an Afghan family of four consisting of mother, father and two minor children); *SAB and SAR* (n 134) (The Court found a violation of art 3 in respect of an Iraqi father and his minor son).
183 Istanbul Convention, art 60(3).
184 *MA v Italy* App no 70583/17 (ECtHR, 31 August 2023).
185 ibid.
186 *MA* (n 184) paras 1 and 41.
187 ibid paras 45 and 47.
188 ibid para 24.
189 ibid para 48.

In its three separate but almost identical judgments in *AD v Greece*,[190] *MB v Greece*,[191] and *ML v Greece*,[192] the Court observed that the three women stayed at the reception centre on the island of Samos between two and a half months and four months. During their stay there, Ms AD, a Ghanian national; Ms MB, a Cameroonian national; and Ms ML, a Sierra Leonean national, needed specialised care due to the advanced stage of their pregnancies and pregnancy-related medical conditions.[193] All women raised issues with considerable shortcomings as regards the accommodation, sanitary facilities, nutrition, and prenatal healthcare.[194] Taking into account the findings of several third parties, the ECtHR concluded that the reception conditions were incompatible with the right to an adequate standard of living.[195] Consequently, there was a violation of Article 3 as the women were subjected to ill-treatment which exceeded the threshold of severity required to engage this provision.[196] The three women were initially accommodated in tents in the informal settlement area, without access to adequate sanitary facilities.[197] Although Ms MB and Ms ML were later placed within the reception centre, Ms MB had to sleep on the floor as she shared the room with another pregnant woman.[198] Further, their accommodation lacked heating and protection against the weather conditions.[199] Ms AD also raised concerns about her unsafe living situation in a tent for three months.[200] When these cases are contrasted with the 2013–2016 Maltese asylum detention cases, it is obvious that the Court has adopted a much more gender-aware approach in its 2023 judgments concerning reception conditions.

6.4.3 Summary Expulsion

The Court has adjudicated several cases concerning border enforcement practices where the respondent State may contest the events described by the asylum applicants or that they expressed their wish to apply for asylum.[201] Three cases concerning summary expulsion in this section illustrate situations where the State denied the applicants a possibility to apply for asylum in its territory or appeal against their summary expulsion. In these cases, the Court does not find the applicants

190 *AD* (n 135) paras 32–33.
191 *MB* (n 55).
192 *ML v Greece* App no 8386/20 (ECtHR, 23 November 2023).
193 The women were between five and seven months' pregnant upon their arrival to Samos. See *AD* (n 135) paras 5 and 34; *ML* (n 191) paras 5 and 37; *MB* (n 55) paras 5, 7 and 35.
194 *AD* (n 135) paras 6 and 8; *ML* (n 192) paras 5 and 7. Ms MB was not provided with the required prenatal healthcare because of a suspected tuberculosis infection. *MB* (n 55) paras 7–8.
195 *MB* (n 55) para 36; *AD* (n 135) para 35.
196 *MB* (n 55) paras 37–38; *AD* (n 135) paras 36–37; *ML* (n 191) paras 39–40.
197 *MB* (n 55) para 5; *ML* (n 192) para 5.
198 *MB* (n 55) para 6.
199 *MB* (n 55) para 6; *ML* (n 192) para 6.
200 *AD* (n 135) paras 5 and 7.
201 Grażyna Baranowska, 'Exposing Covert Border Enforcement: Why Failing to Shift the Burden of Proof in Pushback Cases is Wrong' (2023) 4(4) ECHR L Rev 473, 481.

vulnerable, even if it may find that the children are vulnerable. Instead, the Court is more interested in procedural issues under Article 3 or Article 4 of Protocol 4 (Prohibition of collective expulsion). All three cases analysed in this section concern mothers and children. The 2021 judgment in *MH and Others v Croatia*[202] concerned the expulsion of an Afghan woman, Ms MH, and her six minor children, from Croatia to Serbia.[203] Ms MH claimed that the Croatian police officers ignored her wish to seek asylum in Croatia, escorted them to the border and told them to follow the train tracks back to Serbia. After crossing the border, Ms MH's six-year-old daughter was fatally injured after being hit by a train.[204] While Croatia denied that the family had even entered Croatia, the Court accepted Ms MH's account of the events and found a violation of Article 4 of Protocol 4 in respect of Ms MH and her children.[205] It further found a violation of Article 2 under its procedural limb due to the authorities' failure to conduct an effective investigation into the circumstances leading to her daughter's death.[206] However, the Court did not consider whether Ms MH or her children were vulnerable.

The 2022 judgment in *OM and DS v Ukraine*[207] concerned the removal of two Kyrgyz nationals, Ms OM and her minor son, DS, from Ukraine to Georgia. Ms OM was responsible for the Kyrgyz President's public and media relations until the government forces shot more than 70 people during a protest in the capital city.[208] After the President's resignation, she and over 20 other former public officials were charged with several counts of aggravated murder and abuse of power.[209] After violence erupted in a trial hearing, Ms OM first fled to Kazakhstan and then to Ukraine with her father and her son. Upon their arrival to Ukraine, the authorities removed the family to Georgia on the grounds that her son did not have a passport.[210] Although Ms OM could appeal against the removal decision, the appeal procedure did not have a suspensive effect.[211] The Court found that the Ukrainian authorities failed to discharge their procedural obligation under Article 3 to assess the alleged risks of Ms OM's removal, directly or indirectly, from Georgia to Kyrgyzstan before removing her to Georgia.[212] The Court said nothing about the family's vulnerability in the judgment.

202 *MH* (n 3) (The applicants in the case were the father, Mr RH, his two wives, Ms MH and Ms FH, and their eleven children, most of whom were very young. Only Ms MH and her six children crossed the border to Croatia, whereas the others remained in Serbia).
203 ibid para 7.
204 ibid
205 ibid para 304. See also Baranowska (n 201) 481.
206 *MH* (n 3) paras 163–164 and 303.
207 *OM and DS* (n 3).
208 ibid paras 6–7.
209 ibid paras 8–9.
210 ibid paras 22 and 24 and 27–28.
211 ibid para 28.
212 ibid paras 95–98.

The 2023 judgment in *SS and Others v Hungary*[213] concerned a similar situation as in *OM and DS*. In this case, the asylum applicants were two mothers with their children, one from Yemen and the other from Afghanistan.[214] Hungary initiated criminal proceedings against both mothers after their arrest at the border crossing point at Budapest international airport. The charges were based on the use of counterfeit travel documents, whereas Article 31 of the 1951 Refugee Convention prohibits penalising an asylum seeker for entering the territory of a contracting State to claim asylum.[215] After expressing their wish to request asylum in Hungary, they were removed to Serbia.[216] The Court noted that it was undisputed that the families had expressed their wish to seek asylum in Hungary.[217] Noting that both families arrived at an official border crossing point at the airport via a non-European country,[218] the Court contrasted their situation with asylum seekers, who cross a land border in an unauthorised manner, without using the official border crossing points.[219] It also stated that it could not ignore the fact that asylum seekers were often compelled to travel without appropriate travel documents, and consequently, they might sometimes resort to the use of false or fraudulent documentation.[220] The Court concluded that although the families' removal to Serbia was not motivated by their use of false documentation, they were removed without an effective opportunity to submit arguments against their removal.[221] Consequently, Hungary violated Article 4 of Protocol No 4.[222]

Even though the Court highlighted the vulnerability of the Yemeni family's minor children, noting that their needs were not assessed before their removal to Serbia,[223] it was silent about the vulnerability of the adults in these cases. Ganty has argued that the Court does not view educated asylum seekers sufficiently

213 *SS* (n 3).
214 The Yemeni mother and her five children left Yemen due to the war and because one of the children needed access to specialist medical care unavailable in Yemen. The Afghan mother and two adult children left Afghanistan owing to their fear of persecution related to one of the applicant's job at a human rights NGO, which campaigned for the criminalisation of violence against women and forced marriages.
215 *SS* (n 3) para 15.
216 ibid paras 10 and 16.
217 ibid para 49.
218 The Yemeni family flew to Budapest via Istanbul and the Afghan family arrived via Dubai. See ibid paras 5, 13 and 49.
219 See eg *ND and NT v Spain* App nos 8675/15 and 8697/15 (ECtHR, 13 February 2020), paras 209-210 and 231 (No violation of art 4 of protocol 4 on the prohibition of collective expulsion in the case of a group of irregular migrants from Melilla to Morocco. The Court stated they should have made use of a legal pathway instead). For a factually similar case concerning Ceuta, see *MB and RA v Spain* App no 20351/17 (ECtHR, 5 July 2022).
220 *SS* (n 3) para 50. See also *OM and DS* (n 3) paras 21, 33 and 77–100.
221 *SS* (n 3) para 50.
222 ibid paras 51–52.
223 ibid para 49.

vulnerable.[224] The Court reached such a conclusion in the highly controversial *Sow v Belgium* case, concerning the risk of becoming the victim of FGM for a second time, where it observed that as Ms Sow was educated and she was opposed to FGM, she could not be regarded as a particularly vulnerable woman.[225] It is also worth noting that the Court said nothing about the Afghan family's vulnerability, despite the fact that many EU Member States have, since December 2022, granted refugee status to all asylum-seeking women from Afghanistan, based exclusively on their gender.[226] However, the States have not taken a consistent approach in this.

6.5 Conclusion

The obligation not to return anyone to a country where they may face a risk to their life or freedom is widely considered the most critical of the States' obligations under international law.[227] Yet, the Court's asylum jurisprudence demonstrates that the principle of *non-refoulement* contained both in the ECHR and the 1951 Refugee Convention[228] does not mean that asylum seekers are guaranteed access to asylum procedures in the destination States in practice. It is obvious from the case law analysis that the CoE States repeatedly violate their obligations under both the ECHR and the 1951 Refugee Convention. It also seems that in some States the authorities' decisions to expel asylum-seeking women and their families summarily to States where asylum protection is weaker, or to confine them for lengthy periods in prison-like border transit zones and detention centres, are frequently based on arbitrary criteria, such as, the nationality or religious beliefs of the asylum seeker.

Positively, there is a visible change in the Court's asylum jurisprudence in 2023, which is welcome. The jurisprudence reveals that the ECtHR's judges are starting to demonstrate more awareness of gender-sensitive interpretation of the ECHR and the vulnerability of asylum-seeking women, especially women who are pregnant; have minor children; women who are detained or confined to border transit zones; or women who have experienced sexual, psychological, and physical violence. Although the Court has noted that it may sometimes refer to other international and regional instruments,[229] it has not explicitly referred to the provisions of the Istanbul Convention in its asylum case law. This is an important omission, considering that the Istanbul Convention opens the possibility for refugee status under the 1951 Refugee Convention as it provides that gender-based violence against women is a form of persecution and serious harm based on which States may

224 Sarah Ganty 'Poverty as Misrecognition: What Role for Antidiscrimination Law in Europe?' (2021) 21(4) HRL Rev 962, 997.
225 *Sow* (n 67) para 68.
226 Warin (n 76) 100; Kaya (n 170) 7.
227 See Nadine El-Enany, 'On Pragmatism and Legal Idolatry: Fortress Europe and the Desertion of the Refugee' (2015) 22 Intl J Minority and Group Rts 7, 16.
228 See Refugee Convention, art 33. See Roels (n 11) 79.
229 See, eg, *FG* (n 54) para 117.

also grant temporary protection.[230] Further, the Istanbul Convention requires a gender-sensitive interpretation to be applied to each of the five grounds in the 1951 Refugee Convention.[231]

What emerges from the case law analysis is that the ECtHR focuses on whether an asylum seeker is more vulnerable than others in a similar situation.[232] Although it recognises that an asylum-seeking woman's particular vulnerability deserves heightened protection under the ECHR, the consequence of the Court's focus on compound vulnerability[233] is that the Court ignores the applicants' gender in many of its judgments and decisions. Additionally, the Court's understanding of who is vulnerable is narrow. In general, it fails to see adults who are assumed not to have any additional vulnerabilities as particularly vulnerable asylum seekers.[234] Building on Hudson's concept of compound vulnerability, this chapter has conducted a case law analysis on asylum-seeking women. In this context, compound vulnerability seems to arise in cases where an asylum seeker fulfils two conditions. First, they are either a minor,[235] a pregnant woman,[236] or an LGBT individual,[237] or suffer from poor health.[238] Second, they have been subject to a lengthy[239] or unlawful detention upon their arrival to the CoE State.[240] Although the ECtHR does not consider single parents with their minor children who have been subject to summary expulsion as vulnerable, these applicants are seemingly vulnerable as demonstrated by the specific circumstances of the cases concerning summary expulsions. Additionally, Afghan women can be seen vulnerable due to the systematic human rights violations faced by women in Afghanistan after August 2021.[241]

The Court's 2023 case law regarding the reception conditions has produced by far the most gender-sensitive judgments as yet. This could be argued to demonstrate that the Court is in the process of developing and further elaborating the CoE human rights standards in order to address the difficulties that vulnerable women, unaccompanied minors, and victims of various forms of violence face as asylum-seekers. However, this is a relatively recent development. What the case law analysis brings to light are the new dimensions of vulnerability. This chapter expands and develops the notion of compound vulnerability by recognising that the intersections of gender and nationality, age, race or ethnicity, religious beliefs, or even

230 Istanbul Convention, art 60(1). See also Warin (n 76) 98.
231 Istanbul Convention, art 60(2).
232 Hudson (n 44).
233 ibid 30.
234 *MH v Finland* App no 42255/18 (ECtHR, 16 June 2020), paras 57–58 (The Court found no violation of art 3 if a 22-year-old Hazara Afghan male, who had lived in Iran with his foster parents since the age of five, was returned to Afghanistan). See also Roels (n 11) 78.
235 *RR* (n 135).
236 *Ahmed* (n 4); *RR* (n 135); *HM* (n 163).
237 *OM* (n 153).
238 *Ahmed* (n 4).
239 See eg ibid.
240 See eg *RR* (n 135); *HM* (n 163).
241 Warin (n 76) 100; Kaya (n 170) 7.

marital status can impact on an asylum seeker's vulnerability. For instance, single mothers and their minor children should be considered vulnerable. It is also possible that some CoE States are targeting asylum-seekers particularly from majority Muslim countries by placing them in border transit zones with the aim that they will seek asylum elsewhere.

It is disappointing that the ECtHR readily removes a pending case out of its register in cases where the States provide minimal guarantees that the individual is not at imminent risk of expulsion by the respondent State to avoid a formal finding of a violation of the rights of an asylum seeker and paying out the compensation awarded by the Court.[242] Even though the outcome may be, in some cases, positive for the asylum applicant, especially if they are granted a permanent residency permit. However, in other cases the Court has accepted a tolerated stay, which appears to be inconsistent with the ECHR.[243]

References

Anderson A, 'There Should Be Equality in Opinions': Political Opinion in Intimate Partner Violence Claims' (2024) 36(1–2) IJRL 123.

Ballin S, 'Four Challenges, Three Identities and a Double Movement in Asylum Law: Queering the 'Particular Social Group' after *Mx M* (2023) 49(1) Australian Fem L J 141.

Baranowska G, 'Exposing Covert Border Enforcement: Why Failing to Shift the Burden of Proof in Pushback Cases is Wrong' (2023) 4(4) ECHR L Rev 473.

Baumgärtel M and Ganty S, 'On the Basis of Migratory Vulnerability: Augmenting Article 14 of the European Convention on Human Rights in the Context of Migration' (2024) 20(1) Int JLC 92.

Benslama-Dabdoub M, 'Epistemic Violence and Colonial Legacies in the Representation of Refugee Women: Contesting Narratives of Vulnerability and Victimhood' (2024) 20(1) Int JLC 54.

Bernardini L, '*HM and Others v Hungary*: Immigration Detention, Burden of Proof and Principle of Necessity: Weakening Safeguards at the Borders?' (*Strasbourg Observers*, 19 August 2022) <https://strasbourgobservers.com/2022/08/19/h-m-and-others-v-hungary-immigration-detention-burden-of-proof-and-principle-of-necessity-weakeaning-safeguards-at-the-borders/> accessed 15 August 2024.

Cheikh Ali H, Querton C and Soulard E, *Gender Related Asylum Claims in Europe: Comparative Analysis of Law, Policies and Practice Focusing on Women in Nine EU Member States* (European Parliament 2012) <www.europarl.europa.eu/RegData/etudes/etudes/join/2012/462481/IPOL-FEMM_ET(2012)462481_EN.pdf> accessed 30 March 2024.

Crenshaw K, 'Mapping the Margins: Intersectionality, Identity Politics and Violence Against Women of Colour' (1991) 43(6) Stan L Rev 1241.

Danisi C and others, *Queering Asylum in Europe: Legal and Social Experiences of Seeking International Protection on Grounds of Sexual Orientation and Gender Identity* (Springer 2021).

Dauvergne C, 'Women in Refugee Jurisprudence' in Costello C, Foster M, and McAdam J (eds), *The Oxford Handbook of International Refugee Law* (OUP 2021).

Dauvergne C and Lindy H, 'Excluding Women' (2019) 31(1) IJRL L 1.

242 Lambert Abdelgawad (n 125) 20.

243 *Khan* (n 126) dissenting opinion of Judge Sajó.

Davis L, 'Gay Asylum Seekers European Court of Human Rights (Third Section): Judgment of 17 November 2020' (2021) 2 EHRLR 218.

Delaney EF, 'Analysing Avoidance: Judicial Strategy in Comparative Perspective' (2016) 1 Duke L J 66.

Eckert G, 'Caught in Limbo: The Precarious (Legal) Situation of Non-Removable Migrants Stranded in Europe' (2021) 35(3) JIANL 252.

El-Enany N, 'On Pragmatism and Legal Idolatry: Fortress Europe and the Desertion of the Refugee' (2015) 22 Intl J Minority and Group Rts 7.

Emmenegger P and Stigwall K, 'Women-Friendliness in European Asylum Policies: The Role of Women's Political Representation and Opposition to Non-EU Immigration' (2019) 52(9) Comp Pol Stud 1293.

Ferreira N, 'An Exercise in Detachment: The Council of Europe and Sexual Minority Asylum Claims' in Mole RCM (ed), *Queer Migration and Asylum in Europe* (UCL Press 2021).

Fineman M, 'The Vulnerable Subject: Anchoring Equality in the Human Condition' (2008) 20(1) Yale J L Fem 1.

Freedman J, *Gendering the International Asylum and Refugee Debate* (2nd edn, Palgrave Macmillan 2015).

Freedman J, 'Women's Right to Asylum: Protecting the Rights of Female Asylum Seekers in Europe?' (2008) 9 Hum Rts Rev 413.

Ganty S, 'Poverty as Misrecognition: What Role for Antidiscrimination Law in Europe?' (2021) 21(4) HRL Rev 962.

Gifani N, 'The Code of Gender in Judgments of the European Court of Human Rights: The Case of Traditional Harmful Practice' (2016) 10(2) Helsinki L Rev 12 <https://journal.fi/helsinkilawreview/article/view/74533> accessed 31 March 2024.

Ginés Martín D, 'In Limbo: Divergent Conceptualisations of Ill-treatment by European Courts and the Creation of Non-removable Migrants' (2021) 9(2) Eur Papers 1173.

Glas LR, 'Changes in the Procedural Practice of the European Court of Human Rights: Consequences for the Convention System and Lessons to be Drawn' (2014) 14 HRL Rev 671.

Helfer LR and Ryan C, 'LGBT Rights as Mega-Politics: Litigating before the ECtHR' (2021) 84 LCP 59.

Helfer LR and Voeten E, 'International Courts as Agents of Legal Change: Evidence from LGBT Rights in Europe' (2014) 68(1) Intl Org 77.

Honkala N, ''She, Of Course, Holds No Political Opinions': Gendered Political Opinion Ground in Women's Forced Marriage Asylum Claims' (2017) 26 Social and L Stud 166.

Hudson B, 'Asylum Marginalisation Renewed: 'Vulnerability Backsliding' at the European Court of Human Rights' (2024) 20 Int JLC 16.

Jakulevičienė L and Biekša L, 'Trends in The Qualification of Asylum Claims Related to Gender-Based Violence Under International and European Law' (2021) 26(5) IJHR 833.

Kapur R, 'The Tragedy of Victimisation Rhetoric: Resurrecting the "Native" Subject in International/Postcolonial Feminist Legal Politics' (2002) 15 Harv Hum Rts J 1.

Karagiannopoulou C, Tastsoglou E and Petrinioti S, 'Gender and Asylum Seeking in a European Borderland: Intersectional Discriminations and "Lessened" Citizenship' (2024) 40(1) Refuge 1. doi:10.25071/1920-7336.41162.

Kaya H, 'Afghan Women Are Under Threat from the Taliban: A Great Test of the Turkish Government and the Courts (2024) 36(1–2) IJRL 6.

Kim SY, '*Les Vulnérables*: Evaluating the Vulnerability Criterion in Article 14 Cases by the European Court of Human Rights' (2021) 41(4) LS 617.

Lambert Abdelgawad E, 'The Practice of the European Court of Human Rights When Striking Out Applications' (2018) 36(1) NQHR 7.

Middelburg A and Balta A, 'Female Genital Mutilation/Cutting as a Ground for Asylum in Europe' (2016) 28(3) IJRL 416.

Moreno-Lax V and Vavoula N, 'Vulnerability's Legal Life: An Ambivalent Force of Migration Governance' (2024) 20(1) Int JLC 1.
Querton C, 'Non-State Actors of Protection and the Sliding Scale of Protection for Refugee Women' (2022) 41(3) Refugee Survey Q 444.
Reyhani A-N and Golmohammadi G, 'The Limits of Static Interests: Appreciating Asylum Seekers' Contributions to a Country's Economy in Article 8 ECHR Adjudication on Expulsion' (2021) 33(1) IJRL 3.
Roels L, 'Rape Myths in the European Court of Human Rights' Non-Refoulement Case Law on Sexual and Gender-Based Violence' (2024) 36(1–2) IJRL 77.
Singer D, 'Falling at Each Hurdle: Assessing the Credibility of Women's Asylum Claims in Europe' in Arbel E, Dauvergne C, and Millbank J (eds), *Gender in Refugee Law: From Margins to the Centre* (Routledge 2014).
Spijkerboer T, 'Gender, Sexuality, Asylum and European Human Rights' (2018) 29 Law Critique 221.
Spijkerboer T, 'Stereotyping and Acceleration: Gender, Procedural Acceleration and Marginalised Judicial Review in the Dutch Asylum System' in Noll G (ed), *Proof, Evidentiary Assessment and Credibility in Asylum Procedures* (Martinus Nijhoff 2005).
Viljanen J and Heiskanen HE, 'The European Court of Human Rights: A Guardian of Minimum Standards in the Context of Immigration' (2016) 34(2) NQHR 174.
Warin C, 'Gender in EU Asylum Law: The Istanbul Convention as a Game Changer?' (2024) 36(1–2) IJRL 93.
Welfens N, ''Promising Victimhood': Contrasting Deservingness Requirements in Refugee Resettlement' (2023) 49(5) J Ethnic and Migration Stud 1103.
Wessels J, 'The Boundaries of Universality: Migrant Women and Domestic Violence Before the Strasbourg Court' (2019) 37(4) NQHR 336.
Wessels J, *The Concealment Controversy: Sexual Orientation, Discretion Reasoning and the Scope of Refugee Protection* (CUP 2021).
Wieland R and Alessi EJ, 'Do the Challenges of LGBTQ Asylum Applicants Under Dublin Register with the European Court of Human Rights?' (2021) 30(3) Social and L Stud 405.

7 Gendering Family Reunification Case Law

7.1 Introduction

This chapter focuses on the family reunification jurisprudence of the European Court of Human Rights (ECtHR), using an intersectional feminist lens. Even though in its case law,[1] the ECtHR repeatedly highlights the fact that the European Convention on Human Rights[2] (ECHR) does not guarantee the right of a non-national to enter or settle in a particular country, the jurisprudence of the Court has had a profound impact on family reunification in Europe. In all its cases concerning admission of non-nationals,[3] the Court considers it important to stress the principle established in customary international law according to which a State is entitled, subject to its international obligations, to control the entry of non-nationals into its territory and their residence there.[4] Although the right to family reunification is the only exception to the absence of the right to enter a country, the right to family reunification is not an unconditional right.[5] Consequently, the Court grants States a wide margin in relation to their immigration policies.[6] The Court has long maintained a restrictive approach to the admission of non-nationals in the Council of Europe (CoE) for the purpose of family reunification.

1 See eg *Pajić v Croatia* App no 68453/13 (ECtHR, 23 February 2016), para 79.
2 European Convention for the Protection of Human Rights and Fundamental Freedoms (European Convention on Human Rights, as amended).
3 Dividing individuals based on their European and non-European ethnicity, race or religion is argued to be based on colonial ideas about the world. Therefore, reference is made to 'nationals' and 'non-nationals' of a State. See eg Alana Lentin, 'Europe and the Silence About Race' (2008) 11(4) Eur J Social Theory 487.
4 See eg *MA v Denmark* App no 6697/18 (ECtHR, 9 July 2021), para 131.
5 Jean-Baptiste Farcy, 'Equality in Immigration Law: An Impossible Quest?' (2020) 20(4) HRL Rev 725, 741. For instance, CoE States have no obligation to grant family reunification to individuals who enjoy temporary protection status and whose family members remain outside the territory of the State. See eg Hélène Lambert, 'Family Unity in Migration Law: The Evolution of A More Unified Approach in Europe' in Vincent Chetail and Celine Bauloz (eds), *Research Handbook on International Law and Migration* (Edward Elgar 2014); Patrycja Dabrowska-Klosinska, 'The Right to Family Reunion vs Integration Conditions for Third-Country Nationals' (2018) 20(3) EJML 251. Due to constrains of space, cases concerning family reunification for refugees and those who hold temporary protection status are excluded from the scope of this chapter.
6 Farcy (n 5).

DOI: 10.4324/9781003435099-7

The Court's initial approach was developed in the 1985 landmark judgment in *Abdulaziz, Cabales, and Balkandali v UK*,[7] which saw the Court apply a legal test according to which in cases where family reunification was available outside the respondent State, the family members should develop their family life in the country of origin.[8] In *Abdulaziz*, the UK denied family reunification with the husbands of three non-national women who were permanent residents in the UK. The Court considered whether the married couples could enjoy their right to family life in the women's countries of origin. As the Court found that no real obstacles existed for family reunification outside the UK, it concluded that the UK did not violate Article 8 ECHR (Right to respect for private and family life).[9] It did, however, find that the UK unjustifiably favoured settled migrant men in its family reunification policy, making it easier for men to bring their wives to the UK in a violation of Article 8 in conjunction with Article 14 ECHR. Despite the finding of gender discrimination, the CoE States have long enacted national migration policies that assume that the primary migrant is typically a man who is migrating to take up employment or seeking employment opportunities in the territory of the State to support his family.[10]

The 1988 judgment in *Berrehab v Netherlands*[11] seems to have created conditions for recognising the residence rights of a non-national parent whose children have acquired the nationality of the respondent State at birth. In this case, the Court found that the expulsion of a Moroccan citizen, Mr Abdellah Berrehab, after his divorce from his Dutch wife with whom he had a minor Dutch national daughter, on the sole reason that the couple no longer lived together violated Article 8. The case is significant because before this, the Court had rejected similar cases as inadmissible for almost three decades.[12] Scholars have noted that the Court essentially allowed a non-settled migrant to remain in the territory of the State by regularising his stay, while the States had never intended to extend the protective reach of the ECHR to migrants.[13] *Berrehab* did not, however, make it any easier for

7 *Abdulaziz, Cabales, and Balkandali v UK* App nos 9214/80, 9473/81, and 9474/81 (ECtHR, 28 May 1985).

8 Matteo Bottero, 'Integration (of Immigrants) in the European Courts' Jurisprudence: Supporting a Pluralist and Rights-Based Paradigm'? (2023) 24(4) J Intl Migration & Integration 1719, 1732.

9 As the UK government was required to change its family reunification legislation, it made family reunification with spouses and fiancés virtually impossible for the settled non-white Commonwealth citizens, regardless of their gender. See eg Dia Anagnostou, 'Does European Human Rights Law Matter? Implementation and Domestic Impact of Strasbourg Court Judgments on Minority-Related Policies' (2010) 14(5) IJHR 721, 733.

10 Eleanor Morris, 'Family Reunification and Integration Policy in the EU: Where Are the Women?' (2015) 16 Int Migration & Integration 639, 640.

11 See eg *Berrehab v Netherlands* [1989] 11 EHRR 322, para 29.

12 Stefan Salomon, 'Citizenship and Unauthorised Migration: A Dialectical Relationship' (2020) 83(3) MLR 583, 601.

13 ibid 602 referring to Daniel Thym, 'Respect for Private and Family Life under Article 8 ECHR in Immigration Cases: A Human Right to Regularize Illegal Stay?' (2008) 57 Intl & Comp L Q 87,103; Marie-Bénédicte Dembour, *When Humans Become Migrants: Study of the European Court of Human Rights with an Inter-American Counterpoint* (OUP 2015).

non-national parents to be reunited with their children who had stayed behind in the parent's country of origin.

The 2001 judgment in *Şen v Netherlands*,[14] marked a major milestone in the admission and residence of non-national family members. It centred on the admission to the Netherlands of Sinem Şen, a nine-year-old daughter of a Turkish couple with legal right to residence in the Netherlands.[15] The ECtHR unanimously determined that the Netherlands violated Article 8. While the Court repeated the criteria applied in its earlier inadmissible decisions, it distinguished the facts of *Şen* from the previous decisions as her parents had had two minor children in the Netherlands who were Dutch citizens.[16] The Court found that requiring the entire family to move to Türkiye to develop family life with the family's eldest daughter was impossible for two principal reasons; namely because her parents had been legally residing in the Netherlands for several years, and her two siblings had no links with Türkiye.[17] In his separate opinion, Judge Riza Türmen indicated that the presence of the family's two younger children in the Netherlands was the decisive factor in *Şen*.[18]

However, even after *Berrehab* and *Şen*, States have retained a restrictive approach to family reunification. Several inadmissible complaints against the Netherlands concerning family reunification applications submitted by non-national parents were often refused on the grounds that the effective family bond between the child and their parents were broken.[19] Although the case law analysis in this chapter highlights the centrality of children in family reunification cases, there are some conditions to this. The presence of children with the nationality of the respondent State has, indeed, emerged as a significant factor that restricts the States' margin of appreciation in the matters relating to the entry and residence of non-national family members in more recent case law. However, the Court's approach is not entirely consistent, even though it considers the best interests of the child and children's rights as important. It has, in fact, stated that in cases involving minors, a broad European consensus supports the idea that the best interests of a child must be afforded significant weight, even if these interests alone are not decisive.[20] Therefore, stating that the presence of minor children with the nationality of the State always obliges the CoE State to allow family reunification, or that it prevents the State from deporting the non-national parent, is an oversimplification. The issue depends on the individual circumstances of the case. Such a piecemeal

14 *Şen v Netherlands* App no 31465/96 (ECtHR, 21 December 2001).

15 ibid.

16 *Şen* (n 14) paras 36 and 40. See also Sarah van Walsum, 'Against All Odds: How Single and Divorced Migrant Mothers Were Eventually Able to Claim Their Right to Respect for Family Life' (2009) EJML 295, 302.

17 *Şen* (n 14) para 40.

18 van Walsum (n 16) 302.

19 Fore detailed commentary, see van Walsum (n 16) 302.

20 *MA* (n 4) para 133.

approach is likely to influence the progressive protection of the rights of children and non-national women in migration case law.[21]

It is worth noting that although the countries, which are member States of both the CoE and the European Union (EU), are under the supervision of the ECtHR, their immigration legislation is influenced by the EU.[22] This has meant that these States' margin of appreciation in the area of family reunification is dependent on their EU membership. The Court's jurisprudence in this area implies that the Court allows respondent States a wider margin of appreciation in cases when the respondent State is not an EU Member State as in the case of Switzerland and Norway. This is because EU law obligations under the EU Citizens Directive[23] limit EU Member States' discretion regarding the admission and right of residence of EU citizens and their family members in their territory.[24] While examining the similarities between the ECtHR's approach to family reunification and that of the Court of Justice of the European Union (CJEU) is outside this chapter, the latter court has established that the principle of free movement applies to family members of EU citizens, including same-sex partners, under EU law.[25] The applicability of free movement rights to same-sex couples was confirmed in the CJEU's 2018 judgment in *Coman*.[26] Therefore, the two Courts' jurisdictions have some considerable overlap. Their on-going judicial dialogue has resulted in considerable convergence in areas where their jurisdictions overlap, including family reunification law.[27]

This chapter is structured the following way. Section 7.2 explains the general principles governing family reunification as established in the case law of the ECtHR. Section 7.3 covers the types of family reunification cases that are the most relevant for the purposes of this chapter. Section 7.4 analyses the Court's engagement with family reunification rights of same-sex couples, and Section 7.5 provides a conclusion.

7.2 General Principles on Family Reunification

The Court's family reunification jurisprudence revolves around the questions of how the protection of family life should be reconciled with immigration control; whether the refusal to grant family reunification is contradictory to Article 8

21 Jukka Viljanen and Heta-Elena Heiskanen, 'The European Court of Human Rights: A Guardian of Minimum Standards in the Context of Immigration' (2016) 34(2) NQHR 174, 178.

22 ibid 182.

23 Directive 2004/38/EC of 29 April 2004 on the right of citizens of the Union and their family members to move and reside freely within the territory of the Member States OJ [2004] L158/77.

24 Heli Askola, '(No) Migrating for Family Care in Later Life: *Senchishak v Finland*, Older Parents and Family Reunification' (2016) 18 EJML 351.

25 For commentary, see eg Alina Tryfonidou, 'The ECJ Recognises the Right of Same-Sex Spouses to Move Freely Between EU Member States: The *Coman* Ruling' (2019) 44(5) EL Rev 663.

26 Case C-673/16 *Coman and Others* ECLI:EU:C:2018:385.

27 Paolo Pinto de Albuquerque and Hyun-Soo Lim, 'The Cross-Fertilisation between the Court of Justice of the European Union and the European Court of Human Rights: Reframing the Discussion on Brexit' (2018) 6 EHRLR 567.

ECHR, and the extent of the State's obligations to admit to its territory relatives of non-nationals residing there.[28] The Court has summarised the general principles concerning family reunification in its case law.[29] Generally, it has been prepared to find that the respondent State has a positive obligation to grant family reunification when some of the following five conditions are fulfilled. First, the non-national is a settled migrant or has strong ties with the respondent State.[30] Second, family life existed at the time when the non-national secured settled status in the State.[31] Third, both the settled non-national requesting family reunification, and the family member concerned, are already staying in the State.[32] Fourth, children are involved.[33] Fifth, insurmountable or major obstacles exist in the way of the family living in the country of origin.[34]

In the absence of a cross-cultural definition of the term family in the Convention, CoE States have adopted a narrow approach in order to seek to limit family migration rights to a couple and their minor children, where possible.[35] This means that much of the case law with successful outcomes focuses on the traditional nuclear family.[36] Lambert has argued that as the case law in the context of Article 8 is based on the existence or non-existence of strong or close personal ties between individuals, the ECtHR uses a wide definition of the family, which includes children, spouses, registered, and unmarried partners.[37] Therefore, it could be expected that the Court's understanding of families is wider than a married opposite-sex couple with genetic children.[38] Strong personal ties are recognised to exist even in situations when the family relationship has broken down due to the dissolution of a marriage or where one of the parents no longer lives with their children.[39] Although the Court has recognised that family ties between a child and their parent may only be broken in exceptional circumstances, its inadmissible decisions issued between 1996 and 2005 indicate otherwise. These decisions concern the refusal of

28 Helena Wray, *Article 8 ECHR, Family Reunification and the UK's Supreme Court Family Matters?* (Bloomsbury 2023).

29 *MA* (n 4).

30 See eg *Butt v Norway* App no 47017/09 (ECtHR, 4 December 2012), paras 76 and 87.

31 See eg *Berrehab* (n 11).

32 ibid para 29.

33 See eg *Rodrigues da Silva and Hoogkamer v Netherlands* [2007] 44 EHRR, para 44; *Nunez v Norway* App no 55597/09 (ECtHR, 28 June 2011), para 84; *Jeunesse v Netherlands* [2015] 60 EHRR 17 paras 119–120.

34 See eg *Şen* (n 14) para 40; *El Ghatet v Switzerland* App no 56971/10 (ECtHR, 8 November 2016), para 49.

35 Askola (n 24) 356.

36 Lambert (n 5).

37 Mark Klaassen, 'Between Facts and Norms: Testing Compliance with Article 8 ECHR in Immigration Cases' (2019) 37(2) NQHR 157.

38 Alice Margaria, 'Trans Men Giving Birth and Reflections on Fatherhood: What to Expect?' (2020) 34(3) IJLPF 225, 234.

39 Lambert (n 5). However, when the family members do not a have genetic link, the case law concerning second parent adoption and cross-border surrogacy demonstrates that the Courts do not usually find a violation of Article 8 on grounds of right to family life. See ch 4.

the Netherlands to grant family reunification with the children of non-national parents residing on its territory.[40] The ECtHR consistently found that the family bond between a non-national parent residing in the Netherlands and their minor children, who remained in the country of origin, had ceased to exist.[41] Additionally, the 2021 inadmissible decision in *Jallow v Norway*[42] reveals that more than a genetic link is needed to recognise the right to family reunification where a parent-child relationship has not had a chance to develop due to residence in different countries. In *Jallow*, the ECtHR reiterated that as a rule, cohabitation was a requirement for the recognition of a relationship amounting to family life under Article 8. The case concerned family reunification between a genetic father, Mr Ebrima Pa Jallow, who lived in the Gambia, and his 10-year-old son, G, who resided in Norway with Mr Jallow's ex-wife, Ms KJ. Mr Jallow applied for family reunification with G after Ms KJ's death.[43] The Court stated that a biological kinship between a parent and a child alone, without any further legal or factual elements indicating the existence of a close personal relationship, was insufficient to attract the protection of Article 8.[44] Although other factors may serve to demonstrate that a relationship had sufficient constancy to create *de facto* family ties,[45] Mr Jallow's contact with G was limited. He had met G only once when the latter was four and visited the Gambia on a two-week holiday.[46] The Court found Mr Jallow's complaint manifestly ill-founded.[47]

In cases where the issue concerns family reunification between family members outside the nuclear family, such as, parents of adult children, their siblings, and family members of the third degree and more, the Court generally holds that further elements of dependency must exist involving more than the normal emotional ties.[48] In most family reunification cases, a relationship between extended family members, such as, a niece and an aunt can constitute family life only in exceptional circumstances.[49] However, the Court has not insisted on further elements of

40 *Ahmut v Netherlands* App no 21702/93 (ECtHR, 28 November 1996) (The refusal of the nine-year-old son living in Morocco to join his father in the Netherlands after his mother died did not violate art 8).

41 *Knel and Veira v Netherlands* App no 39003/97 (ECtHR, 5 September 2000); *PR v Netherlands* App no 39391/98 (ECtHR, 7 November 2000); *IM v Netherlands* App no 41226/98 (ECtHR, 25 March 2003); *Chandra and Other v Netherlands* App no 53102/99 (ECtHR, 13 May 2003); *Ramos Andrade v Netherlands* App no 53675/00 (ECtHR, 6 July 2004); *Benamar and Others v Netherlands* App no 43786/04 (ECtHR, 5 April 2005). See also Fulvia Staiano, 'Good Mothers, Bad Mothers: Transnational Mothering in the European Court of Human Rights' Case Law' (2013) 15 EJML 155, 159.

42 *Jallow v Norway* App no 36516/19 (ECtHR, 2 December 2021).

43 ibid para 74.

44 ibid.

45 ibid.

46 ibid.

47 ibid.

48 *Senchishak v Finland* App no 5049/12 (ECHR, 18 November 2014) (The Court found no violation of the rights under art 3 of a Russian mother was not allowed to remain in Finland with her adult daughter who was a naturalised Finnish citizen).

49 *Butt* (n 30).

dependency in cases concerning young adults, who still live with their parents and do not yet have a family of their own.[50]

The ECtHR has also addressed the issue when States are not under a positive obligation to grant family reunification. Factors that may weigh in favour of exclusion include a history of breaches of immigration law or considerations of public order.[51] Additionally, where the family members are aware that one person's immigration status was precarious when they developed family ties, the removal of the non-national will constitute a violation of Article 8 only where the circumstances of a case are exceptional.[52] Consequently, the State is under an obligation to allow the residence in limited instances.[53] Scholars have criticised the Court for using terms, such as, precarious immigration status as anyone who is on a temporary work visa or a student visa, or is an asylum seeker awaiting the decision on their asylum application can be considered to have a precarious immigration status.[54] Additionally, it is often challenging for a case to meet the threshold of the requirement that the circumstances of the case should be exceptional.[55]

7.3 Admission and Residence

Existing literature in the field of legal and socio-political studies has examined the gendered impact of the Court's family reunification case law under Article 8.[56] Previous case law analyses have focused on three specific areas, including the right to family life as a ground for challenging an expulsion of a non-national parent; spousal family reunification, and single and divorced migrant parents' access to family reunification with their children born in the country of origin.[57] Article 8 is relevant in the context of complaints concerning the admission, expulsion, and residence of a non-national.[58] It has been argued that in contrast to cases concerning expulsion of a settled or irregular migrant, the situation in family reunification cases in what Klaassen has characterised as cases concerning solely the question of whether a non-national should be admitted to the territory of the State typically involves the right

50 See eg *Yesthla v Netherlands* App no 37115/11 (ECtHR, 15 January 2019), para 32 (The Court found no violation of the rights of naturalised Dutch citizen, Ms Emabet Yeshtla, under art 8 when her adult son, who was Ethiopian, could not obtain a family reunification in the Netherlands to live with her).
51 *MA* (n 4) para 132.
52 For cases concerning exceptional circumstances, see eg *da Silva* (n 33) para 39; *Jeunesse* (n 33) para 108.
53 Klaassen (n 37) 165.
54 Salomon (n 12) 605.
55 ibid 604. See also Klaassen (n 37) 165.
56 Staiano (n 41) 158.
57 See eg Betty de Hart, 'Love Thy Neighbour: Family Reunification and the Rights of Insiders' (2009) 11 EJML 235; van Walsum (n 16).
58 Adel-Naim Reyhani and Gloria Golmohammadi, 'The Limits of Static Interests: Appreciating Asylum Seekers' Contributions to a Country's Economy in Article 8 ECHR Adjudication on Expulsion' (2021) 33 (1) IJRL Law 3.

of residence in and admission to the territory of the CoE State.[59] In the latter types of cases, the family has already been separated through the immigration of one or both of the parents.[60] Therefore, the question for the Court in family reunification cases is often whether the respondent State is under a positive obligation to allow the entry of the non-national family member in order for the family to develop or strengthen their family life.[61] However, the ECtHR has decided only a handful of complaints where the case concerns admission such as *Şen*.[62]

There are views that the expulsion of a non-national, on the other hand, does not strictly concern family reunification, unless the ECtHR considers that nothing prevents the other family members from relocating to the country of origin of non-national parent, partner, or spouse subject to the expulsion measure, to develop or strengthen family life there.[63] In its assessment of whether the expulsion of a non-national amounts to a violation of Article 8, the ECtHR balances multiple factors, such as the length of the family relationship; the duration of residence; the extent to which family life would be effectively ruptured; past breaches of immigration law; knowledge of precarious immigration status; whether there are children in the marriage, and if so, on the interests and well-being of the children.[64] Viljanen and Heiskanen argue that national authorities do not always assess the personal circumstances of the individual in expulsion cases, but the authorities' decision may have been made as a result of the CoE State's overall immigration policy which is aimed at restricting net migration.[65] They further argue that when there is evidence that national authorities' decisions concerning immigration are arbitrary, the ECtHR is willing to shift the burden of proof onto the government.[66]

Salomon is of the opinion that the States' restrictive migration policies often impact on racialised individuals, and these policies habitually, although not in every case, create intersecting inequalities on grounds of the individuals' class and gender.[67] Salomon notes that most of the existing legal scholarship remains silent on the intrusion of immigration law into the right to family life of the national whose partner or spouse is subject to expulsion.[68] This highlights an important omission both in the scholarly literature and the Court's jurisprudence. According to him, in cases concerning expulsion, the ECtHR does not engage in a substantive assessment of the interests of the family member whose spouse or partner is subject to an expulsion order.[69] Of the several factors considered by the Court in these

59 Claire Fenton-Glynn, *Children and the European Court of Human Rights* (OUP 2020). See also Klaassen (n 37) 162.
60 Fenton-Glynn (n 59).
61 ibid.
62 Klaassen (n 37) 162.
63 ibid.
64 See eg *da Silva* (n 33) para 39.
65 Viljanen and Heiskanen (n 21) 193.
66 ibid 192–193.
67 Salomon (n 12) 587.
68 ibid 601–602.
69 ibid 603.

cases, only two factors potentially make allowances for the interests of that family member.[70] The Court may usually consider whether the family member, who is often a national of the respondent State, would face any difficulties in the country of origin of their non-national spouse or partner subject to the expulsion measures if they had to follow the latter there, and whether the national of the respondent State was aware of the precarious immigration status of their spouse or partner.[71] Salomon further argues that expulsion exacerbates structurally disadvantaged legal positions of non-white family members who are nationals of the CoE State as they are more likely to encounter restrictions on family life by the possible expulsion of their spouses or partners.[72] They may also be affected by the reduction of social benefits for nationals that aim to deter irregular migration.[73] This may well mean that the partner or spouse who holds the nationality of the respondent State is forced to follow their partner or spouse to the country of origin of the latter, not only because they wish to continue to maintain a family life, but because of the family's changed economic situation. Therefore, the ECtHR's role in this area is critical due to its ability to hold governments accountable for a variety of arbitrary measures taken against non-national family members in their territory, such as, immigration detention, exclusion from social benefits, or administrative or penal sanctions for irregular stay.[74]

The next three sections utilise the framework of Klaassen, who has categorised family reunification cases of the ECtHR into three types depending on so-called compliance tests used by the Court to determine of whether the respondent State complies with its obligations under Article 8.[75] The first category of cases includes the determination whether the State is under a positive obligation to allow for the entry and residence of the non-national seeking family residence permit when the State has not yet allowed their entry or residence. Second, the Court determines whether the State is under a negative obligation to refrain from interfering with Article 8 when it seeks to terminate the lawful residence of a settled migrant. The third category involves cases which *de facto* concern the termination of residence on the territory of the State of a person who has not been granted the right of entry or residence.

The next sections analyse, through an intersectional feminist lens, the case law concerning women who have applied for family residency permits either for themselves or for their minor children (Section 7.3.1) and women who are subject to an expulsion order. The analysis in Section 7.3.2 focuses on three cases concerning

70 ibid. See also de Hart, 'Love Thy Neighbour' (n 57) 247.

71 Salomon (n 12) 603.

72 ibid 611.

73 ibid.

74 For arguments concerning the role of the regional courts to hold national governments into account, see Matilda Gillis, 'Can We Talk? The Application of the Public Law Democratic Dialogue Model to the Interactions between Domestic Legislatures and the European Courts' (2022) 23 German LJ 56.

75 See Klaassen (n 37) 157.

the expulsion of a settled migrant mother, and the analysis in Section 7.3.3. focuses on cases concerning an expulsion of a non-settled migrant woman. An additional dimension of family reunification for same-sex couples is discussed in Section 7.4. Strikingly, most of the cases in Section 7.3.3 concern a situation where the individual has entered a CoE State without appropriate authorisation or has overstayed a short-term visa.[76] It is also worth noting that surprisingly, the cases that concern an irregular stay of a mother of a minor child who holds the nationality of the CoE State have been the most successful in persuading the ECtHR overall. This chapter will deal with cases concerning these issues in turn.

7.3.1 Entry and Residence of a Non-National

The complaints concerning the entry and residence of a non-national family member are often argued to be the most relevant for the purposes of family reunification. However, many of these cases have often been unsuccessful. In many cases, the minor child with whom their parents seek family reunification has arrived in the CoE State using a temporary visa. The Court is unlikely to find a violation of Article 8 when the non-national staying in the territory of the State has limited ties to the State due to having stayed in there for a short time or having stayed there irregularly.[77] Even if the Court does not find an interference with the right to respect for family life of the family members under Article 8, it nevertheless seeks to ascertain whether the State is under a positive obligation to allow for the entry and residence of the minor child of the non-national parent.[78] In many of these cases the Court has concluded that the family members can continue to strengthen family life outside of the respondent State because no insurmountable obstacles exist in the way of the family living in the country of origin.[79] The reasoning behind this is, that when a State has not permitted the entry or residence of a non-national child, the refusal does not interfere with established family life under Article 8 as the State has not allowed the establishment of private and family life within its territory.[80] Consequently, this does not trigger the justification test of Article 8(2).[81] The Court bases its reasoning on the right of a State to control immigration.[82]

The analysis in this section focuses on cases of parents who are seeking family reunification with their minor child born outside the territory of the CoE. In a series of complaints against the Netherlands, the non-national parents found themselves in very similar, if not identical, situations. They alleged a violation of their right to

76 Klaassen (n 37) 162.

77 This applies to individuals who enjoy temporary protection. See *MA* (n 4) para 134.

78 Klaassen (n 37) 158.

79 See eg *Gül v Switzerland* App no 23218/94 (ECtHR, 19 February 1996); *Ahmut* (n 40); *Chandra* (n 41); *Berisha v Switzerland* App no 948/12 (ECtHR, 30 July 2013); *IAA v UK* App no 25960/13, (ECtHR, 8 March 2016).

80 Klaassen (n 37) 158 and 162.

81 ibid 162.

82 ibid.

family life on the grounds of being excluded from family reunification with their children under the Dutch immigration law.[83] The national authorities' arguments centre around the position that because the parents left their children in the care of relatives or friends in their country of origin upon their emigration, the family bond was broken.[84] What is striking about these cases is that the Court's descriptions of the single mothers' decisions to migrate included explicit references to new marriages or partnerships in the Netherlands and the young children's dependence on the care of others while their mothers left them behind.[85] Staiano has argued that the mothers were portrayed as promiscuous women and bad mothers who abandoned their husbands and children while pursuing a relationship with a new partner in the Netherlands. Yet, there is a recognition in the scholarly literature focusing on the Court's jurisprudence on single mothers that gender and the lack of economic privilege make single mothers vulnerable.[86]

One of the inadmissible decisions is particularly worthy of a closer look. In its 2003 decision in *IM v Netherlands*,[87] the Court noted that Ms IM left her nearly two-year-old daughter, S, behind in Cape Verde to marry a Dutch citizen, Mr NAS, and settled in the Netherlands with him. The Court specifically noted that as her new husband did not wish that her minor daughter would travel to the Netherlands to stay with the couple, Ms IM agreed that her daughter would remain in Cape Verde.[88] Significantly, after her arrival in the Netherlands, Ms IM and her husband had a son, E, who acquired Dutch citizenship at birth.[89] By the time Ms IM applied for family reunification with her 8-year-old daughter, S, she and Mr NAS had divorced.[90] A significant issue in the case was that Ms IM mentioned the fact that her son, E, was a Dutch citizen and he maintained a regular contact with his father in her complaint to the ECtHR, but not before the national courts.[91] The ECtHR stated that it could not take this into consideration.[92] *IM* should, and could, have been a landmark case along with *Şen*. However, Ms IM was unable to convince the ECtHR that her son's presence in the Netherlands was an important argument

83 Staiano (n 41) 157.
84 See van Walsum (n 16) 308; Staiano (n 41) 157 and 160.
85 Staiano (n 41) 162–163. The Court never mentioned the age of the children when it evaluated the fathers' decisions to migrate and it described the consequence of the fathers' decisions to migrate as 'living apart' from their children, rather leaving their children behind. See, eg, *Mensah v Netherlands* App no 47042/99 (ECtHR, 9 October 2001); *Lahnifi v Netherlands* App no 39329/98 (ECtHR, 13 February 2001); *Adnane v Netherlands* App no 50568/99 (ECtHR, 6 November 2001); *Ahmut* (n 40) para 70: 'The fact of the applicants' living apart is the result of Salah Ahmut's conscious decision to settle in the Netherlands rather than remain in Morocco'.
86 See *Garib v Netherlands* App no 43494/09 (ECtHR, 6 November 2017) (A dispute concerning inability of a single mother relying on social benefits to access moderate-cost rented housing due minimum income requirements).
87 *IM* (n 41).
88 ibid.
89 van Walsum (n 16) 307.
90 ibid.
91 ibid.
92 ibid.

against the possibility of family reunification in Cape Verde.[93] What *IM* and the long line of cases before and after it demonstrate is that if the national authorities have adopted a systematic approach to limit net migration, every mistake will be used against the individuals.

The 2013 judgment in *Berisha v Switzerland*[94] concerned a family reunification request submitted by a married couple, Mr Sait Berisha and Ms Selvije Berisha, with their three minor children, who had remained in Kosovo with their grandmother. Mr Berisha obtained a permanent residence permit in Switzerland in 2005 after marrying a Swiss citizen in 2000. After the couple divorced in 2006, Mr Berisha married the mother of his three children, who was granted a five-year residence permit in Switzerland. The couple's youngest son, E, was born in Switzerland in 2010. Their application for residence permits for their three children born in Kosovo before their marriage was rejected on the grounds that the couple had not mentioned that they had three children when they entered Switzerland. The children subsequently arrived at Switzerland irregularly. The Court considered that although the children had become well integrated in Switzerland, their period of stay there was not long enough for them to have lost their solid social and linguistic ties to Kosovo. Furthermore, the couple's oldest son, R, who was 17, and their oldest daughter, L, who was 19, could be supported at a distance. Lastly, the couple were not prevented from travelling or even staying with their ten-year-old daughter, B, in Kosovo to ensure that she was provided with the necessary care and education so that her best interests as a child were safeguarded. The Court concluded that although the couple may prefer to develop their family links with their three children in Switzerland, Article 8 did not guarantee them a right to choose the most suitable place to do this. Therefore, there was no violation of Article 8.

The following two cases show how sceptically national authorities treat family reunification requests involving older women. In the first case, the issue is that an elderly mother of a naturalised Finnish citizen is expected to be able to obtain care in the country of origin with the financial assistance of her daughter, if necessary. In the second case, the age difference between a married couple when the husband was much younger than the wife caused the national authorities to question the genuineness of the relationship. The 2014 judgment in *Senchishak v Finland*[95] concerned a family reunification request between a naturalised Finnish citizen and her 72-year-old Russian mother, Ms Marina Senchishak. After suffering a stroke which left her right side paralysed, she travelled to Finland with a short-term tourist visa.[96] She unsuccessfully applied for a residence permit based on family ties to her daughter.[97] The Finnish appeal court concluded that just because Ms Senchishak's care in Russia would be more expensive than in Finland, this was not a reason to

93 ibid.
94 *Berisha* (n 79).
95 *Senchishak* (n 48).
96 ibid paras 8–9.
97 ibid para 10.

grant her a residence permit as her daughter could help her financially and could also visit her in Russia.[98] The Court concluded Ms Senchishak's deportation to Russia did not violate Article 3.[99]

In the 2017 inadmissible decision in *Schembri v Malta*,[100] the Court suspected the genuineness of the marriage between a 73-year-old Maltese national, Ms Concetta Schembri, and her 30 years younger husband, Mr S, a Pakistani citizen, who had unsuccessfully applied for asylum in Malta in 2004. The couple travelled to Italy and married there in 2008.[101] Mr S unsuccessfully applied for an entry visa to Malta at the Maltese embassy in Rome.[102] Ms Schembri claimed that he was not issued with a written decision refusing his application nor was he informed about the possibility of appeal.[103] Instead, the embassy staff suggested that he should return to Pakistan to apply for an entry visa.[104] Although Mr S returned to Pakistan, he was unable to obtain an entry visa to Malta from there.[105] The Court essentially confirmed the conclusion of the domestic courts that the couple's marriage was not genuine and did not, therefore, attract the protection of Article 8.[106]

It is remarkable that none of the cases in the analysis have been successful. Klaassen has suggested that the Court may be more willing to find that the State has a positive obligation to allow family reunification when the family member remains outside the respondent State at the time when family reunification application is made.[107] Whether that is the case remains to be seen, as *Şen* appears to be the only successful case in the area. The decision to not allow Ms IM to rely on the fact that her son was Dutch seems like a mere technicality. Cases like these highlight the significance of the specific legal expertise of the lawyers presenting individuals like Ms IM in both EU law and the ECHR because litigation under EU citizenship case law may have resulted in a different outcome. The fact that very few cases have been successful in this area is indicative of the restrictive approach adopted by the CoE States towards admission and residence of non-national children and spouses of the nationals of the CoE State or non-nationals who enjoy long-term residency rights in the State.

7.3.2 The Termination of Residence of a Settled Migrant

The cases in this section can be characterised as cases where a mother, who is subject to an expulsion measure and an accompanying re-entry ban, has a settled

98 ibid para 17.
99 ibid para 46.
100 *Schembri v Malta* App no 66297/13 (ECtHR, 19 September 2017).
101 ibid paras 7 and 9.
102 ibid.
103 ibid para 9.
104 ibid.
105 ibid para 11.
106 ibid para 52.
107 Klaassen (n 37).

migration status in the respondent State. However, they have not become nationalised after having resided there lawfully for a long time. Their children may or may not be the nationals of the respondent State. Although settled migrants with a right of residence enjoy a higher level of protection compared to non-nationals seeking entry or requesting to regularise their irregular migration status,[108] in its jurisprudence concerning expulsion of a non-national due to criminal activities, the Court has accepted that a long-term resident can be expelled when their crimes are serious.[109] It has consistently found that the expulsion does not violate the settled migrant's rights under the Article 8, even if the individual has family members, including their own parents, siblings, or children who live in the territory of the State. Even if the Court was to find that the termination of lawful residence of a non-national amounted to an interference of Article 8, this may be justifiable under Article 8(2).[110] In such cases, the Court addresses the question of whether the State seeking to determine the residency is under a negative obligation to refrain from interfering with Article 8.[111]

The ECtHR has decided three cases concerning the expulsion of a settled migrant woman after criminal convictions.[112] All three women argued that their children would be forced to leave the State territory if an expulsion order against them was enforced. In none of the cases, which focus on arguments that the rights under Article 8 will be violated by the separation from their children and spouses, has the ECtHR considered this an obstacle for expulsion or the accompanying re-entry ban, even where the child is a national of the CoE State. Although the State can lift the re-entry ban, the Court frequently sides with the State, if the State is unwilling to do so. Therefore, the jurisprudence is still very much influenced by the States' interest to control the entry and residence of non-nationals to their territory. The 1998 judgment in *Dalia v France*[113] provides an apt illustration. It concerned an Algerian national, Ms Aïcha Dalia, who had resided in France after a successful family reunification with her mother at the age of 15. She complained that her permanent exclusion from the French territory meant that her minor French national son, Karim, would be forced to leave France. She was permanently excluded from France after she was sentenced to 12 months' imprisonment for acquiring, possessing, and selling heroin.[114] Despite this she remained in France after her release from prison and married a French national.[115] Although she was expelled to Algeria in

108 ibid 158.
109 ibid.
110 Interferences must be in accordance with law, must pursue one of the legitimate aims set out in art 8(2), and must be necessary in a democratic society. The legitimate aims are national security, public safety or the economic well-being of the country, the prevention of disorder or crime, the protection of health or morals, and the protection of the rights and freedoms of others.
111 Klaassen (n 37) 158.
112 For an overview of cases concerning expulsion decisions against settled male migrants, see Bottero (n 8).
113 *Dalia v France* App no 26102/95 (ECtHR, 19 February 1998), para 52.
114 ibid para 8.
115 *Dalia* (n 113) paras 12–14.

1987, she returned to France two years later, using a temporary tourist visa.[116] She subsequently made three unsuccessful applications to have the permanent exclusion order lifted, relying on the fact that her minor son acquired French citizenship at birth.[117] Although a temporary residence permit could have been issued to her as the mother of a French national child,[118] France refused to do so. The Court concluded that as the refusal to lift her exclusion order was proportionate to the aim of prevention of drug trafficking, there was no violation of Article 8.[119]

The 2007 judgment in *Konstatinov v Netherlands*[120] concerned a temporary exclusion order imposed on a Serbian citizen of Roma origin, Ms Jadranka Konstantinov. She arrived in the Netherlands after a successful family reunification following her marriage to Mr G, who was a long-term resident in the country.[121] After the birth of their son in 1989, Ms Konstantinov was convicted on six occasions of aggravated theft and robbery and sentenced to terms of imprisonment varying from six weeks to 12 months. The Court acknowledged that a temporary exclusion order could be lifted after a limited number of years of Ms Konstantinov's residency outside of the Netherlands. However, the Dutch government was unwilling to do so. The Court adopted a strict approach towards arguments that she could not be deported because her son, who was now 18, may have to leave the territory of the State as a result. Although Ms Konstatinov attempted to rely on the fact her son had suffered from asthma since birth, the Court did not consider that this constituted a further element of dependency for her deportation to violate Article 8.

The 2024 judgment in *Wangthan v Denmark*[122] concerned an exclusion of a Thai national, Ms Karnchana Wangthan from Denmark for the period of six years. Following her marriage to a Danish man in 2017, she and her two minor children from her previous relationship were granted a family residence permit in Denmark.[123] In 2021, she was sentenced to six months' imprisonment for attempted aggravated violence against her husband and physical violence against her son.[124] Ms Wangthan complained that her expulsion and the accompanying entry ban violated Article 8 because her ability to access mental health treatment in Thailand was uncertain.[125] The Court observed that the societal considerations in favour of her expulsion outweighed the considerations against her expulsion based on her private and family life, considering the nature and seriousness of her

116 ibid para 13.
117 ibid paras 15–16 and 54.
118 ibid para 50.
119 ibid paras 54–55.
120 *Konstatinov v Netherlands* App no 16351/03 (ECtHR, 26 April 2007).
121 ibid para 6.
122 *Wangthan v Denmark* App no 51301/22 (ECtHR, 9 April 2024).
123 ibid para 5.
124 ibid para 6.
125 ibid para 8.

offences, combined with her strong ties with Thailand.[126] It further observed that as her ten- and 12-year-old children were brought up in Thailand, they would not encounter serious difficulties there, and her husband could visit her in Thailand.[127] Accordingly, there was no violation of Article 8.[128]

The Court has no qualms about allowing States to expel a woman sentenced to imprisonment, even though it ensured in *Wagnthan* that Denmark did not violate its international obligations when seeking to expel and exclude a wife of a Danish national for several years from its territory due to marital violence and violence against a child. Even though in all cases the expulsion of the mother would have led to a situation where other family members would have had to leave the territory of the State as well, the societal considerations in favour of the expulsion seemed to outweigh other considerations.

7.3.3 The **De Facto** *Termination of Residence*

The third category of cases includes a situation where the immigration status of a non-settled migrant has been precarious from the outset.[129] In the analysis, the women subject to the deportation order are either childless or they are a mother of a minor child, who holds the nationality of the respondent State, and their residence in the State is irregular. Many of the cases analysed in this section involve women who have overstayed their visa or they have entered the State with forged identity documents or without appropriate family residence permits. They may have also applied for asylum on arrival or they have married a national of the respondent State and established family life when their stay immigration status was precarious. Usually, the non-national woman complains that their expulsion would result in their family members, such as spouses and minor children, being forced to leave the CoE State of their nationality in violation of Article 8. A non-settled migrant's position in relation to the State's right to control entry, stay, and expulsion of a migrant has been argued to be very weak.[130]

The Court's approach to these types of cases has not been entirely consistent. The inadmissible decisions from the turn of the millennium demonstrate that the Court has provided a wide margin of appreciation for the States to pursue deportation of the non-national parents, both mothers and fathers, of a minor child born in the territory of the CoE State when they are deemed to have precarious migration status and may have breached immigration rules.[131] Cases after the mid-2000s suggest that the presence of the non-national mother is in the best interest of the child when the child is a national of a respondent State, regardless whether the State is an

126 ibid para 9.
127 ibid paras 29–30.
128 ibid para 34.
129 Klaassen (n 37).
130 Reyhani and Golmohammadi (n 58) 10.
131 See eg *Theodora Ajayi and Others v UK* App no 27663/95 (ECtHR, 22 June 1999); *Solomon v Netherlands* App no 44328/98 (ECtHR, 5 September 2000).

EU Member State or not, when the mother has overstayed the territory of the State without a valid residence permit.[132] In contrast, the Court has not considered that the absence of a non-national father in a similar situation would cause some form of hardship for the spouses and children who are likely to remain in the CoE State, despite the fact that their spouses would effectively become single parents as the fathers would be absent during the early years of their children's lives.[133]

De Hart argued in 2015 that in comparison with non-settled migrant fathers whose children are nationals of the respondent State, non-settled migrant mothers in a similar situation are more likely to be granted residence in CoE States, even where they may have a history of breaches of immigration rules.[134] According to her, the Court's case law demonstrates that the demands of motherhood override the State's interests to restrict migration.[135] Yet, she did not make the argument about the impact of these decisions on the spouses of the non-settled migrant men who turn into single mothers overnight as a result of the Court's judgments. This highlights the vulnerability of the spouses or partners who must raise the couple's children as a single parent when the non-national spouse or partner is deported, even though the couple have children who are nationals of the respondent State.

The following judgments and decisions delivered between 1999 and 2022 involving non-settled migrant mothers demonstrate the Court's varying approach. In some of these cases the Court has addressed exceptional circumstances where it has been prepared to find that the State has a positive obligation to grant family reunification.[136] This is so, even if a non-national parent has overstayed their temporary tourist visa or entered the State using a forged passport. In the 1999 inadmissible decision in *Theodora Ajayi and Others v UK*,[137] the Nigerian wife of a British man was subject to an expulsion order for having breached her visa conditions by working contrary to immigration rules. Even though she gave birth to three children, who became British citizens at birth, the UK authorities were not prepared to revoke the deportation order against her until the entire family relocated to Ireland for a period while her husband worked there for a little over a year. Upon the family's return to the UK, the expulsion order was finally withdrawn, and his wife was granted a residence permit in the UK as a family member of an EU citizen. The impact of the EU free movement law on family reunification cases

132 *da Silva* (n 33); *Jeunesse* (n 33); *Nunez* (n 33).

133 See eg *Darren Omoregie and Others v Norway* App no 265/07 (ECtHR, 31 July 2008); *Antwi and Others v Norway* App no 26940/10 (ECtHR, 14 February 2012).

134 Betty de Hart, 'Superdads: Migrant Fathers' Right to Family Life before the European Court of Human Rights' (2015) 18 Man and Masculinities 448, 464.

135 ibid. See eg *Berrehab* (n 11); *Bghial El Hach Houch v Finland* App no 61558/00 (ECtHR, 21 May 2002); *Yousef v Netherlands* App no 33711/96 (ECtHR 5 November 2002); *Useinov v Netherlands* App no 61292/00 (ECtHR, 11 April 2006); *Omoregie* (n 133); *Anayo v Germany* App no 20578/07 (ECtHR 21 December 2010); *Antwi* (n 133).

136 *MA* (n 4) para 134.

137 *Ajayi* (n 131).

in the countries which are Member States of both the EU and the CoE is visible in *Ajayi*, even though the case was decided by the ECtHR.[138]

In its landmark 2006 judgment concerning a parent of a minor child born in the Netherlands in *Rodrigues da Silva and Hoogkamer v Netherlands*,[139] the Court developed a test to determine whether a non-national, who remained in the CoE State without a right of residence for a considerable time, should be allowed to remain there based on Article 8.[140] The case concerned a Brazilian national, Ms Solange Rodrigues da Silva, who cohabited there with her unmarried partner, Mr Daniël Hoogkamer. Her minor son from her previous relationship, five-year-old Carlos, joined the couple who subsequently had a daughter, Rachael, who obtained Dutch nationality at birth.[141] After the couple's relationship ended, Mr Hoogkamer was granted parental responsibility over Rachael.[142] De Hart argues this was to prevent Ms da Silva from taking the child with her to Brazil.[143] Ms da Silva applied for a residence permit, which would allow for her and her son to reside in the Netherlands, either to have access to her daughter or to reside with her.[144] The authorities rejected her application and sought to deport her. The Court found a violation of Article 8, concluding that Ms da Silva's expulsion would have far-reaching consequences on Ms da Silva's responsibilities 'as a mother, as well as on her family life with her young daughter', and that it was in the daughter's best interests that she stayed in the Netherlands.[145] In effect, the ECtHR granted her a residence permit.[146]

The 2011 judgment in *Nunez v Norway*[147] concerned an expulsion order and two-year re-entry ban adopted against a Dominican national, Ms Mirtha Ledy de Leon Nunez. She was first deported from Norway at the age of 21 while staying there on a tourist visa after her arrest on suspicion of shoplifting. She returned to Norway only after four months in breach of her re-entry ban, using a forged passport. Ms Nunez married a Norwegian national and obtained a residence permit. After her divorce, she moved in with Mr O, a Dominican national, who had

138 In cases where a national of an EU Member State moves to another EU Member State, their family members can benefit from the right of residence in the Member State where the EU citizen has migrated to, as well as upon the return of the EU citizen to the Member State of origin as established in the case law of the CJEU. See eg Case C-267/83 *Diatta v Land Berlin* [1986] 2 CML Rev 164; Case 370/90 *Surinder Singh* [1992] ERC I-4265; Case C-127/08 *Metock and Others v Minister for Justice, Equality and Law Reform* [2008] ECR I-06241.

139 *da Silva* (n 33).

140 Klaassen (n 37) 164.

141 Her three-year-old son remained in Brazil with his grandparents. See *da Silva* (n 33) paras 9–11.

142 ibid para 12.

143 de Hart, 'Superdads' (n 134).

144 *da Silva* (n 33) paras 11 and 13.

145 ibid para 44.

146 Lambert (n 5).

147 *Nunez* (n 33). See also the 2012 parallel judgment decided by the Norwegian court in *Antwi* (n 133) where the expulsion of a father, who had used false identity to obtain residence in Norway, did not violate art 8.

held a settlement permit in Norway, and the couple had two children. Ms Nunez's residence and work permits were revoked after the authorities discovered that she had provided misleading information about her identity to obtain the permits. In its analysis, the Court noted that considering that Ms Nunez's links to Norway were formed through irregular residence, a violation of Article 8 would only be found in exceptional circumstances.[148] It found that the couple's children would remain in Norway with their father, who was granted sole parental responsibilities after the couple's separation following the adoption of Ms Nunez's second expulsion order. The Court made an explicit reference to the best interests of the child, noting that the couple's children's interests overrode all other considerations. It, therefore, concluded that Ms Nunez's expulsion would violate Article 8.

The 2011 judgment in *Yoh-Ekale Mwanje v Belgium*[149] is an example of an unsuccessful family reunification case, which highlights the absence of a stable relationship and children. The case concerned a Cameroonian national, Ms Khaterine Yoh-Ekale Mwanje, who was threatened with expulsion to Cameroon in 2009 on the grounds that her residence in Belgium was irregular, and she was in possession of a false passport. At the time of her proposed expulsion, she was at the advanced stage of HIV, without certainty that appropriate medical treatment was available in Cameroon, and she was also placed in detention. As her state of health had stabilised due to medication, the Belgian authorities considered her fit to travel.[150] In 2006, Ms Mwanje began a relationship with a Dutch national living in Belgium. The couple's two applications for permission to marry were refused on the grounds that the authorities questioned the genuineness of the couple's relationship. The Court concluded that Ms Mwanje's deportation did not violate Article 3.[151] It considered that no distinct question arose under Article 8 and, therefore, there was no need to examine her complaint.[152] In this case, the fact her unmarried partner was an EU citizen residing in an EU Member State other than that of his nationality was irrelevant because the couple was not married and the ECtHR does not consider issues of EU law. In cases concerning irregularly residing non-nationals who have health care needs, the ECtHR usually recognises the interests of the States to limit the irregular migrants' access to various public services, including heath care and social advantages on the grounds that they have not contributed to the funding of these services.[153]

The 2012 judgment in *Butt* v *Norway*[154] concerned expulsion of two adult children of a Pakistani woman, Ms Butt, who was expelled to Pakistan in September

148 Klaassen (n 37) 165.

149 *Yoh-Ekale Mwanje v Belgium* App no 10486/10 (ECtHR, 20 December 2011).

150 ibid para 83.

151 ibid para 85.

152 ibid para 128.

153 *Ponomaryovi v Bulgaria* App no 5335/05 (ECtHR, 21 June 2011), para 54. See also Diego Ginés Martín, 'In Limbo: Divergent Conceptualisations of Ill-treatment by European Courts and the Creation of Non-removable Migrants' (2021) 9(2) European Papers 1173.

154 *Butt* (n 30).

2005 for misleading the Norwegian immigration authorities about the family's whereabouts during their early years of residence there.[155] Her children, Ms Fozia Butt and Mr Johangir Abbas Butt, arrived in Norway at the ages of four and three. The family was granted a residence permit on humanitarian grounds and they were later granted a settlement permit.[156] After their father unsuccessfully applied for family reunification with the siblings in Norway, the immigration authorities discovered that the siblings had spent almost three years in Pakistan shortly after arriving to Norway.[157] The family's settlement permit was withdrawn and an expulsion order was adopted against them.[158] The expulsion was not enforced as the siblings were teenagers at the time and their mother had gone missing.[159] They subsequently moved in with their mother's brother and sister in Oslo.[160] In 2005, an expulsion order was adopted against both siblings, who were young adults at the time, on the grounds that their residence in Norway had been irregular since 1999.[161] Mr Butt was subject to an indefinite expulsion order due to his criminal conviction.[162] Although the ECtHR held that it would not be incompatible with Article 8 to expel him to Pakistan, it concluded that the siblings' expulsion would entail a violation of Article 8 as they had lived most of their lives in Norway and their circumstances were exceptional.[163]

The 2015 judgment in *Jeunesse v Netherlands*[164] concerned an expulsion of a Surinamese national, Ms Meriam Jeunesse, who had lived in the Netherlands for 18 years with her husband and three minor children who were all Dutch citizens.[165] She had overstayed her short-term entry visa and her residence in the country was never based on a residence permit. Rather than applying the test in *da Silva*,[166] the Court identified four elements which made the case exceptional, based on which it came to the conclusion that Article 8 would be violated if Ms Jeunesse would not be allowed to continue to reside in the Netherlands.[167] First, it considered the fact that all her family members were Dutch nationals and had the right to enjoy their family life in the Netherlands.[168] The Court noted that Ms Jeunesse herself held Dutch nationality at birth, and only lost this when Suriname gained independence from the Netherlands.[169] Therefore, it was relevant that she did not lose

155 ibid para 88. The siblings' mother died two years after she was expelled to Pakistan.
156 ibid paras 6–7.
157 *Butt* (n 30) paras 7–8.
158 ibid paras 8–9 and 19.
159 ibid paras 9 and 14.
160 ibid para 9.
161 ibid para 14.
162 ibid paras 10 and 14.
163 ibid paras 89–91.
164 *Jeunesse* (n 33) paras 71–72.
165 ibid
166 ibid para 107.
167 Klaassen (n 37) 168.
168 *Jeunesse* (n 33) para 115.
169 ibid.

her Dutch nationality by her own choice.[170] According to the Court, her position was different from the position of non-nationals who had never held Dutch nationality.[171] A second consideration for the Court was the fact that her presence in the Netherlands was seemingly tolerated by the authorities, who had not tried to remove her, enabling her to develop strong family, social, and cultural ties in the country.[172] Third, although no insurmountable obstacles existed for exercising family life in Suriname, the family's relocation there would entail some difficulties.[173] Fourth, in the context of the best interests of the child, the Court noted that Ms Jeunesse was the children's primary carer, whereas her husband had a full-time job that involved shift-work, it was obvious that the children's interests were best served by not disrupting their present circumstances.[174]

A noteworthy development is seen in the 2017 strikeout decision in *Madiani v Netherlands*,[175] which concerned an unsuccessful application for a residence permit for the purpose of stay with her Dutch husband by Ms Mimi Bongo Madiani, a national of the Democratic Republic of the Congo (DRC).[176] The couple had their first child while Ms Madiani's migration status was irregular.[177] She complained that not exempting her from the obligation to hold a provisional residence visa issued by the Dutch embassy in the DRC before she was able to apply for a residence permit was contrary to Article 8. Ms Madiani pointed out that her husband and their four children were Dutch;[178] her husband had income from work; and due to her post-traumatic stress disorder caused by traumatic events in DRC, it was impossible for her to return to the country or to settle there with her family.[179] Ms Madiani's expulsion was postponed pending the outcome of her objection filed with the Deputy Minister due to mental health problems.[180] The Deputy Minister concluded that no medical emergency would arise in the short term if she no longer received psychiatric treatment.[181] The decision was struck out of the Court's register after Ms Madiani was granted a retrospective five-year residence permit.

The 2022 judgment in *Alleleh and Others v Norway*[182] concerned an expulsion order with a two-year re-entry ban against a 39-year-old Djibouti national, Ms Neima Alleleh. She arrived in Norway as an asylum applicant in 2001. She gave a detailed account of her personal history claiming that she was Somali.[183]

170 ibid.
171 ibid.
172 ibid para 116. See also Klaassen (n 37) 168.
173 *Jeunesse* (n 33) para 117.
174 ibid para 119. See also Klaassen (n 37) 168.
175 *Madiani v Netherlands* App no 29381/11 (ECtHR, 16 March 2017).
176 *Madiani* (n 175) para 4.
177 ibid paras 3–4.
178 ibid para 6.
179 ibid para 7.
180 ibid.
181 ibid.
182 *Alleleh and Others v Norway* App no 569/20 (ECtHR, 23 June 2022).
183 ibid para 5.

Her asylum application was rejected on the grounds that she had no well-founded fear of being persecuted in Somalia.[184] Despite this she remained in Norway and unsuccessfully requested that the decision to refuse her asylum be revised.[185] After she married a Norwegian citizen, Mr Rolf Kristensen, she successfully applied for a residence permit on the basis of her marriage and obtained Norwegian citizenship.[186] The couple had four children who became Norwegian nationals at birth. Ms Alleleh was later found guilty of immigration-law breaches on the grounds that she had provided a false explanation and presented false identity papers during her asylum application process, with the consequence that she lost her Norwegian citizenship.[187] The ECtHR noted that her stay in Norway had no valid legal basis as she had repeatedly given incorrect information about her identity over a long period.[188] Further, her expulsion was based on the assumption that her family would stay in Norway as her 55-year-old husband could take care of their four children who were between 9 and 17.[189] Although the Court noted that Ms Alleleh's expulsion impacted on her children more than her, it was proportionate to the means sought and the re-entry was limited to two years and could be reviewed, if necessary.[190] Consequently, there was no violation of Article 8.[191]

In cases like *da Silva*, *Nunez*, and *Jeunesse*, the Court clearly has established that a broad European consensus supports the idea that the best interests of a child must be afforded significant weight,[192] and in some cases their interests may supersede the interests of the State to control migration in their territory. *Alleleh* is a deviation from this line of case law. Even though in *Alleleh* the ban on return was limited to two years, the Court considered that the husband was able to care for the couple's four children as a single father. This ignores the fact that the expulsion threatens to break the close ties between the mother and her children, considering the youngest child's age. *Mwanje* demonstrates that when there are no children involved and the national authorities suspect that the relationship is not genuine, the proposed expulsion of an unmarried partner is unlikely to constitute a breach of Article 8, as the Court did not even examine her complaint under Article 8.

7.4 Same-Sex Couples and Family Reunification

The Convention organs have dealt with complaints that CoE States discriminate against same-sex couples in their family reunification policies. These cases are not separated into three different categories identified in Section 7.3, as the case law in

184 ibid para 6.
185 ibid para 7.
186 ibid para 8.
187 ibid paras 16–17.
188 ibid para 99.
189 ibid para 95.
190 ibid para 99.
191 ibid para 106.
192 *MA* (n 4) para 133.

this area is not extensive. The Commission's early approach allowed States a wide margin of appreciation. The 1989 Commission decision in *C and LM v UK*[193] concerned an application for a family residency permit in the UK by an Australian citizen, Ms C. At the time she lived together in a property that she jointly owned with her unmarried lesbian partner, Ms E, who was a British citizen. She had worked in the UK for a few years and applied for an extension to her work visa, which was denied. In 1989, Ms C had a daughter, LM, who was born through donor insemination. After her daughter's birth, she became financially dependent on Ms E. She argued that the splitting up of the family would be contrary to Articles 8, 12 and 14. Although the Commission recognised that Ms C's expulsion would have impact on the couple's partnership, which according to it, involved private life, within the meaning of Article 8, her deportation was not regarded as an interference with this provision, given the UK's right to impose immigration controls and limits. The Commission found that no exceptional circumstances existed to justify a departure from these considerations and concluded that there was no interference with Article 8. It further found no discrimination on the grounds of sexual orientation contrary to Article 14, although British immigration policy provided protection for opposite-sex couples but did not recognise a lesbian relationship for immigration purposes.[194]

The 1990 Commission decision in *B v UK*[195] concerned a Cypriot man, Mr B, who had arrived in the UK as a student in the 1980s. After the UK government sought to deport him, he claimed that he was cohabiting with a British man. He unsuccessfully claimed asylum in May 1988 on the grounds of being gay because consensual same-sex conduct was a criminal offence in Cyprus. The Secretary of State did not consider the claim credible as the arrest for a criminal offence in Cyprus would not amount to persecution. The Commission stated that it had previously held that no discrimination existed contrary to Article 8 where the UK immigration rules gave priority to cohabiting, unmarried opposite-sex couples but not to same-sex couples in a similar position.[196] It, therefore, accepted that the difference in treatment between Mr B and another person in the same position with an opposite-sex partner could be objectively and reasonably justified. Accordingly, Mr B's complaint was considered manifestly ill-founded.

It took the ECtHR until 2016 to find a violation in the national family reunification policies concerning same-sex couples.[197] Although it had struck out from its register one case concerning family reunification between a same-sex couple in 2015 in *ME v Sweden*,[198] after Sweden granted a Libyan national, Mr ME, a permanent residence. *ME* concerned an unsuccessful application for a residence permit on

193 *C and LM v UK* App no 14753/89 (Commission decision, 9 October 1989).
194 ibid 5.
195 *B v UK* App no 16106/90 (Commission decision, 10 February 1990).
196 *S v UK* App 1716/85 (Commission decision, 14 June 1986).
197 It seems that the Convention organs did not examine any complaints concerning the issue between 1990 and 2015.
198 *ME v Sweden* App no 71398/12 (ECtHR, 8 April 2015).

account of family ties by Mr ME, who claimed to have married N, a trans woman, who held a permanent residence permit in Sweden. The national authorities and the courts doubted the genuineness of the marriage because N was undergoing gender reassignment when Mr ME first met her. This presumed dishonesty of transgender individuals in marriage is documented in other areas, such as, sexual intimacy and gender identity.[199] According to the authorities, Mr ME should have returned to Libya to wait for family reunification as under Swedish law, a non-national seeking a family residence permit should apply for, and be granted, such a permit outside Sweden.[200] Mr ME argued that upon his return to Libya, his marriage to a trans woman would put him at risk of ill-treatment.[201] The outcome can be considered successful for Mr ME, although it was only possible because Sweden granted the permanent residence under the pressure of the complaint to the Court.

The 2016 judgment in *Pajić v Croatia*[202] concerned an application for a residence permit in Croatia by Ms Danka Pajić, a citizen of Bosnia and Herzegovina, for the purposes of family reunification with her same-sex partner, a Croatian citizen, Ms DB. Her application was refused as it did not meet the requirements of national law which made it possible for unmarried opposite-sex couples to successfully apply for family reunification. Ms Pajić challenged this, arguing that although Croatian law provided no family reunification for same-sex couples, the law should be construed in a manner to ensure there was no difference in treatment based on sexual orientation. The Court concluded that as national law excluded family reunification for same-sex couples, the difference in treatment based on sexual orientation was not justified. It also noted that Croatia's margin of appreciation was narrow. Therefore, it found a violation of Article 14 in conjunction with Article 8.

The 2016 judgment in *Taddeucci and McCall v Italy*[203] dealt with a similar issue. The case concerned an application for a residence permit for family reasons in Italy by a New Zealand national, Mr Douglas McCall, who was the same-sex partner of an Italian national, Mr Roberto Taddeucci. The residence permit was rejected on the grounds that the statutory criteria were not satisfied.[204] The couple had lived in New Zealand with the status of an unmarried couple until 2003 when they decided to settle in Italy on the grounds of Mr Taddeucci's poor health.[205] The Court found that Italy's refusal to grant a family residence permit to the same-sex

199 Alex Sharpe, *Sexual Intimacy and Gender Identity 'Fraud': Reframing the Legal and Ethical Debate* (Routledge 2018); Flora Renz, 'Consenting to Gender? Trans Spouses after Same-Sex Marriage' in Nicola Barker and Daniel Monk (ed), *From Civil Partnership to Same-Sex Marriage 2004–2014: Interdisciplinary Reflections* (Routledge 2015).

200 *ME* (n 198) para 17.

201 ibid para 16.

202 *Pajić* (n 1).

203 *Taddeucci and McCall v Italy* App no 51362/09 (ECtHR, 30 June 2016). For commentary, see Giulia Dondoli, 'An Overnight Success a Decade in the Making: Indirect Discrimination on the Grounds of Sexual Orientation' (2018) 18(1) IJDL 5.

204 *Taddeucci* (n 203) para 9.

205 ibid para 8.

partner breached Article 14 taken in conjunction with Article 8.[206] It noted that the refusal essentially meant that Mr McCall was legally obliged to leave Italy, which prevented the couple from continuing to live together and amounted to an interference with their right to respect for family life as guaranteed by Article 8.[207] The Court can be applauded for not insisting that the situation of a same-sex couple should be compared to that of a married cohabiting opposite-sex couple, as the comparison would have been unjust. The recognition of the right to live together as a same-sex couple and to be treated equally with opposite-sex couples in family reunification case law has taken a long time. Although the Court has now firmly established the right not to be discriminated against in this area of law, it has taken several decades for the Court at arrive to this position.

7.5 Conclusion

This chapter has critically examined the case law of the ECtHR on family reunification through an intersectional feminist lens. While the ECHR is not an instrument enabling migration or the right of residence in Europe as such, the judgments of the Court are vitally important for the progressive development of European human rights standards.[208] The analysis of case law reveals that according to the Court's long-established jurisprudence, settled migrants can be expelled and their entry to the territory of the State can be prohibited for a period of time, when they have been convicted of serious crimes. This is even if they have family members in the territory of the State. The Court still takes a restrictive approach towards entry and residence of non-nationals for family purposes, apart from one area which has seen progressive developments in recent decades. In 2016, the ECtHR found that the refusal to grant residence permits to a non-national same-sex partner is in breach of the Convention.[209] It is worth noting that this is a relatively recent development, considering that it has taken several decades for the Court to arrive at this position. Although many West European States currently provide same-sex marriage in their legislation, the 46 Signatory States to the ECHR have divergent attitudes towards recognition of same-sex unions.[210] Therefore, the Court taking a clear stance to enforce the rights of individuals in this area is a welcome development. The ECtHR has firmly ruled that same-sex couples cannot be discriminated

206 ibid.

207 ibid para 59.

208 Kanstantsin Dzehtsiarou, 'The United Kingdom and the European Convention on Human Rights: Together Until the End?' (2024) 5(1) ECHR L Rev 1; Viljanen and Heiskanen (n 21) 178.

209 *Pajić* (n 1); *Taddeucci* (n 204).

210 Laurence R Helfer and Erik Voeten, 'International Courts as Agents of Legal Change: Evidence from LGBT Rights in Europe' (2014) 68(1) Intl Org 77; Peter Dunne, 'Who Is a Parent and Who Is a Child in a Same-Sex Family? Legislative and Judicial Issues for LGBT Families Post-Separation, Part I: The European Perspective' (2017) 30 J Am Acad Matrimonial Lawyers 27; Elwood D Carlson, Stuart Gietel-Basten, and Marie Digoix, *Same-Sex Families and Legal Recognition in Europe* (Springer 2020).

against in policies on family reunification.[211] This has included same-sex civil partners who have unsuccessfully applied for asylum in Europe.[212]

The most developed case law has thus far concerned the right of residence for non-settled migrant women whose children have the nationality of the respondent State. The outcome is influenced by EU law. Lim and the former judge of the ECtHR, Paolo Pinto de Albuquerque, have argued that the role of the CJEU's case law on similar circumstances has been influential in many of the ECtHR's judgments concerning the right of residence for parents and spouses who do not have a valid residence permit in the territory of the CoE State.[213] The child-centred approach in the family reunification jurisprudence of the ECtHR has emerged through a dialogue between different international and European legal instruments and supervisory organs, demonstrating the significance and effects of the cross-fertilisation of human rights.[214] This approach has particularly impacted the ability of primary carers of the children with the nationality of the CoE State to remain in the State territory. The extension of the right to family life to non-settled migrants is a laudable development for the purposes of recognising the right to family life.[215]

Yet, the Court can be criticised for its stereotypical portrayal of migrant fathers and mothers in its family reunification jurisprudence.[216] The Court case law reinforces the gendered notions that women are often seen as the children's primary carers, whereas men are seen as the main breadwinners. The outdated model of the nuclear family seems to dominate the way in which the ECtHR views families in its family reunification jurisprudence. In the attempt to dismantle national restrictions on family reunification, the ECtHR has understood the term family to include spouses, partners, and children.[217] However, it does not always accept the family unification rights of unmarried couples.[218]

Additionally, the Court can be criticised for justifying its approach in many of the cases in the analysis by stating that the circumstances of the case are exceptional. Although the ECtHR has not provided a comprehensive explanation of circumstances that make a case exceptional, it is worth noting that many such cases have involved minors.[219] However, because in general the respondent State is under an obligation to allow residence for a non-national only in limited instances,[220] the ECtHR still delivers judgments like *Alleleh* which demonstrate that although

211 *Pajić* (n 1).
212 *ME* (n 198); *B and C v Switzerland* App nos 889/19 and 43987/16 (ECtHR, 17 November 2020).
213 Pinto de Albuquerque and Lim (n 27) 573.
214 Viljanen and Heiskanen (n 21) 178.
215 Salomon (n 12) 602.
216 de Hart, 'Superdads' (n 134).
217 Lambert (n 5).
218 *Mwanje* (n 149).
219 For cases concerning exceptional circumstances, see eg *da Silva* (n 33) para 39; *Jeunesse* (n 33) para 108.
220 Klaassen (n 37) 165.

the Court assesses the best interests of the child, the State's interest to control migration surpasses the former. Although it is impossible to state with absolute certainty, the case law concerning mothers with children who hold the nationality of the respondent State seems to imply that when the respondent State is not an EU Member State, it enjoys a wider margin of appreciation. This may mean that a non-settled migrant parent may become expelled even when they will be absent from their children's lives for a lengthy period.

Strikingly, the Court has taken some progressive steps by acknowledging the right of a non-national parent to reside in the respondent State in 1988. The ECtHR may, therefore, have inadvertently created the conditions for the development of a significant EU law principle, according to which a non-national parent of a minor who holds the nationality of the EU Member State and, thus, also enjoys the benefits of EU citizenship, cannot be expelled from the State if it results in a situation where the child is forced the leave the territory of the EU as a whole. Remarkably, the respondent State may also choose to grant a residence permit to the non-national family member, even where this means lifting the entry ban accompanying an expulsion order to avoid a finding of violation of Article 8 of rights of the children and the spouse of the non-settled migrant who has been expelled from the State due to a lengthy prison sentence.[221] However, this was the choice of the respondent State, most likely due to the jurisprudence of the CJEU in recent years, rather than an obligation imposed on the State by the ECHR and the ECtHR.

References

Anagnostou D, 'Does European Human Rights Law Matter? Implementation and Domestic Impact of Strasbourg Court Judgments on Minority-Related Policies' (2010) 14(5) IJHR 721.

Askola H, '(No) Migrating for Family Care in Later Life: *Senchishak v Finland*, Older Parents and Family Reunification' (2016) 18 EJML 351.

Bottero M, 'Integration (of Immigrants) in the European Courts' Jurisprudence: Supporting a Pluralist and Rights-Based Paradigm? (2023) 24(4) J Intl Migration & Integration 1719.

Carlson ED, Gietel-Basten S, and Digoix M, *Same-Sex Families and Legal Recognition in Europe* (Springer 2020).

Dabrowska-Klosinska P, 'The Right to Family Reunion vs Integration Conditions for Third-Country Nationals' (2018) 20(3) EJML 251.

de Hart B, 'Love Thy Neighbour: Family Reunification and the Rights of Insiders' (2009) 11 EJML 235.

de Hart B, 'Superdads: Migrant Fathers' Right to Family Life before the European Court of Human Rights' (2015) 18 Man and Masculinities 448.

221 *Ismail v Netherlands* App no 67295/10 (ECtHR, 26 September 2017) (A Tunisian national, Mr Mounir Ismail, argued that his Dutch wife and Dutch children were unable to accompany him to Tunisia, if he was expelled from the Netherlands. After his expulsion, his family followed Mr Ismail to Tunisia. The case was struck out of the Court's register after the Netherlands granted Mr Ismail a residence permit).

Démbour MB, *When Humans Become Migrants: Study of the European Court of Human Rights with an Inter-American Counterpoint* (OUP 2015).
Dondoli G, 'An Overnight Success a Decade in the Making: Indirect Discrimination on the Grounds of Sexual Orientation' (2018) 18(1) IJDL 5.
Dunne P, 'Who Is a Parent and Who Is a Child in a Same-Sex Family? Legislative and Judicial Issues for LGBT Families Post-Separation, Part I: The European Perspective' (2017) 30 J Am Acad Matrimonial Lawyers 27.
Dzehtsiarou K, 'The United Kingdom and the European Convention on Human Rights: Together Until the End?' (2024) 5(1) ECHR L Rev 1.
Farcy JB, 'Equality in Immigration Law: An Impossible Quest?' (2020) 20(4) HRL Rev 725.
Fenton-Glynn C, *Children and the European Court of Human Rights* (OUP 2020).
Gillis M, 'Can We Talk? The Application of the Public Law Democratic Dialogue Model to the Interactions between Domestic Legislatures and the European Courts' (2022) 23 German LJ 56.
Ginés Martín D, 'In Limbo: Divergent Conceptualisations of Ill-treatment by European Courts and the Creation of Non-removable Migrants' (2021) 9(2) European Papers 1173.
Helfer LR and Voeten E, 'International Courts as Agents of Legal Change: Evidence from LGBT Rights in Europe' (2014) 68(1) Intl Org 77.
Klaassen M, 'Between Facts and Norms: Testing Compliance with Article 8 ECHR in Immigration Cases' (2019) 37(2) NQHR 157.
Krajewska A and Cahill-O'Callaghan R, 'When a Single Man Wants to Be a Father: Revealing the Invisible Subjects in the Law Regulating Fertility Treatment' (2020) 29(1) Social and Legal Studies 85.
Lambert H, 'Family Unity in Migration Law: The Evolution of A More Unified Approach in Europe' in Chetail V and Bauloz C (eds), *Research Handbook on International Law and Migration* (Edward Elgar 2014).
Lentin A, 'Europe and the Silence About Race' (2008) 11(4) Eur J Social Theory 487.
Margaria A, 'Trans Men Giving Birth and Reflections on Fatherhood: What to Expect?' (2020) 34(3) IJLPF 225.
Morris E, 'Family Reunification and Integration Policy in the EU: Where Are the Women?' (2015) 16 Int Migration & Integration 639.
Pinto de Albuquerque P and Lim HS, 'The Cross-Fertilisation between the Court of Justice of the European Union and the European Court of Human Rights: Reframing the Discussion on Brexit' (2018) 6 EHRLR 567.
Renz F, 'Consenting to Gender? Trans Spouses after Same-Sex Marriage' in Barker N and Monk D (eds), *From Civil Partnership to Same-Sex Marriage 2004-2014: Interdisciplinary Reflections* (Routledge 2015).
Reyhani AN and Golmohammadi G, 'The Limits of Static Interests: Appreciating Asylum Seekers' Contributions to a Country's Economy in Article 8 ECHR Adjudication on Expulsion' (2021) 33(1) IJRL 3.
Salomon S, 'Citizenship and Unauthorised Migration: A Dialectical Relationship' (2020) 83(3) MLR 583.
Sharpe A, *Sexual Intimacy and Gender Identity 'Fraud': Reframing the Legal and Ethical Debate* (Routledge 2018).
Staiano F, 'Good Mothers, Bad Mothers: Transnational Mothering in the European Court of Human Rights' Case Law' (2013) 15 EJML 155.
Thym D, 'Respect for Private and family Life under Article 8 ECHR in Immigration Cases: A Human Right to Regularize Illegal Stay?' (2008) 57 Intl & Comp L Q 87.
Tryfonidou A, 'The ECJ Recognises the Right of Same-Sex Spouses to Move Freely Between EU Member States: The *Coman* Ruling' (2019) 44(5) EL Rev 663.

van Walsum S, 'Against All Odds: How Single and Divorced Migrant Mothers Were Eventually Able to Claim Their Right to Respect for Family Life' (2009) 11 EJML 295.
Viljanen J and Heiskanen HE, 'The European Court of Human Rights: A Guardian of Minimum Standards in the Context of Immigration' (2016) 34(2) NQHR 174.
Wray H, *Article 8 ECHR, Family Reunification and the UK's Supreme Court Family Matters?* (Bloomsbury 2023).

8 Conclusion

The arguments presented in this book aim to shift the debate about the composition of the ECtHR, putting the issue of institutional diversity discussed in chapter 3 on the agenda for scholars and policymakers alike. Although empirical work with the judges of the ECtHR exists, there is limited work in this regard from the gendered point of view.[1] What emerges from chapter 4 is that the ECtHR has been grappling to come to terms with intersectional discrimination in areas where Article 14, the main discrimination provision of the European Convention on Human Rights[2] (ECHR), has been invoked, such as, forced sterilisation of Roma women in the context of a caesarean section as well as the requirement to be permanently unable to procreate in the context of legal recognition of gender reassignment. The ECtHR has only occasionally applied an intersectional approach in its previous case law where women have raised the issue of intersectional discrimination on the grounds of gender and race or ethnic origin, or gender and age, or gender and sexuality. It uses this approach so rarely that it has not used the specific term intersectional discrimination in its case law, nor has it made many judgments in the past decade where the existence of multiple discrimination is explicitly acknowledged. Additionally, the ECtHR does not always examine whether Article 14 has been violated if it has established that the individual's rights were violated under another Convention provision. Sometimes it may overlook discrimination in cases that allege violation of this provision. For instance, although the ECtHR has recognised that the lack of legal recognition of the change of gender of post-operative trans individuals is central to complaints under Article 14, it has avoided examining these issues under this provision on the grounds that it has found a violation of Article 8.[3]

1 For empirical interviews with the judges of the ECtHR, see eg Nina-Louisa Arold, 'The European Court of Human Rights as an Example of Convergence' (2007) 76(2/3) Nord J Intl L 305; Ezgi Yildiz, 'A Court with Many Faces: Judicial Characters and Modes of Norm Development in the European Court of Human Rights' (2020) 31(1) EJIL 73; Kanstantsin Dzehtsiarou and Alex Schwartz, 'Electing Team Strasbourg: Professional Diversity on the European Court of Human Rights and Why it Matters' (2020) 21(4) German LJ 621.

2 European Convention for the Protection of Human Rights and Fundamental Freedoms, 4 November 1950, ETS 5, art 8.

3 See eg *Christine Goodwin v UK* App no 28957/95 (ECtHR, 11 July 2002), para 108.

DOI: 10.4324/9781003435099-8

The 2024 judgment in *Allouche v France*[4] concerning the failure of the French authorities to prosecute misogynistic and anti-Semitist hate crimes aimed at a French woman, Ms Myriam Allouche, is a welcome development. Even if the judgment does not use the term intersectionality, it recognises that the abuse that Ms Allouche was subjected to was aimed at her because she was a Jewish woman. The case is important for the development of the body of case law where the Court recognises that women, who are members of diasporic and minoritised groups, experience distinct types of discrimination compared to men who belong to the same groups, even if there are fewer cases concerning women. Unfortunately, the Court has long resisted making a finding of intersectional discrimination in its case law in situations where discrimination occurs based on multiple grounds, such as, gender and race or ethnicity; gender and religious beliefs; and gender and membership of the lesbian, gay, bisexual, and transgender (LGBT) community. Establishing that women and minoritised or diasporic groups experience intersectional discrimination allows the Court to recognise that, for instance, racialised women's experiences of gender discrimination are inseparable from their experiences of racial discrimination because these experiences occur simultaneously.[5] If the Court was to consider intersectional discrimination in its judgments, it would arguably have the capacity to persuade the States to adopt policies that would benefit all disadvantaged applicants.[6]

It was noted in chapter 5 that profound developments have occurred in Europe in several related areas, including LGBT rights; legal recognition of children born through donor insemination and surrogacy; same-sex unions; asylum, and family reunification in the recent decades. Although LGBT rights, especially the ability to obtain recognition of same-sex unions, have enhanced the family reunification rights, not all signatory States to the Convention provide this. Whereas many West European States have provided same-sex marriage in their legislation starting from 2010,[7] it has taken the ECtHR until 2021 to establish that States have a positive obligation to provide for an opportunity for same-sex couples to have their relationships acknowledged.[8] In terms of parental rights of both same-sex couples and opposite-sex couples, problems remain with the recognition of a non-genetic parent's rights in cases concerning surrogacy[9] and especially in terms of same-sex parents in the

4 *Allouche v France* App no 81249/17 (ECtHR, 11 April 2024).

5 Ratna Kapur, 'The Tragedy of Victimisation Rhetoric: Resurrecting the "Native" Subject in International/Postcolonial Feminist Legal Politics' (2002) 15 Harv Hum Rts J 1, 8.

6 One collaborative project concerning intersectional reimagining of the judgments of the ECtHR is in the development. See Intersectional Rewrites: European Court of Human Rights Judgments Reimagined <https://intersectionalrewrites.org/authors-editors/> accessed 24 July 2024.

7 Peter Dunne, 'Who Is a Parent and Who Is a Child in a Same-Sex Family? Legislative and Judicial Issues for LGBT Families Post-Separation, Part I: The European Perspective' (2017) 30(1) J Am Acad Matrimonial Lawyers 27; Elwood D Carlson, Stuart Gietel-Basten and Marie Digoix, *Same-Sex Families and Legal Recognition in Europe* (Springer 2020).

8 *Fedotova and Others v Russia* App no 40792/10 and others (ECtHR, 13 July 2021); *Koilova and Babulkova v Bulgaria* App no 40209/20 (ECtHR, 5 September 2023).

9 See eg *AM v Norway* App no 30254/18 (ECtHR, 24 March 2022).

case of second parent adoption.[10] Although the ECtHR and national authorities have been willing to recognise the parent-child relationship between intended genetic fathers and their children born abroad through surrogacy agreements solely based on the foreign birth certificate,[11] this is not the case for the non-genetic parent.[12] Consequently, the non-genetic parent usually needs to either adopt the child or obtain a court order to exercise joint parental responsibility. The requirement for the non-genetic mothers to adopt the child creates gender asymmetry, which is discriminatory against women.[13] This is significant because the Court fails to recognise the continuous disadvantage that arises from the non-recognition of the filial link between the child and the non-genetic parent. If one of the parents dies or the parents' relationship breaks down, the recognition of the child-parent relationship between the non-genetic parent and the child becomes even more complicated, if not impossible.

It was established in chapter 6 that the ECtHR has rarely considered gender in its asylum case law in the past. This is even though the Court has found gender discrimination in its case law relating to other areas of life, including family reunification.[14] The ECtHR is getting better at recognising the vulnerabilities of asylum-seeking women, especially when they are pregnant or have been subjected to forced marriage or marital and sexual violence. There is still work to do in terms of recognising intersectional discrimination when it comes to asylum-seeking women and LGBT asylum applicants. The Court has been criticised for its long-standing approach according to which asylum-seeking women are categorised as vulnerable and deserving of refugee status only if they lack protection from their male relatives. However, this is an impossible standard to achieve, considering in that both women and men are equally powerless to protect themselves when the population in their country of origin experiences indiscriminate violence due to an armed conflict or collective punishment.[15] Therefore, suggesting that women should invoke the protection of their male relatives when their State of origin is unable to provide sufficient protection falls short of the standards of protection required by international refugee law.[16] As regards LGBT asylum applicants, the Court has rejected all LGBT asylum claims, except for two cases where the Court acknowledged that gay

10 See eg *CE and Others v France* App nos 29775/18 and 29693/19 (ECtHR, 24 March 2022).

11 *D v France* App no 11288/18 (ECtHR, 16 July 2020).

12 Melanie Levy, 'Surrogacy and Parenthood: A European Saga of Genetic Essentialism and Gender Discrimination' (2022) 29 Mich J Gender and L 121.

13 ibid 124–125.

14 Sergio Carrera Nuñez, 'The ECtHR's Judgment in *Biao v Denmark*: Non-Discrimination Among Nationals and Family Reunification as Converging European Standards: ECtHR, *Biao v Denmark*, Judgment of 24 May 2016, Application No 38590/10' (2016) 23(5) MJ 865.

15 Malak Benslama-Dabdoub, 'Epistemic Violence and Colonial Legacies in the Representation of Refugee Women: Contesting Narratives of Vulnerability and Victimhood' (2024) 20(1) Intl JLC 54, 59.

16 Lyra Jakulevičienė and Laurynas Biekša, 'Trends in the Qualification of Asylum Claims Related to Gender-Based Violence Under International and European Law' (2021) 26(5) IJHR 833.

men may face persecution in the hands of their relatives and other private individuals in the country of origin.[17]

Although as a regional human rights treaty, the ECHR, is not an instrument that enables migration or the right of residence in the Council of Europe (CoE) States as such, the ECtHR frequently examines whether a refusal to grant family reunification is contradictory with the requirements of Article 8 (Right to respect for private and family life).[18] It was noted in chapter 7 that in the context of the ECtHR's family reunification case law, no objective or reasonable justification exists for the exclusion of unmarried same-sex couples from family reunification.[19] Additionally, in cases concerning unsuccessful asylum applicants, the ECtHR has recognised that the same-sex union entered into in the State of asylum means that the applicants should be provided with a residence permit for family purposes without requiring them to return to the country of origin to apply for such a permit due to the risk of persecution arising from their sexual orientation.[20] Yet, the States adopt a restrictive approach to family reunification, especially when there are no EU law provisions that require them to issue family permits in line with the EU Citizens Directive.[21]

It also appears that strike out decisions have emerged to be substantial in the area of asylum and, to some extent, family reunification. Sometimes issues relating to asylum and family reunification overlap because the individual may have arrived at the CoE State territory as an asylum seeker. In some instances, the case is struck out from the Court's register because the unsuccessful asylum seeker subject to deportation has formed a family relationship in the country of asylum, which has resulted in a residence permit for family purposes being granted to them.[22] There are also cases where the respondent State has granted a temporary residence permit for other reasons. The ECtHR will strike a pending case out of its register if it is satisfied with the State's promise to grant even a temporary or tolerated residence.[23] It is beneficial for the State to grant a residence permit to the individual in question as the strike out decisions do not result in a violation of the Convention provisions nor are the States obliged to pay damages.

Finally, even though the book does not focus on EU law, the impact of EU law in the jurisprudence of the ECtHR is difficult to ignore, particularly in the area of family reunification. Considerable academic commentary exists on the relationship between the European systems for the protection of human rights under the ECHR

17 *B and C v Switzerland* App nos 889/19 and 43987/16 (ECtHR, 17 November 2020); *MI v Swizerland* App no 56390/21 (ECtHR, 12 November 2024).
18 Helena Wray, *Article 8 ECHR, Family Reunification and the UK's Supreme Court Family Matters?* (Bloomsbury 2023).
19 *Pajić v Croatia* App no 68453/13 (ECtHR, 23 February 2016).
20 *ME v Sweden* App no 71398/12 (ECtHR, 8 April 2015); *B and C* (n 17).
21 Directive 2004/38/EC of 29 April 2004 on the right of citizens of the Union and their family members to move and reside freely within the territory of the Member States OJ [2004] L158/77.
22 *ME* (n 20); *RBAB and Others v Netherlands* App no 7211/06 (ECtHR, 7 June 2016).
23 Elisabeth Lambert Abdelgawad, 'The Practice of the European Court of Human Rights When Striking Out Applications' (2018) 36(1) NQHR 7, 20.

and EU law[24] and the relationship between the ECtHR and the CJEU.[25] It has further been acknowledged that the EU's increasing importance in the human rights sphere has added another layer to the relationship between the two regional courts.[26] The cooperation between the courts is important for ensuring progressive interpretation of human rights protection within the CoE States, and citations to one another's jurisprudence can provide a more contemporary take on the rights contained within the ECHR as the comparable rights in the EU human rights legislation.[27] In the latter case, the rights are also more elaborate.[28] Judicial dialogue between the two courts is, therefore, likely to be beneficial for both courts in order to support their own reasoning in their respective judgments.[29]

It can be argued that some of the ECtHR's judgments concerning family reunification have been influenced by the growing body of case law on EU free movement rights and the accompanying right of residency for non-national family members in the State of the EU citizen's nationality under the EU Treaties and the EU Citizens Directive. The CJEU has seen an increase in the number of cases concerning applications for family residence permits by non-national family members in the past few years. Consequently, there is a significant body of case law on family members of EU citizens who are non-nationals of an EU Member State themselves.[30] Although the CJEU is distinctly not a human rights court,[31] it increasingly adjudicates rights under the Charter of Fundamental Rights and it frequently draws from jurisprudence of the ECtHR. It can be argued that the CJEU's emerging jurisprudence on the residence rights of non-national family members is increasingly progressive. Similarly, the CJEU's recent case law on the rights of asylum-seeking women in the past few years seems to be increasingly gender-sensitive in line with the CoE Istanbul Convention.[32] The case law of the CJEU may persuade the ECtHR

24 See eg Katja S Ziegler, Elizabeth Wicks and Loveday Hodson, *The UK and European Human Rights: A Strained Relationship?* (Hart 2015).

25 See eg Lize R Glas and Jasper Krommendijk, 'From Opinion 2/13 to *Avotiņš*: Recent Developments in the Relationship between the Luxembourg and Strasbourg Courts' (2017) 17 HRL Rev 567; Paolo Pinto de Albuquerque and Hyun-Soo Lim, 'The Cross-Fertilisation between the Court of Justice of the European Union and the European Court of Human Rights: Reframing the Discussion on Brexit' (2018) 6 EHRLR 567.

26 Ziegler, Wicks and Hodson (n 24).

27 Charter of Fundamental Rights of the European Union [2012] OJ C326/391.

28 ibid, art 52(3) stipulates that rights in the Charter that correspond to those in the ECHR must be given the same meaning and scope as those laid down by the Convention.

29 See also Glas and Krommendijk (n 25); Dean Spielmann, 'Foreword' in Kanstantsin Dzehtsiarou and others (eds), *Human Rights Law in Europe: The Influence, Overlaps and Contradictions of the EU and the ECHR* (Routledge 2014) vii–xxi.

30 Kristine Kruma, 'Family Reunification: A Tool to Shape the Concept of EU citizenship' in Maribel Gonzáles Pascual and Aida Torres Pérez (eds), *The Right to Family Life in the European Union* (Routledge 2017).

31 See eg Grainne de Búrca, 'After the EU Charter of Fundamental Rights: The Court of Justice as a Human Rights Adjudicator?' (2013) 20(2) MJ 168.

32 Council of Europe Convention on preventing and combating violence against women and domestic violence (adopted 11 May 2011) CETS No 210.

to embrace a broader definition of the term family, one that promotes a more inclusive understanding of families beyond the traditional nuclear family as well as their rights. In this way, the scope of the right to respect for private and family life under Article 8 ECHR can adapt to the changing interpretations of what constitutes family life. It is important to note that the relationship between the two regional courts is based on dialogue, rather than one-sided influence from the ECtHR to the CJEU or the other way around. The former judge of the ECtHR, Pinto de Albuquerque and his coauthor Lim have argued that the CJEU's judgments have been influential when the ECtHR has adjudicated the right of residence for non-settled migrant parents and spouses in the territory of the CoE State.[33]

The CJEU is also taking strides in the area of gendered asylum. One of the most significant reasons for the EU's commitment to advance gender equality is the EU's accession to the Istanbul Convention in October 2023, after which the CJEU must integrate the Istanbul Convention into its reasoning on gender in asylum law.[34] Reflecting this, the EU has adopted a Directive on Violence against Women,[35] which has been hailed as a significant sign of the EU's dedication to achieving substantial equality.[36] The asylum related case law delivered by the CJEU after its accession reflects this commitment. In January 2024, the CJEU stated that under EU law,[37] in some circumstances, women as a whole from a particular country of origin and more specific groups of women who share an additional common characteristic, may be regarded as belonging to a particular social group for the purposes of refugee status.[38] Additionally, EU Member States should provide subsidiary protection status for women facing a real threat of being subjected to familial violence and femicide due to the alleged transgression of cultural, religious or traditional norms. In June 2024, the CJEU held that refugee status may be granted to women, who during their stay in a State of asylum, have asserted their wish to be treated equally with men as holding such an opinion could constitute as a reason for persecution in the country of origin.[39] The case law analysis demonstrates that the

33 Pinto de Albuquerque and Lim (n 25) 573.

34 Catherine Warin, 'Gender in EU Asylum Law: The Istanbul Convention as a Game Changer?' (2024) 36(1-2) IJRL 93, 101.

35 Directive (EU) 2024/1385 of the European Parliament and of the Council of 14 May 2024 on combating violence against women and domestic violence [2024] OJ L2024/1385.

36 Ceren Kasım, 'Advancing Gender Equality: The EU's Landmark Directive 2024/1385 on Violence Against Women' (*EU Law Analysis*, 21 June 2024) <https://eulawanalysis.blogspot.com/2024/06/advancing-gender-equality-eus-landmark.html> accessed 30 July 2024.

37 Directive 2011/95/EU of the European Parliament and of the Council of 13 December 2011 on standards for the qualification of third-country nationals or stateless persons as beneficiaries of international protection, for a uniform status for refugees or for persons eligible for subsidiary protection, and for the content of the protection granted OJ [2011] L337/9, art 10(1).

38 Case C-621/21 *Intervyuirasht organ na DAB pri MS* (Women victims of domestic violence) EU:C:2024:47, para 61.

39 Case C-646/21 *K and L v Staatssecretaris van Justitie en Veiligheid* ECLI:EU:C:2024:487 (Two Iraqi sisters, Ms K and Ms L, who attained majority while living in the Netherlands, unsuccessfully claimed asylum after arriving to the country in 2015, together with their parents and aunt).

CJEU's recent judgments take a markedly proactive approach towards embracing gender equality. Even if the ECtHR does not yet explicitly reference the Istanbul Convention, it is likely that such references will increase in the future. It has been suggested that the Istanbul Convention is likely to be a game changer for the protection of asylum-seeking women and no doubt also for LGBT asylum seekers.[40]

In terms of future research, there is scope for examining the engagement between the ECtHR and the CJEU in the areas of law beyond family migration and asylum in the area of economic rights through the intersectional lens. Additionally, one area of future research concerns the relationship between the ECtHR and the United Kingdom (UK) courts from an intersectional feminist point of view, as the UK is one of the Contracting States to the ECHR. The engagement may prove important and timely as the UK courts have in some cases arrived at a different conclusion, finding discrimination in cases where the ECtHR may have not done so. For instance, in the case of civil partnerships for opposite-sex couples.

References

Arold NL, 'The European Court of Human Rights as an Example of Convergence' (2007) 76(2–3) Nord J Intl L 305.

Benslama-Dabdoub M, 'Epistemic Violence and Colonial Legacies in the Representation of Refugee Women: Contesting Narratives of Vulnerability and Victimhood' (2024) 20(1) Intl JLC 54.

Carlson ED, Gietel-Basten S, and Digoix M, *Same-Sex Families and Legal Recognition in Europe* (Springer 2020).

Carrera Nuñez S, 'The ECtHR's Judgment in *Biao v Denmark*: Non-Discrimination Among Nationals and Family Reunification as Converging European Standards: ECtHR, Biao v Denmark, Judgment of 24 May 2016, Application No 38590/10' (2016) 23(5) MJ 865.

de Búrca G, 'After the EU Charter of Fundamental Rights: The Court of Justice as a Human Rights Adjudicator?' (2013) 20(2) MJ 168.

Dunne P, 'Who Is a Parent and Who Is a Child in a Same-Sex Family? Legislative and Judicial Issues for LGBT Families Post-Separation, Part I: The European Perspective' (2017) 30(1) J Am Acad Matrimonial Lawyers 27.

Dzehtsiarou K and Schwartz A, 'Electing Team Strasbourg: Professional Diversity on the European Court of Human Rights and Why it Matters' (2020) 21(4) German LJ 621.

Glas LR and Krommendijk J, 'From Opinion 2/13 to *Avotiņš*: Recent Developments in the Relationship between the Luxembourg and Strasbourg Courts' (2017) 17 HRL Rev 567.

Jakulevičienė L and Biekša L, 'Trends in The Qualification of Asylum Claims Related to Gender-Based Violence Under International and European Law' (2021) 26(5) IJHR 833.

Kapur R, 'The Tragedy of Victimisation Rhetoric: Resurrecting the "Native" Subject in International/Postcolonial Feminist Legal Politics' (2002) 15 Harv Hum Rts J 1.

Kasım C, 'Advancing Gender Equality: The EU's Landmark Directive 2024/1385 on Violence Against Women' (*EU Law Analysis*, 21 June 2024) <https://eulawanalysis.blogspot.com/2024/06/advancing-gender-equality-eus-landmark.html> accessed 30 July 2024.

Kruma K, 'Family Reunification: A Tool to Shape the Concept of EU citizenship' in Maribel Gonzáles Pascual and Aida Torres Pérez (eds), *The Right to Family Life in the European Union* (Routledge 2017).

40 Warin (n 34) 105.

Lambert Abdelgawad E, 'The Practice of the European Court of Human Rights When Striking Out Applications' (2018) 36(1) NQHR 7.
Levy M, 'Surrogacy and Parenthood: A European Saga of Genetic Essentialism and Gender Discrimination' (2022) 29 Mich J Gender and L 121.
Pinto de Albuquerque P and Lim HS, 'The Cross-Fertilisation between the Court of Justice of the European Union and the European Court of Human Rights: Reframing the Discussion on Brexit' (2018) 6 EHRLR 567.
Spielmann D, 'Foreword' in Dzehtsiarou K and others (eds), *Human Rights Law in Europe: The Influence, Overlaps and Contradictions of the EU and the ECHR* (Routledge 2014).
Warin C, 'Gender in EU Asylum Law: The Istanbul Convention as a Game Changer?' (2024) 36(1–2) IJRL 93.
Yildiz E, 'A Court with Many Faces: Judicial Characters and Modes of Norm Development in the European Court of Human Rights' (2020) 31(1) EJIL 73.
Ziegler KS, Wicks E and Hodson L, *The UK and European Human Rights: A Strained Relationship?* (Hart 2015).

Index

FSC
www.fsc.org
MIX
Papier | Fördert
gute Waldnutzung
FSC® C083411

Kolibri 360 GmbH
Ferdinand-Jühlke-Straße 7
99095 Erfurt, Deutschland
produktsicherheit@kolibri360.de